GENERATIONAL ACCOUNTING

GENERATIONAL ACCOUNTING

Knowing Who Pays, and When, for What We Spend

——— ■ ———

Laurence J. Kotlikoff

With a New Afterword

THE FREE PRESS
A Division of Macmillan, Inc.
New York

Maxwell Macmillan Canada
Toronto

Maxwell Macmillan International
New York   Oxford   Singapore   Sydney

The Free Press
A Division of Macmillan, Inc.
866 Third Avenue, New York, N. Y. 10022

Maxwell Macmillan Canada, Inc.
1200 Eglinton Avenue East
Suite 200
Don Mills, Ontario M3C 3N1

Macmillan, Inc. is part of the Maxwell Communication Group of Companies.

First Free Press Paperback Edition 1993

Printed in the United States of America

printing number

1 2 3 4 5 6 7 8 9 10

Library of Congress Cataloging-in-Publication Data

Kotlikoff, Laurence J.
  Generational accounting: knowing who pays, and when, for what we spend / Laurence J. Kotlikoff.
    p.   cm.
  Includes bibliographical references and index.
ISBN: 978-0-02-917585-9
    1. Fiscal policy—United States.   2. Budget deficits—United States.
  3. United States—Economic conditions—1981–   I. Title.
  HJ2051.K66   1992
  339.5´0973—dc20   91-44312
                                                               CIP

To Alex, with all my love

CONTENTS

—— ■ ——

	Preface	ix
	Acknowledgments	xvii
1.	Smoke and Mirrors	1
2.	U.S. Economic Malaise	37
3	Blame It on the Deficit	65
4.	Figures Lie and Liars Figure	89
5.	Generational Accounting	115
6.	Deficit Delusion	143
7.	Postwar Generational Policy	165
8.	Social Security and the Baby Boomers	193
9.	Whither Generational Accounting?	217
	Afterword	221
	Notes	225
	Index	255

PREFACE

——— ∎ ———

This book makes the radical argument that the government's budget deficit—the cornerstone of conventional economic policy analysis and management—is a number devoid of economic content and that its use has repeatedly led us astray. By employing this faulty indicator we have repeatedly misjudged the true stance of economic policy and have chosen policies that compound, rather than solve, our critical economic problems.

This book debunks accepted wisdom, but it also offers an entirely new way of thinking about, measuring, and making economic policy. This new fiscal approach, called "generational accounting," addresses all the real issues underlying our concern with deficits. In particular, it reveals how much money the government, now and in the future, is slated to take from each contemporary generation as well as from those generations not yet born.

Generational accounting is forward-looking. It recognizes that people think about tomorrow in deciding how much to work, spend, and save today. Part of their thinking ahead includes thinking about their future tax payments to and their future transfer payments from the government. In contrast to generational accounting, the deficit completely ignores the future, including the government's likely future taxes and transfer payments. In so doing, the deficit leaves out a great deal of what is influencing people's immediate spending decisions. This, in part, is why the deficit has proved to be such a poor guide to stimulating private spending during recessions. The deficit's short-term perspective has also diverted attention from longer-term economic issues and, as a result, inhibited longer-term thinking, planning, and policy-making.

The critical problem with the deficit, however, lies in the fact that its definition is completely arbitrary. Governments are free to label their various receipts and payments with alternative sets of words, each of which produces its own time-path of government deficits but leaves unchanged the underlying treatment of different generations and the underlying stimulus to private spending. While generational accounting reveals the true underlying stance of policy, the deficit, in fact, tells us only about our choice of words. The realization that the deficit is not well grounded has begun to dawn on policy-makers in Washington, who can bear witness to how easy and how often one can change the deficit's definition.

Notwithstanding growing qualms about its meaning, the U.S. federal deficit is widely viewed as our country's number one policy problem. Since the early 1980s the deficit has dominated national economic debate and has greatly influenced the choice of real policy (as opposed to just words). The United States is not alone in paying unwarranted attention to deficits. Budget/fiscal deficits play the central role in economic policy-making in virtually every country around the world. And the deficit is the key variable used by the International Monetary Fund to determine whether countries are complying with its conditions for loans.

Deficit obsession extends beyond central governments and international lending institutions. Financial analysts are convinced, notwithstanding the evidence to the contrary, that fiscal deficits are responsible for keeping interest rates high and causing inflation. Many economists, particularly traditional Keynesian economists (postwar disciples of John Maynard Keynes), agree and argue further (again, despite the evidence) that these official liabilities reduce the nation's saving, investment, and rate of growth.

If, as argued here, the deficit is a figment of language, not economic reality, then this should be of interest to the players in the worlds of business, finance, and economic policy. It should be equally important to everyday citizens who ultimately determine, through their elected officials, the course of economic policy and who are at the receiving end of policy decisions.

The baby boom generation should be especially worried about the validity of the deficit as the yardstick we use for making policy. Their retirement finances as well as the welfare of their children will be profoundly affected by the dramatic aging of the U.S. population that will occur over the next forty years. By the year 2030 the age-composition of the United States will resemble that of present-day Florida. The graying of America raises some tough and touchy questions: Will there be enough young workers (the boomers' children) in 2030 to pay the Social Security and Medicare benefits of retired baby boomers? And will those future workers have any money left over to help their parents (today's boomers) if all their taxes are spent on interest on the official federal debt? Is the baby boom generation in dire straits because of the government's fiscal irresponsibility? Or is the recent buildup of official U.S. liabilities only a small and misleading part of a set of larger generational obligations that the government has failed to face?

Whatever the true answers to these questions, the baby boom generation needs to know the answers and know them now. If government policy, after all the smoke (and mirrors) has cleared, is really endangering the baby boomers' old-age financial security, baby boomers should take immediate steps, such as increasing their saving, to cushion their impending financial crisis. Unfortunately, an understanding of the plight of the baby boomers cannot be achieved, even in part, by considering either the government's reported debt or its change over time (the deficit).

Giving baby boomers, as well as members of all other generations, a clear sense of what the government has in store for them, now and down the road, is a key objective of this book. Generational accounts provide this information. Generational accounts comprise a set of numbers, one for each generation, indicating the net amount members of the generation will, on average, pay the government over their remaining years. Generational accounting also reveals the likely fiscal burden to be imposed on future generations.

Knowing how much their generation is slated to pay will not only help the young, middle-aged, and old decide how much to save for their future. It will also provide them with the information they need to argue against further fiscal encumbrances. And it will help them get policies enacted that they both want and are willing to pay for—that is, policies whose benefits, but also whose costs, accrue to their own generations. Finally, in exposing our intended treatment of future generations, generational accounting may put an end to what, in the United States, has been a four-decade-long process of shifting very sizable fiscal burdens onto our posterity. In the absence of generational accounting this redistribution has gone largely undetected and undebated and has left future Americans to face, over their lifetimes, substantially larger net tax bills than those we ourselves have faced or will face.

Is this book really different from recent books on U.S. fiscal policy? Indeed it is. Most recent books spend hundreds of pages describing the astronomical size of government debts and predicting doomsday. Others question the construction of the deficit and offer elaborate corrections. This book is not about the size of the deficit or how to fix it. This book is about why the government's budget deficit doesn't measure what we think it measures, why it cannot be fixed, and why we must abandon the use of it in favor of generational accounts for purposes of making fiscal policy.

To argue that the deficit is devoid of economic significance and must be replaced by a meaningful measure of fiscal policy is certainly not to apologize for the deficit. Other economists have written that the U.S. deficit is a problem, but not such a big problem. Such statements assume that the deficit is a measure of something economic. Again, the contention here is that it is not. I share many of the concerns of those worried about the deficits, but assert that the deficits tell us nothing about those concerns.

This book contains a radical message, but the microeconomics—the theory of the economic behavior of rational households and profit-maximizing firms—underlying its argument is certainly not radical. The fact that this book departs so dramatically from the entrenched Keynesian macroeconomic view is testimony to how far traditional Keynesian macroeconomics has strayed from the rigorous implications of microeconomics.

Traditional Keynesian economists, for the most part, assume that people are extremely shortsighted when it comes to thinking about the future. Given their assumption of myopia, it's not surprising that Keynesian economists take a cash-flow measure of policy—the deficit—as their centerpiece of policy analysis. But are we really as myopic as these economists seem to believe? Do we just forget about our future Social Security and private pensions when deciding how much to save? Do we really purchase cars or houses and go on vacations oblivious to our future income prospects? Do we put money into IRA accounts because we don't expect to be around tomorrow? Hardly. In contrast to those Keynesians, neoclassical economists, like the author, who base their macroeconomics on microeconomics, assume that the public's behavior, by and large, is more or less rational, which includes thinking and planning resonably about the future.

The assumption that people act rationally doesn't mean none of us makes mistakes in planning for the future, or that all of us foresee the future perfectly, or that the information we have available to plan for the future is necessarily correct. Indeed, the basic premise of this book is that we have been considering misleading information about our government's generational policies. What rationality requires is that, in making our economic choices, we appropriately process what information we have available. In particular, it implies that we neither ignore the future nor *systematically* over- or undervalue our future income prospects. Surely some of us overvalue our future incomes and undersave, and others of us undervalue our future incomes and oversave. But economic behavior, on average, appears to be in accord with the assumption of rationality. While there is no disputing Keynes's famous dictum that "in the long run, we're all dead," most of us will still be here for a while and are prepared to plan for our stay.

Certainly, in making our mistakes none of us does what the traditional Keynesians assume, which is simply to ignore the future. In a Keynesian world full of such irrational people, who consider only their immediate cash-flows, the deficit might have some meaning, but it has no meaning in our world, where people are, in the main, quite rational and think about the government's impact on their cash-flows not only this year but in future years as well. The argument against myopic deficits and in favor of forward-looking generational accounting rests then on the same basic assumption of rationality that underlies virtually all of microeconomic theory and, increasingly, most of macroeconomics (including, by the way, the modern branch of Keynesian economics, called New Keynesian economics).

What does the new approach to fiscal policy reveal about past and current U.S. policy? First, U.S. generational policy is seriously out of balance. Unless current generations agree to accept a larger share of the costs of paying for the government's spending, future Americans will have to pay at least a 21 percent larger share of their lifetime incomes to the government than is the case for today's young Americans. Second, generational accounting reveals that most of the very sizable postwar passing-of-the-generational buck occurred between 1950 and 1979—years that witnessed a marked decline in the ratio of federal debt to the economy's gross national product. Third, the new approach shows that the shifting of generational burdens by policies that leave the government's budget deficit unchanged can be much larger than by policies that substantially increase the budget deficit. Finally, generational accounting succeeds, where the deficit fails, in identifying the significant financial peril to the baby boom generation and its children of permitting, in this decade, either the direct or indirect dissipation of the Social Security Trust Fund or the unbridled growth in Medicare spending.

As most Americans sense, the U.S. economy is at a crossroads. Our nation's paltry rates of saving, investment, and growth will, if they are not very rapidly raised, lead inexorably to second-rate economic status. While the federal government is not the sole cause of our economic woes, the federal government needs to take the lead in averting further economic decline. The first step is for our leaders to recognize that, notwithstanding their "balanced budgets" and "deficit-reduction targets," they—Republicans and Democrats alike—have spent four decades pursuing a generational policy that was destined to lower our nation's saving rate. This policy permitted middle-aged and older generations at the time to pay less and consume more, with the consequence that today's young generations and generations yet to come will pay a great deal more and consume a great deal less than would otherwise have been the case. The second step is for our leaders to abandon their use of misleading and outmoded short-term economic indicators, the most dangerous of which is the deficit. Pulling ourselves out of our economic hole is a task that will take decades, not years, and planning for the long term cannot be based on fiscal measures that tell us precious little about the present and next to nothing about the future. The third important step is for our leaders to put an immediate halt to the ongoing redistribution to current Americans from future Americans. But to stop this redistribution, we first need to measure it, which means we need to do, at an official level, the kind of generational accounting described in this book. The final, and most important, step is for all of us to become generationally conscious—to realize that preserving the economic welfare of our children, grandchildren, and so forth, even at our own sacrifice, is a goal worthy of our great and generous nation.

ACKNOWLEDGMENTS

———— ∎ ————

T|he book owes an intellectual debt to many economists. The largest debt is to Alan Auerbach, Professor of Economics, University of Pennsylvania. Alan and I have co-authored numerous articles and one book on fiscal policy. Much of our research is connected with the argument of this book. Indeed, those of our studies which are co-authored with Dr. Jagadeesh Gokhale, an economist at the Federal Reserve Bank of Cleveland, develop the method of generational accounting and contain many of the numerical findings reported here.

My interest in developing a meaningful and operational measure of generational policy dates to 1974, when I read a seminal paper on unfunded social security written by my thesis adviser, Martin Feldstein, Professor of Economics at Harvard University and President of the National Bureau of Economic Research. Marty's paper showed how the U.S. government, under the guise of a balanced budget, used the social security system to run up enormous implicit liabilities—which must be paid by future generations.

Marty's exposure of those liabilities opened to question the entire calculation of the government's budget deficit. It led to studies correcting the government's debt for inflation, growth, market revaluations, and government assets. Two economists who contributed significantly to that literature are Robert Eisner, Professor of Economics at Northwestern University and former President of the American Economic

Association, and Michael Boskin, Professor of Economics at Stanford University and Chairman of the Council of Economic Advisers.

Those studies were taking place against a backdrop of fiscal policy research that was becoming increasingly concerned with the long-term economic effects of fiscal policy. As part of that research, much of which was conducted in the National Bureau's Project on Taxation, Alan Auerbach and I developed an elaborate fiscal policy computer simulation model to study the effects of fiscal policies not only on current but also on future generations. This research and that of other economists, including Christophe Chamley, Professor of Economics, Boston University; Lawrence Summers, Professor of Economics, Harvard University; and David Bradford, Professor of Economics, Princeton University, and member of the President's Council of Economic Advisers, began to show the structural similarity of a variety of fiscal policies, each of which produced wildly different time-paths of government budget deficits.

The plethora of budget deficits that could be associated with the same fundamental policy stimulated my writing a series of papers on the non-uniqueness of fiscal labels. Those papers exposed the underlying problem with the use of budget deficits and also called for the construction of generational accounts. The actual development of those accounts seemed more formidable than proved, in retrospect, to be the case. My colleagues and I might not have embarked on the construction of those accounts had it not been for the very strong prodding of David Bradford. Other economists who encouraged my research on generational accounting are Armen Alchian, Professor Emeritus of Economics, UCLA; Martin Bailey, Professor of Economics, Emory University; Jagdish Bhagwati, Professor of Economics, Columbia University; Olivier Blanchard, Professor of Economics, MIT; Michael Boskin; Robert Clower, Professor of Economics, University of South Carolina; Rudiger Dornbusch, Professor of Economics, MIT; Robert Eisner; Martin Feldstein; Stanley Fischer, Professor of Economics, MIT; Benjamin

Friedman, Professor of Economics, Harvard University; George Hatsopolous, President and CEO, Thermo Electron; Jane Gravelle, Senior Specialist in Economic Policy, the Congressional Research Service of the Library of Congress; James Hines, Visiting Assistant Professor, Harvard University; Edward Leamer, Professor of Economics, UCLA; Robert Lucas, Professor of Economics, University of Chicago; George de Macedo, Minister of Finance of Portugal; Greg Mankiw, Professor of Economics, Harvard University; William Niskanen, Chairman, Cato Institute; James Poterba, Professor of Economics, MIT; John Riley, Professor of Economics, UCLA; and Marty Weitzman, Professor of Economics, Harvard University.

This book, like most others, has a number of human sine qua nons. Erwin Glikes and Peter Dougherty of The Free Press were exceptional publishers at each stage of the book's development. Their great enthusiasm for the project reinforced my own, and Peter's balanced judgment on how to frame the argument proved absolutely invaluable. In addition to Peter, I had another outstanding editor in Ron Boster, Chief of Staff to Representative Bill Gradison. Ron provided line-by-line comments on the entire manuscript. He saved me from a number of sins of omission, commission, and grammar, and his comments greatly influenced the way I wrote the book. I can't thank Ron enough.

I also received extensive and very helpful comments and suggestions from Alan Auerbach, Michael Aaronson, Economics Editor, Harvard University Press; Roger Ballentine, Esq. of Patton, Boggs & Blow; Selma Ballentine, Manager, Child Works; David Bradford; Robert W. Bramlett, Assistant Director of the Federal Accounting Standards Board; Christophe Chamley; Jagadeesh Gokhale; Jane Gravelle; Dennis Hanseman, Vice President and Managing Editor, Southwestern Publishing Company; Barbara Kotlikoff Harman, President, Nina Ricci Perfumes USA; Ruth Helms, Lecturer, Department of History, University of Colorado; Leila Heron, International Trade Specialist, Digital Equipment Corp.; James Keefe, Aquisitions Editor, Southwestern Publishing Company; Vivienne Kotlikoff, President, Kotlikoff Associates; the author Lawrence Leamer; Robert Lucas; Robert Rosenthal, Professor of Economics, Boston University; Judy Schub, Senior Coordinator, Federal Affairs Economic Team, American Association of Retired Persons; Terry Vaughn, Economics Editor, MIT Press; Carolyn Weaver, Resident Scholar and Director of Social Security and Pension Project, the American Enterprise Institute; Moira Bucciarelli, Aquisitions Associate, MIT Press; Andrew Weiss, Professor of Economics, Boston University; and Tom Woodward, Chief Economist for the Minority, House Budget Committee.

I had outstanding help on the preparation of the manuscript from my remarkable secretary, Norma Hardeo, and from my research assistants, Bhashkernand Hardeo and Ritu Nayyar. Jinyong Cai, an economist at the World Bank; Jane Gravelle; and John Sabelhaus, Professor of Economics, Towson State University, provided special, and in many cases quite extensive, data analyses, for which I am extremely grateful.

I also want to thank Boston University and the Massachusetts Institute of Technology for cofinancing my sabbatical year's leave at the MIT Department of Economics, which I spent, in large part, writing this book.

My wife, Dayle Ballentine, provided just the right mix of advice, constructive criticism, support, and love, and our infant son, Alex, produced a chorus of laughter, giggles, squeals of delight, and da-das that lifted my spirits throughout the book's preparation.

GENERATIONAL
ACCOUNTING

1

SMOKE AND MIRRORS

■

We all remember Hans Christian Andersen's story "The Emperor's New Clothes," in which an entire society believed something because everyone said it was true. The story in this book closely resembles "The Emperor's New Clothes," the principal difference being that it's not a fairy tale. Rather, it is about the mismeasurement and misreading of U.S. economic policy. The main measuring rod for economic policy in the United States and elsewhere is the fiscal, or budget, deficit. Everyone is sure the U.S. deficit is a big, big problem, especially its Washington tailors. But its tailors are having increasing difficulty spinning their yarn. There are loose threads everywhere, and the whole fabric looks as though it could easily come apart.

This book takes a strong tug on the deficit's loose threads. It unravels the perception that the deficit provides a useful guide to our past, current, or future economic policy. It also offers a new perspective on economic policy. The new perspective—entitled generational accounting—goes to the heart of why there is so much concern about the deficit, namely, its alleged impact on the welfare and spending patterns of current and future generations. It also addresses many other concerns associated with budget deficits, in-

1

cluding the level of interest rates, the rate of inflation, and the extent of national saving.

While the book centers on the U.S. economy and U.S. fiscal policy, its underlying messages about misleading policy indicators, faulty economic analysis, and the need for generational accounting are fully relevant to other countries as well. Indeed, most countries of the world, even those comprising the former Soviet Union, have adopted or are adopting a fiscal deficit as their primary gauge of macroeconomic policy. As a consequence, many countries, including Japan, Germany, France, and Great Britain have, like the United States, incorrectly blamed all manner of problems on their deficits and have systematically ignored all manner of problems that don't affect their deficits.

IS THE DEFICIT REALLY WHAT AILS US?

The United States is moving into the 1990s with some very vexing economic problems. Most of them go far beyond the short-run concern about recession that continues to plague our economy and those of other Western countries. Many stem from our insufficient saving. The United States has had a low saving rate since 1970 and a critically low saving rate since 1980. In the 1970s the United States saved, on average each year, only 8.5 percent of its output. Since 1980 it has saved only 4.1 percent of its output. While some West European countries are also over-consuming, West European countries are, on average, saving at roughly twice the U.S. rate. The Japanese appear to be saving at three or more times our rate.[1] As a result, the rest of the industrialized world is piling up income-earning assets at a much faster pace than our own. *Unless our saving behavior turns around, the United States will soon end up the poor kid on the block.*

The current low rate of U.S. saving is particularly surprising coming, as it does, at a time when the sizable baby boom generation (those born between 1947 and 1964) should be starting to put some money aside for its retirement.[2] The propensity of Americans to retire from their main job at earlier and earlier ages (retirement at age fifty-five is now common), coupled with our increasing life expectancies, spells a long period of retirement for baby boomers. If baby boomers are saving less and are likely to retire early, how will they support themselves in old age? If they think Social Security will provide them a generous level of old-age income, they should think again. In 1983 the federal government recognized that paying boomers their full Social Security benefits would require huge increases in payroll tax rates in the early part of the next century, which would fall, in large part, on the boomers' children and grandchildren. To prevent that outcome, the feds scheduled major reductions in Social Security benefits to be phased in after the turn of the century.[3] *This legislation cost baby boomers the equivalent of more than $1 trillion current dollars.*[4] America's saving shortfall is thus particularly problematic for America's boomers.

Saving less also means investing less. If America had to rely solely on its own saving to finance its investment, the addition of new plant and equipment to our existing stock of capital would be meager indeed. As it is, our investment rate, which has averaged only 5 percent of output in the years since 1980, is barely respectable, thanks only to the willingness—perhaps temporary—of Europeans and Japanese to invest their savings in the United States.[5] Increased foreign investment in the United States shows up in our national income accounting as a larger trade deficit. Instead of thanking our European and Japanese friends for adding to the number of machines and factories and jobs in this country, we have taken to "Japan bashing," faulting the level of the dollar, and generally bemoaning the size of the trade deficit. What we haven't done is address the underlying problem, namely our unwillingness to postpone current consumption in favor of saving and the investment that such additional saving would finance.

Workers are more productive when they have more capital—more and better lathes, computers, robotics, trucks, plants, and so on—with which to work. Lackluster U.S. in-

3

vestment has meant, in very concrete terms, giving many U.S. workers a smaller and more out-of-date set of tools to do their jobs than workers in other countries have. The low rate of U.S. investment is partly responsible for the slow-down in productivity growth, which, in plain English, means the slow rate at which workers' real wages have grown.[6] Indeed, many U.S. workers have seen their real wages decline since the mid-1970s as they have been outcompeted by foreign workers with a bigger and better set of tools. Other Americans have seen their wages underbid by low-wage workers in countries like Malaysia and Korea. Our increasingly poor performance in education is another culprit in reducing productivity and real wage growth. Average SAT verbal test scores are 21 points lower, and average SAT math test scores 10 points lower, than their respective averages in 1972.[7]

Disappointing productivity growth; keen foreign competition, especially in labor-intensive commodities; and educational shortcomings have hit some segments of U.S. society much harder than others. Income inequality has increased, poverty rates are up, crime is on the rise, homelessness is rampant, and social segmentation seems the order of the day. In short, America is distressed, and most fingers, at home and abroad, are pointing and have been pointing at the U.S. federal deficit as either the cause of our problems or the reason we can't address our problems.

OUR FIXATION WITH THE DEFICIT

America and the rest of the world are deeply concerned with the U.S. deficit. *Since 1981 U.S. federal debt has more than tripled.* The U.S. government now owes more than $3 trillion in official IOUs. It's hard to fathom three trillion dollars. Stacked in one pile of dollar bills, U.S. debt would rise 203 miles. Placed end to end, U.S. debt would circle the globe 11,687 times.[8] But the 3 trillion dollars aren't to be stacked or placed in a row. They are to be repaid with interest. Measured in terms of the nation's daily rate of consumption, paying off the government's debt is equivalent to all 250 million Americans going more than 300 days without buying food, clothing, or any other consumer goods and services.

Clearly, the debt is big. And it's getting bigger. The 1991 federal deficit exceeded $300 billion, the biggest deficit (to that date) in the nation's 215-year history. As the debt has grown, so has the rhetoric about its supposedly damaging effects. According to Alan Greenspan, Chairman of the Federal Reserve, the debt "has already begun to eat away at the foundation of our economic strength."[9] Prominent commentators like Ted Koppel have called the United States "the world's largest debtor nation."[10] The journalist Lawrence Malkin sees "a national debt of crippling dimensions" and envisions "our country shredding at the edges like a third world nation."[11]

WHO'S RESPONSIBLE?

One of the scariest things about the apparent blatant profligacy that seems to rule in Washington is that it has occurred under the aegis of Republican Administrations. After all, if we can't trust Republicans to be fiscally conservative, whom can we trust? The Republicans, of course, blame the Democrats, who blame the Republicans, who blame the Democrats . . . In between bouts of blaming each other, the politicians have engaged in serious wringing of hands. In 1985 they passed the Gramm–Rudman–Hollings legislation, which "mandated" automatic spending cuts (sequestration by the Administration of appropriated federal expenditures) if the deficits exceeded certain limits.

To understand how well that legislation worked, consider the original $36 billion Gramm–Rudman (short for Gramm–Rudman–Hollings) deficit target for fiscal 1990. Now guess the size of the actual 1990 federal deficit. If your guess is $100 billion or less, your jaundice coefficient is too low. If your guess was $220 billion, which is more than six times the original target, you hit the mark. How could the politicians permit a $220 billion deficit and still report they were

5

meeting the Gramm–Rudman targets? Easy: *They revised the targets.* The revised Gramm–Rudman targets for future deficits are even higher. In the 1990 federal budget agreement the 1992 Gramm–Rudman–Hollings deficit target was set at $328 billion.[12] The original proponents of deficit controls, Representative Phil Gramm, Senator Warren Rudman, and Senator Ernest Hollings, were sufficiently distressed by the moving-targets game that they actually voted against the new targets, which, nonetheless, still bear their names.

THE DEFICIT AS THE ROOT OF ALL ECONOMIC EVIL

These days it's hard to find anyone willing to say a good word about the deficits. Quite the contrary. Recession, high real interest rates, inflation, low rates of saving and investment, lackluster productivity growth, diminished international competitiveness, balance of payment problems—all are blamed on deficits. For many critics, the most alarming feature of federal debt is not its effect on current economic performance but the burden it supposedly imposes on future generations. Surely, they argue, someone will have to pay at least the interest on this debt. And won't this be our children and grandchildren?

Not everyone thinks the deficits are too high. There are still some, including a few Keynesians, who grumble that it is too low. Their belief is that larger deficits stimulate economic activity and that larger deficits are needed to restore the economy to full employment. Others don't mind deficits (increases in the debt), but worry that if the debt gets too high, it will be hard politically to run supposedly economically stimulating deficits during recessions.

Still others say we need more government spending on a variety of programs ranging from helping the poor, to sponsoring more research on alternative energy sources, to building a space shield against nuclear attack. They are dismayed by the continued refrain that, given our large deficits, we can't afford any new programs. Frustrating new spending programs by running up a large debt was, by the way, the not-so-hidden agenda of Ronald Reagan. In that respect, Reagan probably thought he had out-Republicaned even Calvin Coolidge.

THE GOLDEN RULE OF DEFICITS

The federal debt seems so big and has been accused of so many economic crimes that anyone favoring even larger deficits is likely to be strung up. Indeed, virtually all politicians have become fervent believers in, or at at least exponents of, what may be called the "Golden Rule of Deficits," according to which *the only good deficit is a zero deficit.* A zero deficit was the ultimate target of the original Gramm–Rudman–Hollings legislation, and it remains the "natural zero" underlying the ongoing debate about reducing the deficit.[13] What's so special about zero? Don't ask, just obey, or at least say you are trying to obey the Golden Rule.

But it's hard not to ask. If deficits are bad—indeed, very bad—wouldn't surpluses be good, indeed very good? Don't we really want to make the deficit a big negative number? Furthermore, why is the Golden Rule about the deficit— which is the change in the amount of government debt—why isn't it about the *level* of government debt? Having piled up more than $2 trillion dollars of additional debt in the last ten years, are we going to be satisfied if we simply keep the debt from growing, which is implicit in a balanced budget? Don't we want to reduce the outstanding debt?

One reason our deficit credo sanctifies zero may be that any other number, such as $83.67 billion, would invite haggling, jeopardizing unity among the community of believers. If an $83.67 billion deficit were taken as the proper deficit norm, someone would argue for $85.72 billion, and someone else would argue for −$93.17 billion, and someone else . . . Zero has a natural ring to it.

As with other deeply held religious beliefs, tracing the precise origins of the Golden Rule of Deficits is not easy.

One of the earliest statements of the Golden Rule was made by Adam Smith. In his *Wealth of Nations*, published in 1776, Smith wrote that "the only good budget is a balanced budget." Smith felt that governments, like households, should live within their means. David Ricardo, another of the great classical economists, also espoused the Golden Rule, but he tweaked his co-believers by pointing out that deficits may not matter. The government's debt, he argued, was a bill we passed to our descendants. If we care for our descendants, Ricardo asked, won't we also pass to them, in the form of bequests, the wherewithal to pay this bill?

For adherents to the Golden Rule of Deficits, Ricardo's misgivings were a minor heresy. Not so the views of John Maynard Keynes. Keynes wrote his own economics bible and titled it, with all the humility he could muster, *The General Theory of Employment, Interest, and Money*.[14] He wrote the book during the Great Depression, when private enterprise was anything but enterprising. Keynes figured that only the government could jump-start the economy. He advocated increased government spending—even on digging and refilling holes in the ground if necessary—to stimulate economic activity. Yes, there would be bigger deficits, but so what? The most important thing was to get back to full employment. For a world yearning for answers, even the idea of wasting resources started to sound attractive. While Keynes certainly fed the hunger for an answer, how seriously he took this and his other proposed solutions is unclear.[15]

Keynes's disciples, the Keynesians, were and are more circumspect about deficits. In the late 1930s the famous English economist John Hicks developed, and subsequent Keynesians have refined, the famous IS-LM model, a component of which is referred to (no kidding) as the "Keynesian Cross."[16] This model suggests that deficits are useful for stimulating the economy, but they can also harm the economy by raising interest rates and reducing saving and investment. In recent years, when deficit-bashing has been popular, most Keynesians have stressed the harmful effects of deficits.

SCHISMS OVER APPLYING THE GOLDEN RULE

Although the federal deficit is widely viewed as the United States' number one economic policy problem, there is no consensus as to how to measure the deficit. How can one follow the Golden Rule of Deficits if one doesn't know how to measure it? Some, like Senator Daniel Patrick Moynihan of New York, want to leave Social Security taxes and benefit payments out of the calculation. Others want to include the full value of the S&L bailout, while others are concerned about adjustments for inflation, growth, and the government's acquisition and sale of assets.

The debate has not been restricted to politicians. Economists have played a large role in lobbying for their favorite definition of the deficit. Martin Feldstein, Chairman of the Council of Economic Advisers under President Reagan, caused a huge stir in the economics profession in the 1970s by stressing the size and potential effects of the unfunded liabilities of government retirement programs, such as Social Security, and the need to take them into account. Feldstein pointed out that the government's clear promises to current workers to pay them Social Security benefits when they retire represent government liabilities, just as do promises to pay interest and principal on existing government debt.[17] True, unlike bondholders, current workers don't literally hold a piece of paper in their hand indicating their legal title to future Social Security benefits, but that is a legalistic, not an economic, distinction.[18]

Rather than leave Social Security out of the deficit, Feldstein's research suggested including Social Security's unfunded liabilities in the deficit, a treatment completely different from what occurs under the conventional (National Income and Product Account) deficit definition. *Including Social Security's unfunded liabilities would increase the reported level of national debt by $7 trillion—from more than $3 trillion to more than $10 trillion!* [19] Adding in the unfunded liabilities of the government's other major retire-

9

ment programs—the civil service and military retirement programs—would raise the $10 trillion figure to $11 trillion.[20]

Another economist who has taken aim at the measurement of the deficit is Robert Eisner, Professor of Economics at Northwestern University and a past President of the American Economic Association. Eisner spent much of the last decade carefully measuring the amount of government assets and pointing out the need to subtract the government's assets from its liabilities in determining its net debt. Eisner believes that judging the wealth position of the government by looking only at its debts makes no more sense than judging the wealth position of an individual (or a company) by looking only at his or her (its) debts. Eisner's response to Ted Koppel would probably be: "Yes Ted, we are the biggest debtor country in the world. But we're also the wealthiest country in the world, with assets far in excess of our liabilities. Indeed, U.S. net worth currently exceeds $20 trillion.[21] Show me another country with this much net worth."[22]

Unlike the correction suggested by Feldstein's research, Eisner's suggested adjustment would reduce, rather than increase, the reported size of government debt by netting the government assets against its liabilities. According to Eisner's calculations for 1984, the government's net liabilities (gross liabilities minus assets) were only $58 billion, rather than the $1.6 trillion officially reported.[23]

WHY IT MATTERS HOW WE MEASURE THE DEFICIT

Much is at stake in how we measure the deficit. Recall that the Golden Rule requires cutting spending or raising taxes to make the deficit zero. Hence, if we define the deficit in such a way that its value is close to zero, there will be little need either to cut spending or to raise taxes. Alternatively, if we define the deficit so that it is very large, we'll have to reduce spending sharply or dramatically raise taxes to obey the Golden Rule.

There are those who want to define the deficit to make it big, and there are those who want to define the deficit to make it small. While each school advances intellectual arguments, the clear ulterior motive of many of these advocates is to influence the real course of economic policy. Consider, for instance, the underlying motives of those who want to adjust the deficit for inflation and growth. Such adjustments would dramatically reduce the officially defined deficit and, according to the Golden Rule, eliminate the need for the painful spending cuts and tax increases enacted in 1990. To get a sense of the magnitude of the proposed inflation and growth adjustments, consider the 1990 traditional National Income and Product Accounts (NIPA) deficit, calculated by the U.S. Department of Commerce, of $161 billion. *The inflation and growth adjustments transform the 1990 NIPA $161 billion deficit into a $27 billion surplus!*[24] Had everyone agreed in 1990 on those adjustments, and had the government publicly announced that we were running a surplus, enactment of the 1990 budget agreement would not have been likely.

The motives of those who want to leave Social Security taxes and transfers out of the deficit's definition seem much different. Because the large baby boom cohort will be paying substantial amounts of Social Security taxes in this decade and the next, the federal budget, inclusive of Social Security, is projected to show a substantial surplus. The concern of those, like Senator Moynihan, who wish to leave Social Security out of the budget deficit (surplus) calculation is that the Administration and Congress will decide, through adherence to the Golden Rule (the best surplus, like the best deficit, is zero), to eliminate these surpluses by cutting taxes other than Social Security, by increasing transfer payments, or by increasing federal spending on goods and services—in other words, by running a much looser fiscal policy than would be appropriate.

The redefinition of the federal budget deficit to exclude Social Security has actually occurred. In 1985 Congress and

the Administration agreed to leave Social Security surpluses out of the unified budget, but to keep them in the budget for purposes of the Gramm–Rudman deficit targets. In
1990 Social Security surpluses were also excluded from the
new Gramm–Rudman deficit, which differs from the unified
budget deficit because it excludes the costs of the S&L
bailout. On the other hand, the NIPA deficit has historically
included Social Security and still does. The NIPA deficit also
includes, as of 1990, the S&L mess.

If this confuses you, it should. It must also be giving
the willies to believers in the Golden Rule. If there are
three bona fide deficits—the unified budget deficit, the
Gramm–Rudman deficit, and the NIPA deficit—which one
should be set equal to zero? The values of these three deficits are, by the way, quite different. At the end of January
1991, the Congressional Budget Office (CBO) forecast (1) a
unified budget deficit (which excludes Social Security but
includes the S&L bailout) equal to $360 billion, (2) a Gramm–
Rudman deficit (which excludes Social Security and the
S&L bailout) of $256 billion, and (3) a NIPA deficit (which
includes Social Security and the S&L bailout) of $298 bil-
lion.

The CBO also forecast a fourth deficit, namely the NIPA
deficit excluding the S&L bailout. This fourth deficit is $194
billion. The difference between $360 billion, the largest of
the three official deficits, and $194 billion is $166 billion,
roughly 3 percent of GNP. Not so long ago a 3 percent of
GNP peacetime deficit would have been viewed as an economic crime of no small proportion. *Today, the definition of
the deficit is so confused that the choices of deficits alone differ by 3 percent of GNP!*

THE SMOKE AND MIRRORS GAME

The government's official decision to remove Social Security from the deficit is hardly the first instance of redefining
the deficit. Modifying the deficit, typically to avoid hard

12

choices, has become so routine in Washington that the game has even been christened: It's called "Smoke and Mirrors." Many of our elected officials are extraordinarily skillful in playing Smoke and Mirrors. According to Dr. Robert Reischauer, Director of the Congressional Budget Office, "The Gramm–Rudman–Hollings process has ... encouraged reliance on overly optimistic economic and technical assumptions and transparent budget gimmickry."[25] Reischauer indicates that since 1985 fully half of the apparent deficit reduction has been achieved by such gimmicks as "accelerating revenue collections, selling government assets, moving agencies off budget, and altering the rules governing distribution of lump-sum retirement benefits for federal workers." Such gimmickry, by the way, would have been much worse were it not for the determined efforts of a phalanx of outstanding government economists who, together with concerned members of the Administration and Congress, have opposed such schemes and, when unsuccessful, have fought a rear-guard action by exposing the longer-term implications of "Smoke and Mirrors."[26]

One particularly resourceful play of Smoke and Mirrors entailed keeping the S&L bailout off the books and out of the public eye for five long years. Had the public been fully informed of the magnitude of the problem earlier, it might have forced the government to address the causes of the S&L debacle much sooner. That could have limited the bailout costs to about $25 billion. Instead, the problem burgeoned over the course of five years into a roughly $200 billion loss.

The following brief account of how Congress hid the S&L bailout is hard to follow. It was supposed to be. Don't necessarily try to understand the details, just read it for its heuristic value. To quote a senior government economist who generously provided the author with an in-depth written account of the S&L gambit: "If this is confusing it's not my fault; the whole thing from beginning to end has been ridiculous."

THE S&L BAILOUT

FSLIC (pronounced FIS LICK) stands for Federal Saving and Loan Insurance Corporation. Before its dissolution in 1989, FSLIC guaranteed the money we deposited with federally insured S&Ls even if the people running those S&Ls lost the money we entrusted to them. The S&L managers have, indeed, been losing money, and for a long time. Since the mid-1960s S&Ls have found themselves with assets represented by low-interest-paying long-term mortgages, and liabilities represented by high-interest-paying short-term deposits. As the profit picture got worse, particularly in the early 1980s, the S&L managers began to make more and more risky loans in a desperate attempt to salvage their situation.

Government regulators were supposed to keep an eye on the managers and make sure they didn't squander our money. Well, in the 1980s the regulators, for several reasons, including our zest for deregulation, let down their guard.[27] Things got so bad that a number of very high rollers, some of whom were rather shady characters, ended up running quite large S&Ls. (One, by the way, was a magician. He used his depositors' money to add to his personal collection of magic tricks and magic memorabilia.)

By the mid-1980s everyone knew FSLIC had a problem. At that time most experts thought it was at least a $25 billion problem; that is, certain troubled S&Ls, because of bad loans, were short $25 billion. Had their depositors shown up at the banks' doors and demanded their funds, Uncle Sam would have had to shell out $25 billion on the spot. While some depositors in the troubled S&Ls asked for their money immediately, others waited, because they knew the government was standing behind their savings accounts. So the situation was one in which the S&L depositors held pieces of paper, namely their savings account statements, which collectively totaled about $25 billion, all of which was owed directly by the government. Now those pieces of paper, called S&L "savings account statements," were in no important way different from other pieces of paper called "govern-

14

ment treasury bills." Both sets of pieces of paper gave their holders a claim on the U.S. treasury. But the $25 billion owed to S&L depositors was not on the books.

Since the S&L depositors knew that the government stood behind their deposits, they did not move to withdraw their money, which gave the S&Ls wide latitude to invest as they wished. With many of the S&Ls insolvent, their owners had no money of their own to lose, and so actually had an incentive to engage in riskier lending—a recipe for greater losses to the government. But to close down those S&Ls the government would have to pay off the depositors and explicitly recognize the $25 billion of IOUs. Adding $25 billion to the government's official debt would have proved too embarrassing at a time when our leaders in Washington were already publicly acknowledging deficits of more than $200 billion and passing legislation with quixotic titles like "the Balanced Budget Act of 1985." Instead they decided to deal "off budget" with the problem of making good on the saving accounts. They also decided they would publicly acknowledge only $11 billion of the $25 billion problem. The story of the S&L deficit cover-up[28] then became even more complex:

A scheme was prepared under which a quasi-private entity called The Financing Corporation (FICO) would borrow what FSLIC needed and simply hand the funds over to FSLIC. FICO first obtained about $1 billion dollars from the Federal Home Loan Bank System (FHLB). With this FICO bought $11 billion (face value) of 30-year zero-coupon bonds from the Treasury. At the same time it was buying the zeros, FICO sold conventional coupon-bearing securities of its own in the same amount and at the same maturity. The purpose of having FICO hold the zeros was to provide its creditors with an ironclad guarantee that the principal on its borrowings would be repaid. Interest payments on the FICO bonds would come out of higher insurance premiums assessed on the thrifts by FSLIC. This arrangement met the criteria used for keeping the borrowing off-budget, and FSLIC now had $11 billion to spend. Since they were not explicit full-faith and credit obligations of the Government, the FICO obligations carried a higher yield; this was the cost of keeping them off-budget.

This Rube Goldberg funding mechanism operated little more than a year when it became clear that a lot more money would be needed to clean up the mess. A new entity called the Resolution Trust Corporation (RTC) was to replace FSLIC in the job of cleaning up. It would get finances from a FICO-like entity called REFCORP. But, at this point, according to our government economist, ". . . no one could plausibly pretend that enough funds could be collected in increased insurance premiums to cover the interest costs on this much borrowing." So REFCORP would have to get money for interest from the Treasury, which would show up on-budget and, therefore, in the deficit. An amount of $50 billion was the sum designated for the cleanup.

While many members of Congress wanted to put all $50 billion of the S&L debt on-budget, the Administration balked. So a compromise was struck under which $30 billion of the $50 billion would be kept off-budget through additional FICO financing, and the remaining $20 billion would be put on-budget. But there was a problem with this compromise. Putting the $20 billion on-budget would trigger Gramm–Rudman sequestration. So to avoid the sequester the $20 billion was put on-budget in the waning days of fiscal 1989 when it would occur too late to cause any of the enforcement mechanisms in Gramm–Rudman to kick in.

By the Fall of 1990 RTC had used most of the $50 billion. More was needed. By this time the problem had reached upwards of $200 billion. But the spending scheme could not be repeated. The FHLB did not have enough money to advance REFCORP to buy more zeros, so the off-budget, zero-coupon bond laundering scheme could no longer be used. So the decision was made in the 1990 budget agreement to put any new borrowing for the S&L bailout on the books (i.e., to include it in the official deficit). But the substantial additional borrowing needed would easily lead to the violation of the new contemplated Gramm–Rudman targets. So the government simply decided to leave this borrowing out of the new Gramm–Rudman deficit; i.e., to ignore this part of the government's deficit for purposes of Gramm–Rudman.

THE MOUNTING FRUSTRATION WITH SMOKE AND MIRRORS

The public is catching on to the Smoke and Mirrors game. Some people worry that Congress and the Administration are playing the game to avoid hard choices. Others worry that they are playing the game to invent problems that don't really exist. Still others question whether Congress and the Administration, in their deficit-definition game, have completely lost sight of our real economic problems and policy. In a Time/CNN poll[29] during the 1990 budget debate, five hundred adult Americans were asked: "If the Bush Administration and Congress reach agreement on a deficit plan, do you expect A) one that avoids the real issue or B) a meaningful accord?" Fully 70 percent of the respondents chose A. In the same poll 30 percent of respondents responded "no" to the question "Do you think the budget deficit really does matter?"

The public is also getting angry. In President Bush's September 12, 1990, address to a joint session of Congress he stated: "America is tired of phony deficit reduction, or promise-now, save-later plans. Enough is enough. It is time for a program that is credible and real." Many Americans may find the idea of Congress playing definition and other games with the deficit outrageous. "Just leave it alone!" they might say. "The deficit's definition has served this nation well for over two hundred years." The problems with this view are first that the deficit hasn't served this nation well in the past, and second that the definition of what is the deficit has evolved over time. In 1776 we didn't have such institutions as the unfunded civil service retirement program, which raise difficult issues about defining the deficit.

The Smoke and Mirrors game is a troubling commentary on Washington. But it also raises doubts about the usefulness of the deficit as a measure of fiscal policy. If there are so many different ways to define the deficit, how can we be sure we've chosen the correct one? Why are we changing

17

both the unified deficit and the Gramm–Rudman deficit? Did we have the wrong definition in the past? *Why are we trying to set the deficit to zero if we aren't even sure what it measures, let alone why it should be zero?*

THE DEFICIT—A NUMBER IN SEARCH OF A CONCEPT

Is there a fundamental economic concept that the deficit measures? If so, there should be a single conceptually correct way to measure it. If not, we need to ask what concept the deficit is supposed to measure and then determine a measure consistent with that concept. Unfortunately, from the perspective of standard (neoclassical) economic theory the deficit is not a well-defined economic concept. This is meant in a mathematical sense.[30] Neoclassical models of the economy invariably consist of a set of equations describing the behavior of households, firms, and the government over time. But there is an infinite number of different ways to label the terms entering the models' equations, each of which produces a different time sequence of deficits, with no implication for the models' predictions about the effects of government policy.[31] While we have already discussed a bewildering variety of different definitions of and adjustments to the deficit, *economic theory tells us that by choosing the right words we can literally make the deficit anything we want.*

As an analogy, take the case of two economics professors, one American and one French, presenting the same model (set of equations) to their students. The American will refer to the terms in the equations using English and the Frenchman will use French, but the real workings of the model will be the same. From the perspective of economic theory, the fiscal labels one applies to one's model and the resulting deficits are just as arbitrary and noneconomic as is the choice of whether to use French or English to discuss the model.

A good example of the arbitrary nature of fiscal labels arises in the case of Social Security. The government can (and does) label our Social Security contributions "taxes" and our Social Security benefits "transfers." Suppose, instead, it called our Social Security contributions "loans to the government" and our Social Security benefits "return of principal and interest" on those "loans," plus an additional "old-age tax" equal to the difference between actual benefits and the "return of principal plus interest" on the "loans." In this case, which makes every bit as much sense as the standard labels, the reported deficit would be entirely different—not only with respect to its level, but also with respect to its changes over time. Had the government, historically, simply used different words to describe Social Security, but otherwise kept its policies the same, we would have had an entirely different postwar sequence of deficits. And the government's stock of debt would now be roughly $7 trillion larger than its currently reported value.

Would you care if the government changed its words but didn't change the amount it took from you when you were young or gave back to you when you were old, nor change the likelihood that you would pay and receive those sums?[32] Not if you are rational. If you are rational all you will care about is how much you have to give the government and how much it gives you back. You don't really care what words it attaches to the money it gives you or the money you give it.

This is not an isolated example. Every dollar the government takes in or pays out is labeled in a manner that is economically arbitrary. As a consequence, the unified federal deficit is simply one of countless possible deficits, each of which depends on the economically unimportant issue of what words (not actions) the government chooses. While the government now has three different official deficit definitions, there is no limit to the number of official or unofficial deficit definitions Congress and the Administration could adopt.

Thus the problem of defining the deficit runs far deeper than most people, including most economists, have believed to be the case. While several of the adjustments recommended by economists, such as those for growth and infla-

19

tion, do not involve the question of labeling receipts and payments, other recommended adjustments do. For example, the suggestion that the $7 trillion of unfunded Social Security liabilities be put on the books corresponds to using the words "government borrowing" to label workers' contributions to these programs and using the words "repayment of principal plus interest" to label most of the benefits paid by them.

If you are starting to doubt whether the government's deficit is likely to have any value as an indicator of the stance of U.S. fiscal policy, you are getting the point. Anyone trying to relate the deficit to the economy's past performance, be it economic growth, interest rates, inflation, investment, or saving, must face the fact that there is an infinite array of alternative historical series of deficits that could be used in such analyses. The fact that only a small subset of historical deficit series, namely those put out by the government, have been written down and are easy to look up, does not imbue such deficits with any special value for analytical purposes. A countless number of additional historical deficit series are sitting in the wings waiting to be constructed and mistakenly related to issues of substance.

WHAT KIND OF ECONOMIC POLICY MEASURE DO WE SEEK?

Obviously, any measure of economic policy whose value depends on the government's vocabulary, rather than its behavior, is not going to get us very far. If we are going to replace the deficit with a meaningful metric, we need first to ask what question about government behavior the deficit is supposed to answer. The question, quite simply, is which generations are going to pay for the government's current and projected spending on goods and services?[33] Will those of us alive today (current generations) pay a reasonable share of this spending, or will we foist most of the bill onto our children, grandchildren, and so on (future generations)? And given the amount we agree to shoulder, how will that amount be divided among those of us who are young, middle-aged, and old? As discussed in Chapter 4, the question: Which generations will pay? is one of four fundamental questions about fiscal policy the government needs to be asking.

Raising the question "Who will pay?" gets to the point that the public understands, but most politicians love to avoid—namely, that letting one set of Americans off the hook in meeting the government's bills means putting some other set of today's or tomorrow's Americans on the hook. Our politicians are fond of telling us whom they are helping but are nowhere required to state whom they are hurting. The desire to force politicians to disclose the costs as well as the benefits of their proposals underlies initiatives for a balanced budget amendment as well as the "pay-as-you-go" provisions of the 1990 budget agreement. Unfortunately, as described later in the book, neither the balanced budget amendment nor the "pay-as-you-go" strictures of the recent budget deal will necessarily impose any discipline on the policy process. What is needed to help instill real fiscal discipline is full and direct disclosure of the gains and losses from public policies to different generations.

Knowing which generations will pay is also critical for economic stabilization policy. Obviously, reducing fiscal burdens on current generations at the price of increased burdens on future generations will immediately stimulate the spending of current generations on consumer goods and services—what economists term consumption. In addition, policies that redistribute solely among those now alive can expand current consumption demand. The reason is that older generations, because they have fewer years left to live, have larger propensities to consume their available resources than do younger generations. Hence, taking money from the young and handing it to the old will, on balance, raise aggregate consumption. Stimulating current consumption demand may be needed, periodically, to pull the economy out of recessions. But if deficits can't answer the question of which generations pay, then they can't be of much use in stabilizing the economy.

One reason the deficit is deficient as a measure of economic stimulus is that, as a cash-flow concept, it completely ignores the future. If the government were to announce a small tax cut this year coupled with a very large tax increase in future years, the deficit would increase, but the public may feel a lot poorer and reduce its spending. Another reason is that "revenue-neutral" tax changes and "pay-as-you-go" tax–transfer schemes can leave the deficit unchanged but nonetheless redistribute huge sums from generations with small consumption propensities to those with large consumption propensities, and thereby greatly stimulate private spending on goods and services—what economists call "aggregate demand."

GENERATIONAL ACCOUNTING

Generational accounting measures directly the amount current and future generations can, under existing public policies, be expected to pay over time in net taxes (taxes paid less transfer payments received) to the government. This type of analysis is essential if we really want to know the burden we are imposing on future generations. It is also critical for understanding how economic policy directly affects national saving and collaterally influences investment, interest rates, and growth. As just indicated, the smaller the share of the government's ongoing spending bill that we current generations agree to pay, the more those of us alive today will spend on immediate consumption, and the smaller will be our nation's saving.

Generational accounting is neoclassical economic theory's prescription for how to measure who will pay for the government's spending. The theory is quite clear about what does and does not enter into the calculation of the generational stance of economic policy. Hence, it indicates precisely how to deal with each of the deficit bugaboos (the objections/corrections that have been raised/offered concerning the measurement of the deficit). The point should be stressed, however, that generational accounting is not some type of fix-up for the deficit. As a measure of the government's generational policy or of any other aspect of economic policy, the deficit is, quite simply, hopeless.

Advantages of Generational Accounting

Generational accounting has the following attractive features:

1. Unlike deficit (cash-flow) accounting, generational accounting is not an arbitrary accounting exercise. Rather, it answers the following two well-defined economic questions: How does the projected fiscal burden on future generations compare with that on current generations? and How do changes in policy alter the fiscal burdens facing different generations of Americans? Since it addresses economic questions, generational accounting, properly applied, is invariant to the words with which we choose to label government receipts and payments.

2. Generational accounting considers the entire gamut of government economic policies. The deficit, in contrast, has missed, in the case of the United States, most of the fiscal policy action in the postwar period, including the dramatic "balanced budget" growth in government spending in the 1950s; the huge expansion of "pay-as-you-go" federal government retirement programs in the fifties, sixties, and seventies; the major switch in the last four decades away from consumption taxation toward income taxation; the elimination, through the 1983 amendments to the Social Security system, of almost $1 trillion dollars' worth, in present value, of baby boomer Social Security retirement benefits; and the very significant generational impact of the "revenue-neutral" Tax Reform Act of 1986.

3. Generational accounts change only when policy really changes. The deficit, in contrast, can change even though economic policy hasn't changed. As indicated, Congress is now scrambling to redefine the federal deficit in fear of the spending spree that could arise when, later this decade, Social Security surpluses push the traditional federal deficit

(which includes Social Security) into surplus. Congress wants to hide these surpluses, because it knows, in its heart of hearts, that the impending surpluses will not really reflect a more generationally responsible economic policy.

4. Generational accounting obeys the "No Free Lunch" dictum. Somebody has to pay for the government's spending, and somebody has to pay for the government's beneficence to particular generations. Generational accounting makes clear who is being hurt as well as who is being helped. Any policy that lets some generations pay less shows up, explicitly in the generational accounts, as placing a commensurately larger burden on other generations. Imagine Congress and the Administration being forced to state publicly not only which generations it intends to help with its proposals, but also which generation(s) it intends to hurt by the same proposals!

5. Generational accounting would bring into the light of day legislative time bombs politicians often enact in the dark of night. In their zeal to protect Social Security recipients from inflation, Richard Nixon, Wilbur Mills, and the rest of the Congress, apparently inadvertently, double-indexed Social Security against inflation in the early 1970s. The Nixon-Mills pas-de-deux made the Social Security benefits of successive new retirees rise at a rate faster than the real growth rate of the economy. That couldn't be sustained, so in 1977 the government reformed Social Security and planted another, rather hidden, time bomb. This time bomb cut the real benefits of new retirees starting in 1981.[34] It produced the outrage voiced in recent years by the so-called notch babies. The notch babies are recent retirees who feel they should be as well treated by Social Security as those who had recently retired under the Nixon-Mills era rules. Time bombs are not just a thing of the past. Baby boomers face two Social Security time bombs, both of which were created by the 1983 Social Security legislation. The first is fairly well known. Starting in 2000 there will be a gradual two-year increase in the age Americans must attain in order to be eligible for full normal retirement benefits. The second

24

time bomb concerns the income taxation of baby boomers' Social Security benefits; the government has sneakily chosen not to index for inflation the level of retiree's income beyond which Social Security benefits are taxable under the federal income tax. As a consequence, a much greater share of baby boomers' Social Security benefits will be taxed away by the feds than is the case for current retirees.

6. Generational accounts personalize the government's behavior. There are a lot of zeros in our almost 6,000,000,000,000-dollar ($6 trillion) economy and our roughly 300,000,000,000-dollar ($300 billion) federal deficit. What do all the zeros in the government's statistics mean to you and me? Wouldn't it be better if the government simply indicated how much it intends to take from each of us, both now and in the future? Generational accounting heads in that direction. In specifying the average amount members of each generation will have to pay, it provides Americans with a much better sense of their personal treatment by the government.

7. Generational accounting can help both individuals and the government plan for the future. Each of us faces lots of economic uncertainty. The government should be in the business of mitigating, not magnifying, that uncertainty. But in obsessing on its current cash flow, the government rarely looks into the future. In the case of Social Security, where long-term planning is really required, the politicians seem to need a short-run financial crisis to get them even to raise the subject. This head-in-the-sand mentality leaves uncertain precisely how policy will evolve. Generational accounting forces us to talk today about what we intend to do tomorrow.

8. Finally, generational accounting automatically deals with each of the major concerns raised by those who, unlike your author, think the deficit is conceptually sound but simply needs adjustment. It deals with inflation by measuring all payments and receipts in inflation-adjusted (constant) dollars. It nets all the government's real assets against all its real liabilities (including liabilities such as the S&L bailout)

25

to form the value of government net worth, which is ultimately used to help determine the burden on future generations. It directly considers the government's implicit obligations to make future transfer payments (e.g. on food stamps) and to carry out future spending (e.g. on national parks) and the public's implicit obligations to pay future taxes. It accounts for state and local as well as federal government fiscal policy. Finally, in projecting transfer payments, spending, and taxes through time and the implied burden on future generations, generational accounting deals with how the levels of these fiscal variables will grow through time, including growth arising from demographic change.

Understanding Generational Accounting

Microeconomics argues that the decisions we make today take into account how the government is treating us right now, but also how it is likely to treat us in the future. For example, our current consumption and saving decisions should reflect not only this year's taxes, but also future taxes and transfers, such as Social Security benefits. Hence, understanding the government's influence on our current behavior requires considering how it is likely to treat us in the future. And this is true no less for those of us who are poor than for those of us who are rich.

The idea of generational accounting is to summarize with one number the net amount we are currently paying the government (federal, state, and local) along with the net amount we are likely to pay the government down the road. A generational account is the difference between all current and future taxes (payroll taxes, income taxes, sales taxes, and so forth) paid to the government and all current and future transfers (welfare, Social Security, Medicare, unemployment insurance, and so on) received from the government, combined as a present value and averaged over all members of a specific age group. "Present value" means "the equivalent amount of money that would have to be paid today." To understand present value, consider the value today (the

26

present value) of receiving x dollars at a particular date in the future. This is determined by calculating how much money one would have to invest today, say in a money market account, so that at the specified date in the future the principal plus interest earned on the money would equal x. Thus if the annual interest rate is 10 percent, the present value of $110 received a year from now is $100, since investing $100 today will yield $110 a year from now.

To grasp in concrete terms the notion of a generational account, consider the $176,224 account for forty-year-old males in 1989. This figure is the difference, in present value, between the average amount of taxes forty-year-old males could expect to pay to the government over their remaining lives and the average amount of transfers from the government they could expect to receive over their remaining lives.[35] Thus the government's treatment of forty-year-olds in 1989 was equivalent to the government's taking $176,224, on average, from forty-year-olds in 1989 and never bothering them (taxing them or transferring to them) again.[36]

According to the neoclassical model, in making his 1989 consumption and saving decisions, the average forty-year-old male would primarily consider his lifetime treatment by the government (the $176,224) and would not be particularly concerned by policies that changed the timing of his net tax payments, provided those policies left the present value of his net payments (his lifetime treatment) the same. For example, if the government took more from him this year, but returned in the future the additional amount taken with interest, this would leave both the present value of his net payments and his economic position unchanged. Thus, microeconomic theory tells us that as long as the government is properly adjusting for interest, individuals don't care when they pay, but rather how much they pay. (This statement ignores the issue of uncertainty, but an analogous statement holds when people's future treatment at the hands of the government is uncertain.) Micro theory also tells us that individuals don't care what words the government attaches to the monies it takes and hands back. Again, what matters is not the words used, but how much (in present value) is given and how much (in present value) is received. But the words the government uses make all the difference in the world to the deficits it reports through time.

Using Generational Accounts to Determine the Burden on Future Generations

The Economics Nobel Laureate Milton Friedman's famous line "There is no free lunch" applies in spades to the government's activities. The government, like any individual or household, must pay for what it spends, both today and in the future, on goods and services. This includes copy machines, the White House telephone operators, and upkeep of the national parks. Where does the government get the money to pay for its consumption spending through time? Well, the government may have some net assets (assets less liabilities) on hand. The remainder it needs to get from either current or future generations.

A simple equation, $A = B + C + D$, summarizes the above statements. The term A stands for the value today (the present value) of the government's current and future spending (its spending through time). B stands for government's net assets. C stands for the value today (the present value) of the current and future net tax payments of generations alive right now. And D stands for the value today (the present value) of the future net tax payments of generations yet to come.

This equation is what economists call the "government's intertemporal (over time) budget constraint." If we have dollar amounts for the terms A, B, and C, we can subtract B plus C from A to determine D, the amount, in present value, future generations will have to pay in the aggregate, that is, the total burden we are foisting on future generations.

With a little bit of effort one can determine values of B (the government's net wealth) and A (the projected present value of government consumption). Now the term C (the amount in present value paid by current generations) is simply the sum of all the generational accounts of different age groups currently alive multiplied by the number of people in those age groups. This term can also be calculated. Hence, one can arrive at the value for D, the present value charged to future generations.

A tougher question is how the total bill handed to future generations will be spread over the particular generations showing up in the future. No one knows for sure, but let's assume the burden is spread smoothly across all future generations so that each new generation's burden keeps pace with the economy's rate of productivity growth. Then, knowing the total amount future generations will pay and projecting the number of people in the future, one can determine the growth-adjusted bill, or generational account, for average Americans born in the future.

As described in subsequent chapters, the generational accounts (lifetime net tax burdens) of future generations appear to be about 21 percent larger than those of current newborn generations. This means that U.S. generational policy is considerably out of balance. Unless U.S. economic policy (federal, state, and local) is changed, and changed radically, future young generations will bear a much bigger burden than will current newborns.

Future generations will already pay more because their taxes will depend, in large part, on their incomes, and their incomes will be higher simply because of real (after inflation) economic growth. Making them pay yet an additional 21 percent larger lifetime tax bill may not be politically feasible. After all, why should our children and grandchildren agree to pay a much bigger share of their lifetime incomes than we intend to shoulder? The reaction of our children, when they reach voting age, is likely to be to try to use the tax-transfer system to shift a portion of their burden back onto us. We baby boomers (your author is one, too) need to be concerned about the implications of what is learned from generational accounting. If we don't deal with them now, they are likely to come back to haunt us in our old age.

While generational policy needs our concerted attention, the situation is not quite as bad as many alarmists have made out. There are policies, discussed later in the book, that can correct the generational imbalance in ways that will cause pain, but not extreme pain. The point is to adopt those policies as soon as possible and to stick with them for a number of decades. This is particularly important in light of the impending Social Security surpluses. By using generational accounts, rather than the deficit, to track progress in reducing the burden on future generations, we will avoid misinterpreting the impending federal budget surpluses (caused by the Social Security surpluses) as indicative of a reduced fiscal burden on our descendents.

IF THE DEFICIT IS NOT GROUNDED IN BASIC ECONOMICS, WHY IS IT SO POPULAR AMONG ECONOMISTS?

There are several reasons why the deficit continues to be used by economists to discuss fiscal policy. To begin with, many economists, including virtually all economists talking to the media about the economy, are Keynesian economists, and the government's deficit plays a key role in Keynesian economics. As previously mentioned, the traditional Keynesian model is not grounded in microeconomics, which deals with the economic behavior of individual households and firms.[37] Rather, it represents a set of *a priori* postulates about the interrelationship of macroeconomic variables, such as employment or saving. In effect, Keynesian economics simply asserts that the deficit influences this or that macro variable in a particular manner.

Since there is no fundamental theory underlying the Keynesian model, the definition of the deficit is up for grabs. Most Keynesian economists simply rely on the official deficit, although which official deficit to use is becoming increasingly unclear. Others consider what is called the "full employment deficit"—the conventional deficit adjusted to reflect the difference between taxes and spending if the economy were at full employment. Still others prefer a deficit that is corrected for inflation, growth, and government

30

assets. While Keynesian economists disagree about which deficit to use, they are all sure their choice of the deficit provides a meaningful index of the economy's economic policy.

If pressed, Keynesians will assert that the households that inhabit their paradigm are either so extremely myopic or so highly cash-constrained that their consumption decisions are based only on their immediate cash-flow, namely, their immediate disposable incomes. In a world of such households, a cash-flow measure of economic policy like the deficit might make some sense. Given this underlying view about household behavior, the failure of Keynesian economists to question the value of the deficit is not surprising.

The same is not true of neoclassical economists. Unfortunately, neoclassical economists are just beginning to understand that the deficit's definition is entirely arbitrary from the standpoint of the economic theory they utilize. These economists, including the author, were so inured to the notion that the terms "deficit," "taxes," and "transfer payments" were meaningful economic concepts that they failed, until recently, to realize that different words could be applied to the same government behavior. This extremely simple point was right in front of everyone's eyes, but was so close that it was very hard to see. Your author tripped over the point in the course of studying, within formal models, the dynamic effects of different fiscal policies on saving, growth, and generational welfare.[38] He learned that fiscal policies featuring radically different deficits could have identical effects on all economic variables. He then realized that the fiscal policies being studied were identical, and that the different deficits were resulting solely from different choices of how to label government receipts and payments.

Moving the economics profession and the policy-makers away from using the deficit as a measure of fiscal policy will not be easy. As in "The Emperor's New Clothes," there are a lot of tailors who have specialized in this material. Even neoclassical economists (your author included) have mistakenly believed that the Keynesian model provided a good shorthand for neoclassical economic policy analysis. The rational expectations revolution in economics in the 1970s, spearheaded by Professors Robert Lucas of the University of Chicago and Thomas Sargent of Stanford University, successfully discredited Keynesian empirical research because of its implicit assumption that households form irrational expectations about the future. But the problems with using the Keynesian model for correctly gauging the true stance of fiscal policy have largely gone unnoticed.[39]

Another reason neoclassical economists find it hard to abandon the deficit in their policy discussions is that the entire postwar generation, including members of the media, has been educated in college to believe the deficit measures something economic and something important. Even though people may have doubts about the deficit, especially when they see so many different definitions of it, their sense that the deficit tells them something about the economy is deeply ingrained. Rather than try to reeducate the public, many neoclassical economists have taken the easy route of talking to the public in the language the public knows—which, in this case, is the conventional language of taxes, transfers, and the deficit. Given the Golden Rule of Deficits and the fact that following the Golden Rule doesn't always lead in the policy direction these economists desire, they respond by doing what members of Congress have done, namely, manipulating the definition of the deficit. Of course, talking down to the public in this manner ends up reinforcing the notion that a deficit, somehow defined, tells us something useful.

ARE PEOPLE AS MYOPIC OR CASH-CONSTRAINED AS THE KEYNESIANS SUGGEST?

According to the Keynesians, households decide how much to consume and save primarily on the basis of their current disposable income; if the government cuts taxes and runs deficits, consumers will experience an increase in their disposable incomes and will therefore increase their current consumption. While considering one's current income sounds sensible, the Keynesian model also assumes that households partly or fully ignore their future incomes in making their current consumption decisions. Hence, if consumers learn with absolute certainty that their incomes in the future will be lower by precisely the amount (adjusted for interest) of their current tax break, they will, according to the Keynesian model, always increase their current consumption anyway.

Keynesians justify this assumption about behavior by asserting that households are either irrationally myopic or that they are cash-constrained—that they have no savings to use to finance current consumption, nor can they borrow against future income to finance current consumption. According to Keynesians, households value a dollar today more highly than a dollar plus interest tomorrow. Given its focus on current cash-flows, it is not surprising that a cash-flow measure of government activity—the deficit—should play such an important role in the Keynesian model.

In contrast to the Keynesian model, the microeconomics underlying the neoclassical model is based on the premise that people make consumption and saving decisions rationally, which means, among other things, that they fully consider their future incomes as well as their current incomes in making these decisions. This is not to say that we foresee with certainty our future incomes, only that we think rationally about what our future incomes may be. Thus, the neoclassical view considers how we act today, taking into account, rather than ignoring, the future, including our future treatment at the hands of the government.

Neoclassical economists also question the notion that the United States is living hand-to-mouth, in other words, that the population is severely cash-constrained. They point out that even if everyone in the United States completely stopped working, the country as a whole could finance its current rate of consumption for roughly five years without borrowing a cent. How? By spending its more than $20 trillion in net worth (assets less liabilities). Certainly the United

States as a whole is not cash-constrained, nor, according to virtually all empirical studies, is more than a small segment of American society.[40]

A QUICK GUIDE TO THIS BOOK

Concern about the deficits and the broader issue of generational policy has arisen against the backdrop of our very disturbing economic problems. While the U.S. economy stayed out of recession for almost a decade, many Americans experienced declines in their living standards in the 1980s, and others worry if they will be next. Our national rates of saving, investment, and productivity growth are too low and have been too low for too long. The optimism of the Reagan years seems to have given way to a gnawing pessimism about America's future economic position, particularly its relative standard of living. The next two chapters discuss U.S. economic malaise and the widespread view that the U.S. federal deficit is chiefly responsible for our economic woes.

Chapter 4 looks through the deficit angst to our underlying concerns about economic policy. It identifies the four fundamental types of economic policy that we should, according to economic theory, be worried about. This discussion puts generational accounting in context. Generational accounting describes one of the four policies, namely, the government's treatment of different generations. As such, it doesn't pretend to answer all policy questions.

Chapter 4 also points out (1) that none of the four types of policy bears any relationship to the deficit and (2) that our government is either not measuring or not measuring correctly any of these policies. From the perspective of economic theory, our conduct of economic policy is akin to driving in Los Angeles with a map of New York. Our map of New York is highly detailed, with multiple overlays and exquisite coloring, but its use will surely get us lost.

Chapter 4 also draws the potential connections between

generational policy and the critical problems plaguing the U.S. economy. Chapter 5 discusses the use of generational accounts to measure the generational stance of U.S. policy. It presents baseline accounts for 1989 and considers how alternative policies, including the 1990 budget agreement, alter those accounts. The tables in that chapter permit each reader to look at his or her demographic group and obtain a personal understanding of the economic impact of different policy options.

While Chapter 5's policy experiments with generational accounts dispel the myth that deficits have any intrinsic relationship to generational policy, Chapter 6 shows why the deficit's definition is up for grabs; it addresses directly the fundamentally noneconomic character of government deficits. It asks the reader to consider U.S. fiscal affairs from the perspective of a Martian who hovers over the United States, observes transactions between the public sector and the public, but, to his great fortune, can't understand English and therefore can't understand what the government says it's doing. Playing Martian is helpful for seeing that the government's reported deficit depends entirely on the words it uses, not on the economic policies it conducts.

If the words our government used to produce its deficits somehow coincided with the policy it was conducting, Chapter 6's castigation of the deficit could be dismissed as a useful point of theory, but not one with real-world significance. Such is not the case. Chapter 7 examines postwar U.S. economic policy and demonstrates that enormous deficits have been reported when generational policy was relatively tight (conservative), and tiny deficits have been reported when generation policy was very loose (liberal).

Chapter 8 applies the new generational perspective to the issue of Social Security's prospective treatment of the baby boomers. The chapter examines a range of alternative Social Security scenarios, including Senator Moynihan's recently debated proposal to cut payroll taxes, as well as several variants. It also considers the implications for baby boomers of

35

failing to gain control of health care costs. Finally, Chapter 9 summarizes the book's main argument and expresses the hope that Hans Christian Andersen's sobering conclusion to his fairy tale will not be echoed in the government's response to this book.

2

U.S. ECONOMIC MALAISE

———— ∎ ————

T he Teflon President is the name we gave to smiling, self-assured Ronald Reagan. Was this really a man to whom no problem would stick, or were we simply letting his problems—which were our problems—slide out of sight? After worrying through the Johnson, Nixon, Ford, and Carter years, we were just as eager in the 1980s to have a reassuring Ronald Reagan coat us in Teflon as he was to have us coat him. And the coating helped. Collective optimism is a powerful force for coordinating economic actions, and the spell of optimism that Reagan cast on the country fueled the longest peacetime recovery on record.

But down deep many Americans worried about what the late Walter Heller described as a "haunted prosperity." They worried about businesses financed with "junk" bonds, the number of corporate takeovers, the inevitable housing market crash, the trade deficits, the volatility of the stock market, our failure to save, our treatment of the poor, the continued decay in inner cities, the potential for inflation, and the timing and severity of the next recession. They also wondered when their real pay would start to increase.

If we felt secure in "staying the course" by electing George Bush, we certainly weren't sure the course could be stayed. Few of us saw more than a handful of the President's "thousand points of light," and even the President seemed to have problems with his "vision thing." As the 1990s began, we also started feeling poor. Governments at all levels were telling us they were out of money and needed to raise taxes and cut services. The federal government came up with a five-year half-trillion-dollar deficit-reduction package that went far beyond the rather benign "revenue enhancers" of recent years. Then the recession came. A good fraction of those hard hit were white-collar workers, many of whom had never dreamed of standing on unemployment lines.[1]

Feeling poor is bad enough, but the government's alleged debt problems have also made us feel that we've lost control. Addressing our problems costs money, but none of us seem to have any money we're willing to give, either now or in the future. Worse yet, we seem unable or unwilling to pay for things the government has already purchased. Past federal borrowing has, we are told, saddled us with more than $12,000 in debt per man, woman, and child in the country. Even those Americans still brave enough to call themselves "liberals" have bought into the need for budgetary restraint. *The New Republic* in 1989 could only muster the lament: "Even if big initiatives must be postponed to pay for the Reagan deficit, that doesn't mean Democrats have to stop talking about them."[2]

Have we lost control of the economy as well as economic policy? Could the debt overhang keep the economy from growing? Listen to *Newsweek's* economics columnist, Robert Samuelson: The "threats are real. The burden of repaying all our debts could cripple economic growth and even trigger a banking crisis."[3] Could the debt keep the economy from investing? Listen to Wall Street's Peter Peterson: The "United States has acquired a structural deficit economy, meaning at no stage of the business cycle can we generate the amount of savings necessary for minimally adequate investment."[4] Could the debt keep interest rates high? Listen to Princeton's Alan Blinder: "In the aftermath of the 1981 tax cuts . . . many economists [have] warned that massive government budget deficits would keep real interest rates very high, thereby creating an unfavorable climate for investment."[5]

These statements and thousands like them have taken their toll on our Teflon. Some religious leaders have become so exercised about the state of the economy and our failure to confront our debts that they have taken up sermonizing about economics. The Reverend Robert Schuller is co-author with Paul Dunn of *The Power of Being Debt-Free* with such chapters as "Stealing From Our Children" and statements like this: "A debt-free America is a big, bold, beautiful dream!" We certainly have very real problems in this country, but "blame it on the deficit" has become such an easy out that it could be the title of a Broadway musical.

Our concerns are short- and long-term. In the short term we are worried about avoiding deep and recurring recession. Beyond the short term we wonder when, if ever, real wage growth will return to the United States. We also ask whether our stagnating economy masks a longer-term process of economic and social disintegration, in which one segment of society continues to prosper and the other continues to lose ground. For the long haul, we baby boomers need to consider how we are going to fare in old age, given that we are saving so little, that we have so few children on whom to rely, that our Social Security benefits have been cut, and that what Social Security benefits we have left could be dissipated, directly or indirectly, through the chicaneries of government finance.

This chapter examines our short-term concerns about recession and dismisses the deficit as anything more than a psychological factor in causing recession. The rest of this chapter turns to our longer-term problems. The relation or nonrelation of these problems to the federal deficit is taken up in the following chapter.

CAN ECONOMIC HISTORY REPEAT ITSELF?

Were the 1980s like the 1920s—a time of fast deals, high living, self-indulgence, and misplaced optimism? And will the 1990s, heaven forbid, resemble the 1930s? Many modern-day sooth-

39

sayers find the parallels striking.[6] They see Ronald Reagan as Calvin Coolidge reincarnate. They see the stock market crash of 1987, like the crash of 1929, as an early warning siren. They look at the financial and banking crisis of the last few years and see the banking panics of the early 1930s. They observe our trade conflicts with Europe and Japan and envision new trade barriers, which, like the 1931 Smoot–Hawley tariffs, will lead to a collapse of world trade. And they tell us the recent bankruptcies of some of the nation's oldest and most prominent businesses, including Pan Am, the Bank of New England, and Bloomingdale's, are just the tip of the iceberg.

Our current economic circumstances do bear some rather spine-chilling resemblances to those of the early 1930s. But the U.S. and international economies of the 1990s are radically different from those of the 1930s. America is increasingly becoming a country that assembles foreign-made components, and markets, organizes, and plans production, rather than the country in which production itself occurs. In 1930 more than one-fifth of the labor force worked in agriculture. Today less than 3 percent of the labor force is so employed (and they produce more).[7] Employment in manufacturing has also declined (though manufacturing has maintained its share of total output). In 1930 manufacturing accounted for one in five jobs; today it accounts for only one in six.[8] As agriculture and manufacturing have declined, service-producing industries (including the government sector) have expanded. Today, more than three-quarters of the nonagricultural labor force is employed in the service sector.[9]

The world is also more economically integrated. In 1929 the United States exported only 7 percent of its total output; today it exports 12 percent. General Motors now has manufacturing operations in thirty-nine countries. It builds engines in Australia, fuel injection systems in Brazil, trucks in Canada, and brakes in Brazil, and it assembles cars in Mexico. America's fastest-growing automaker is Honda, and Honda is also America's leading exporter of cars to Japan. McGraw-Hill is the biggest publisher of textbooks in Spanish in the Spanish-speaking world.

While the structure and international integration of the world economy differ greatly from that of sixty years ago, the differences may be insufficient to preclude a repetition of economic history. What will keep us from repeating the 1930s are the lessons we learned from that decade and the governmental institutions we constructed as a result of that experience. In particular, the world is well aware of the critical importance of international trade. The economic integration of Europe, which will culminate in the 1992 liberalization of professional and financial services, is testimony to the world's strong support for free trade. A collapse of world trade, as in the 1930s, arising from squabbles over remaining trade barriers, is exceedingly unlikely.

Nor will financial markets collapse. The last few years have sorely tested the U.S. government's insurance of commercial bank deposits and saving and loan deposits. True, several very large institutions have failed, but, thanks to deposit insurance, there has been no panic and no great implosion of lending. While the regulatory failures of the FSLIC (Federal Saving and Loan Insurance Corporation) and FDIC (Federal Deposit Insurance Corporation) will cost current and future Americans many times more than the Gulf War, the U.S. banking system remains intact.

A final reason to doubt economic doomsday is that international central bankers have learned an important lesson from the 1930s, namely, the importance of substantial and timely injections of money into the financial system to lower interest rates and to ward off a severe contraction of economic activity. The actions of central bankers—most importantly the Chairmen of the U.S. Federal Reserve—in the postwar period have been chiefly responsible for reducing the frequency and severity of economic fluctuations.

IS FEAR THE ONLY FEAR TO FEAR?

What caused the latest recession? Well, why not blame it on the deficit? The fact that we had seven straight years before 1991 in which we reported comparably large deficits with no recession shouldn't stop us. Some Keynesians, as alluded to before, would argue that the deficit was too small; according to them, had we only run even larger deficits, there would never have been a recession. Our Broadway musical and those Keynesians aside, let us suppose, as argued here, that the official deficit is completely arbitrary and bears no fundamental relationship to the underlying economic policy. Then it is surely hard to see how something real—namely, the economy's performance—could depend on this errant measure. Saying the deficit caused the recession would, in this case, be akin to saying the increase in the number of entries in the yellow pages caused the recession.

If there was a real connection between the officially reported deficit and the recession, it was probably the month after month of deficit hysteria that led up to the 1990 budget agreement. We Americans have a penchant for frightening ourselves that dates back to the Salem witch trials. More recent examples are the communist scares of the 1950s, the fallout shelters of the 1960s, and the run on gas masks by U.S. civilians at the beginning of the Gulf War.[10] Getting the country overwrought about the deficit at the same time it was learning about the FSLIC's and the FDIC's colossal problems, seeing the housing price bubbles burst, facing dramatic increases in energy costs, and watching some of our top computer firms and banks, like Digital and Bank of Boston, laying off workers, was hardly going to improve consumer and business confidence.

Ours is a big economy with tens of thousands of businesses. Lining up what Keynes called the "animal spirits" of the managers and owners of these businesses so that everyone hires his full contingent of workers, instead of holding back to see how things turn out, is no easy task. Economists aren't too eager to admit it publicly, but there is an important element of psychology embedded in their recent models of "coordination failures," which feature "multiple equilibria"—multiple positions in which the economy may land, some of which feature full employment and some of which do not. These models take seriously the fact that economic markets are not synchronized; there is no Walrasian (named after the French economist Léon Walras) auctioneer who simultaneously clears and coordinates the thousands of markets for different goods and services so that demands always match supplies at a single market price. As a consequence, "animal spirits" play a key role in coordinating beliefs about which equilibrium the economy is in.

Our previous recession, the one from July 1981 through November 1982, also seemed to have had a strong psychological stimulus. The blow to "animal spirits" in that recession was Federal Reserve Chairman Paul Volcker's announcement in October 1979 of a new and much tighter course of monetary policy. Financial markets, which had been thoroughly programmed by economists to believe that tighter money would raise interest rates, reacted with sharp increases in interest rates. The prime rate, which was 9.1 percent in 1978, rose to 12.7 percent in 1979 and 15.3 percent in 1980.[11] The interesting thing is that it is hard to see in the data any significant reduction in the growth of the monetary base (the money directly supplied by the Federal Reserve) until 1981. From 1977 to 1978 the monetary base rose by 8.9 percent. It rose by 8.5 percent from 1978 to 1979, when Volcker's policy took effect, and by 8.1 percent from 1979 to 1980, the first full year of the Volcker policy.[12] Apparently, the markets were more involved in what they heard Volcker saying than with what he actually did. Could our highly sophisticated financial markets have overreacted and precipitated the 1981–82 recession? You bet. Could we also be letting the government's deficit numbers tell us more than they do?

IS AMERICA FALLING BEHIND?

What really worries most Americans is not Paul Erdman's fantasy of economic Armageddon but the steady erosion of the United States' economic position in the world. In a 1990 Gallup Poll, only 32 percent of Americans said they felt good about where the country was heading.[13] According to the *Boston Globe*, Americans think "the nation is being eclipsed by Japan,

43

West Germany, and other emerging economic powers."[14] What troubles us is not that other countries are catching up with the United States—this was, after all, General George Marshall's plan for Europe and General Douglas MacArthur's plan for Japan. What troubles us is that we could be left in the dust.

The British know about losing one's economic position in the world. At the beginning of this century they had the world's strongest economy and a per capita level of income second to none. Right now they rank seventeenth among OECD (Organization of Economic Cooperation and Development) countries in per capita income, just above Italy and just below Australia.[15] The Argentines are also familiar with losing ground. In 1895 their per capita income was 55 percent of U.S. per capita income.[16] Today it is only 13 percent.[17]

Are we really heading the way of Britain or, worse yet, Argentina? Many economists seem to think so. Consider the titles of some recent books and articles by distinguished economists: *The Age of Diminished Expectations*, by MIT's Paul Krugman;[18] *Day of Reckoning*, by Harvard's Benjamin Friedman;[19] *The Zero Sum Society*, by MIT's Lester Thurow;[20] and "The Morning After," by Peter Peterson.[21] Each of these authors has a particular concern. For Krugman, it is the U.S. trade deficit: "With no relief from our persistent trade deficit, the United States could become the third-ranked economic power by the end of the decade." For Friedman it is the federal deficit: "America as a nation will watch others take its place in the world order. These are the real costs of our current fiscal policy." For Thurow it is the economy's growth rate: "In our entire history we have never grown even half as rapidly as the Japanese." For Peterson, it is economic decline: "The 1980's and 1990's may be remembered as a turning point in America's fortunes—a period when we took the British route to second-class economic status."

THE DISMAL ECONOMY

These economists are right to be alarmed about America's economic position in the world, although their connection of this decline to the federal deficit needs to be questioned. *In terms of per capita income, the United States has dropped, since 1970, from first place to ninth place among the major industrialized countries.*[22] Why is the United States falling behind? Certainly, as discussed in Chapter 1, a large part of the answer has to do with the failure of Americans to save and invest at anything close to the rates of Europeans and Japanese. As we all know from personal experience, the more we save, the more assets we accumulate. And the more assets we accumulate, the more asset income we add to the income we earn from working to raise our total income. The same holds true for the country as a whole; after all, the country's total income is just the sum total of our collective incomes.

U.S. SAVING AND INVESTMENT

Figure 2–1 shows how America's annual net saving and net investment rates have varied since 1950. While each of those performance indices has fluctuated over time, their values since 1980 have been considerably smaller than they were between 1950 and 1980. The saving rate is the share of the nation's net national product (or NNP, output less depreciation of the nation's capital goods) that is not consumed in a given year.[23] It averaged 8.9 percent between 1950 and 1979, but only 4.2 percent since 1980. The saving picture is, if anything, getting worse. Since 1986 the U.S. saving rate has averaged less than 3 percent. Considering that the bottom has dropped out of U.S. saving, U.S. net investment as a share of net output has held up rather well; during the 1980s the U.S. investment rate fell by only a third, although the saving rate fell by more than half. The reason the investment rate held up is simple: Foreigners increased their investment in the United States.

Will foreigners continue to invest at the same rate in the United States? Probably not. For one thing, countries with excess saving (saving in excess of domestic investment which is available to invest abroad), like Japan and Germany, are starting to save less. In the case of Japan, which is

45

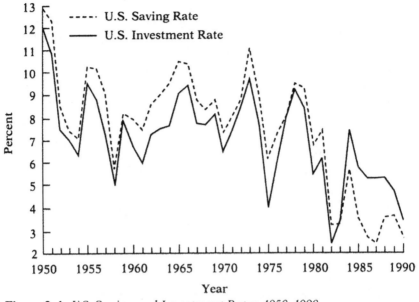

Figure 2-1 *U.S. Saving and Investment Rates, 1950–1990*

aging much more rapidly than either the United States or Western Europe, saving rates are likely to fall dramatically over the next twenty years as young and middle-aged Japanese, who save at a very high rate, decline in number relative to older Japanese, who save at a much lower rate. Even if the saving of our foreign investors remains high, they may invest proportionately less of it in the United States. Their excess saving is likely to be diverted, in good part, to more profitable investments in Eastern Europe. The decline in foreign investment in the United States may already have begun. The ratio of foreign investment to U.S. output was 40 percent smaller in the last three years than in the previous five.

THE U.S. TRADE DEFICIT

As mentioned in Chapter 1, foreign investment is referred to as the "trade deficit."[24] Unlike the fiscal deficit, the trade deficit is a well-defined economic concept. One can also use

Figure 2–1 to determine the size of the trade deficit relative to U.S. net output.[25] This is simply the distance between the investment rate and saving rate curves. The trade deficit was negative (that is, it was in surplus) for most of the 'fifties, 'sixties, and 'seventies (the saving curve was higher than the investment curve), meaning that the United States was saving more than it needed for domestic investment and therefore invested the rest of its saving abroad. Just the opposite has been true since roughly 1980. In recent years the trade deficit as a share of net national product has been as large as 2.8 percent.[26]

The fact that foreigners in recent years have been increasing the stock of capital in the United States to the tune of 1 to 2 percent of U.S. net output per year should be welcomed by all Americans. *What is disturbing is not the size of the trade deficit but, to repeat, the low level of U.S. saving.* Since U.S. saving plus the U.S. trade deficit adds up to total investment in the United States, the fact that U.S. saving has declined and the trade deficit has grown means that an increasing share of the capital in the United States is being owned by foreigners. Yes, this means that some of our companies have names like Honda, but would the Honda workers in Marysville, Anna, and East Liberty, Ohio, be better off if their Japanese employers picked up their $2.2 billion worth of automobile and motorcycle plants and took them back to Japan? Obviously not.

Thinking about Honda's physically transporting $2.2 billion worth of capital to the United States is the right way to view the trade deficit. Unfortunately, the word "deficit" in "trade deficit" is loaded, because it implies that a country running a trade deficit is actually borrowing. That is not the case. While Americans are saving a paltry amount, our saving, nonetheless, is positive. Hence, collectively we are *not* borrowing to consume beyond our incomes. But because we are saving so little, we are adding little to the factories, machine tools, and other capital goods available to be used in the United States. So foreigners are, in effect, bringing capital goods to our country. This is the sense in which a larger portion of the capital goods in the United States is being owned by foreigners. The picture, in the aggregate, is not one of our selling off America to have a big party, but rather it is one of foreigners putting their assets to work in America.

This picture is easy to miss in all the headlines about the Japanese buying up Rockefeller Center, the British buying up the New York *Daily News*, the Saudis buying up Citicorp, and so on.[27] What we miss in those headlines is the fact that Americans are also buying up firms abroad—both large and small. The Overseas Fund of Fidelity Investments, which invests in Japan and Southeast Asia and which is just one of Fidelity's international mutual funds, alone totals $1 billion. And Fidelity is only one of the nation's large institutional investors. We also miss the point that when foreigners buy into American companies they are, in part, getting the funds to do so by selling to Americans some of their holdings of companies in their own countries. Indeed, economic theory strongly predicts this international diversification of investors' portfolios. The saying "Don't put all your eggs in one basket" applies equally to Japanese investing in Japan and Americans investing in the United States.

The bottom line here is that we should stop worrying about what foreigners are doing and start worrying about what we aren't doing, namely coming up with the saving needed to acquire additional total assets, whether they be assets we place in the United States or assets we place outside the country. Because most of any additional U.S. saving would probably end up being invested in the United States, more saving would improve our investment picture, which would, in turn, raise workers' productivity and stimulate economic growth.

U.S. PRODUCTIVITY GROWTH

Figure 2–2 indicates how U.S. productivity growth has changed since 1950. Productivity growth is measured here quite conventionally as the annual percentage change in out-

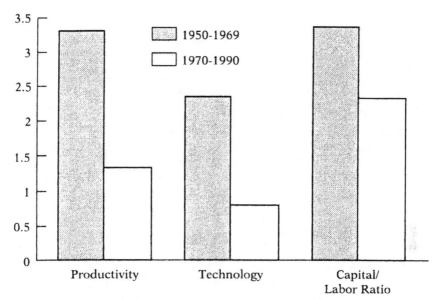

Figure 2–2 *Average Annual Growth Rates in U.S. Productivity, Technology and Capital/Labor Ratio, 1950–1990*

put per unit of labor input. The chart also shows how the growth in capital per hour of worker employment (the Capital/Labor Ratio) and the rate of technological change have fared in the last four decades.[28] *Since 1970 the productivity of U.S. workers has increased at just over 1 percent per year, which is 60 percent less than the productivity growth rate recorded from 1950 through 1969. It's only about a third of the Japanese rate during the same period.*[29] One would have expected the Japanese to have faster productivity growth during the first few decades after World War II as a reflection of the restoration of their economy. Although their increase in productivity has slowed, Japanese productivity at present is growing at more than one and a half times the rate in the United States.[30]

As mentioned in Chapter 1, the U.S. productivity slowdown may be traced, in part, to a decline in U.S. investment, because workers' productivity depends on the amount of equipment, plant, and other types of capital with which they have to work. Between 1950 and 1969 the ratio of capital input to labor input in the nonfarm business sector increased by 64 percent. Between 1970 and 1989 this ratio increased by only 45 percent.[31] Another factor in the productivity slowdown is the rate of technological change, which is measured as the change in output that cannot be ascribed to increases in inputs. Since 1970 technology has been improving by only 0.57 percent per year, as against 1.79 percent per year between 1950 and 1969.[32] These are the figures for the total nonfarm business sector. Within manufacturing the rate of technological change has held fairly steady.[33]

IS AMERICA PULLING APART?

In addition to worrying about falling behind, many wonder if America is pulling apart. The journalist Lawrence Malkin sees a growing polarization in America—a "two-tier society" in which the rich are getting richer, the middle class is being squeezed, and the poor are being offered "hamburger jobs" in our increasingly service-oriented sector.[34] The Harvard political economist Robert Reich writes that America's elite—the upper one-fifth of society—has retreated into a private utopia and forsaken its stake in the national good. According to Reich, America's elite have left the rest of society to fend for itself, particularly when it comes to warding off crime and educating its children.[35]

While certain facts support the view of an economically and socially separating society, others do not. Particular care is needed in assessing changes in the incomes of workers relative to those of the rest of society. Since 1975 average real hourly wages have fallen by 9 percent, and average real weekly earnings have fallen by 12 percent.[36] Those figures seem to suggest that real incomes of workers declined in the last fifteen years, which actually is not the case. The reason is that while workers' real wages have declined, their fringe benefits (such as employer-provided health insurance) have increased. Total compensation (wages plus fringes) per employee in the United States has actually increased in real terms, albeit by less than 3 percent, since 1975. Without question, this is a terribly poor record considering that in the fifteen years up to 1975 total real compensation per worker rose by 35 percent.[37] Still, it's better than some have made out by ignoring fringe benefits.

At the same time that real pay per worker has barely risen, U.S. real income per person has increased by 21 percent.[38] Does this mean that workers have not fared as well as other Americans? Not really. Total compensation paid to labor (including the self-employed) is the same 73 percent of total national income it was in 1973.[39] So workers, at least as a group, are getting the same share of the pie. The reason real per capita income has increased while real income per worker has hardly changed is that a larger percentage of Americans are now working. In 1975, 40 out of every 100 Americans was employed. In 1990 the figure was 47 out of 100 Americans.[40]

This 18 percent (7 over 40) higher employment rate reflects two things. First, a somewhat larger fraction (4 percent) of the population is in its working years, and second, there has been a considerable increase in the labor force participation of married women. In 1975 half of women ages 25–44 participated in the labor force. In 1988 more than two-thirds were in the labor force.[41] Much of the increase occurred for married women 18–35. Have women been forced into the labor market to maintain their families' standards of living? Certainly some have. But in the main, women have gone into the labor markets to raise, not simply to maintain, their families' living standards. Their efforts are primarily responsible for the 21 percent rise in U.S. per capita income since 1975. *Thus the average real income of working families has continued to rise, not because we are more productive, but because so many of us are working harder.*

A TWO-TIER SOCIETY?

If workers have, as a group, maintained their share of the nation's income, is the "two-tier society" so much myth? An-

51

swering this question requires (1) distinguishing what has happened to the real incomes of different types of workers, (2) considering changes in indices of U.S. income inequality, and (3) examining changes in poverty rates.

The real incomes of different groups of workers have indeed diverged in the last ten to fifteen years. Since 1979 real wages of high school grads relative to those of college grads have fallen by about 13 percent, and real wages of high school dropouts relative to high school grads have fallen by about 5 percent. Hence, the college–high school dropout real wage differential has increased by almost 20 percent.[42]

The data on the distribution of income in the United States reinforce the notion of increasing economic inequality. In 1975 the one-fifth of U.S. households with the highest personal incomes accounted for 41.1 percent of total U.S. personal income.[43] In 1987 they accounted for 43.7 percent. The poorest one-fifth of U.S. households lost ground, with their share of total income declining from 5.4 percent in 1975 to 4.6 percent in 1987.

There are problems with using these figures, because the definition of personal income, like the definition of the deficit, is economically arbitrary.[44] Contributions by firms to their workers' pension plans are, for example, excluded from personal income, although contributions by workers to their savings accounts are included. A better way to assess changes in inequality is in terms of actual consumption expenditures. Daniel Slesnik, an economist at the University of Texas in Austin, has studied consumption patterns of American households going back to the early 1960s. According to Slesnik, the 20 percent of households engaging in the most consumption in 1972 were responsible for 39 percent of total expenditures; in 1987 they were responsible for 42 percent. During this period the share of consumption of the 20 percent of households with the lowest expenditures fell from 7 percent to 6 percent.[45] Thus, whether one looks at income or consumption data, there is evidence of increased inequality.

Measures of poverty also suggest increasing economic

disparities, although the extent of the recent increase in poverty rates depends on the measure used. Based on the traditional measure of poverty, which uses pretax income, 11.8 percent of Americans were poor, on average, through the 1970s, and 14.0 percent were poor, on average, from 1980 through 1988. Slesnik has developed a consumption-based poverty line that reflects family consumption needs. Based on this measure of poverty, 9.2 percent of Americans were poor in the 1970s, and 10.0 percent were poor from 1980 through 1988.[46]

The increase in poverty rates is no surprise to welfare caseworkers and others who assist the poor. Demographics, the deterioration of our education system, the worsening of the drug problem, a reduction in work incentives, and a decline in the generosity of welfare have all conspired to raise the fraction of Americans who are poor. The contraction in government aid per poor person is particularly striking. For example, since 1975 real AFDC (Aid to Families with Dependent Children) payments per family receiving AFDC have fallen by more than 25 percent.[47]

LOOKING LONGER-TERM: THE BABY BOOMERS' DEMOGRAPHIC DILEMMA

In today's economic climate many baby boomers are struggling just to keep their jobs and to keep their heads above water. Over the longer haul, boomers can expect to be fully employed, but at very slow-growing wages. This dismal forecast is particularly troubling because the boomers will face their economic futures, to a large extent, alone. Like virtually all developed economies, the United States is projected to experience a dramatic demographic transition over the next fifty years. This reflects the remarkable increase in the number of children born in America, Western Europe, and Japan in the twenty or so years after World War II and the equally remarkable decline thereafter in the number of births. In the United States the fertility rate (the number of births a woman could expect based on current age-specific births per female) increased from 2.9 to 3.8 between 1946, the year before the boom began, and 1957, the peak year of the boom. Between 1957 and 1965, the first year after the boom, the U.S. fertility rate fell from 3.8 back down to 2.9. U.S. fertility has remained low. In the 1970s and 1980s the fertility rates averaged 1.7 and 1.8, respectively.[48]

Because there are so many boomers with relatively few children, the boomers will continue to make big waves in the U.S. age distribution. Today, only 12 percent of Americans are sixty-five and older. In 2030, when the baby boomers are in their seventies, more than one-fifth of Americans will be sixty-five and older, and almost a third will be fifty-five and older. Nursing homes and retirement communities will be packed; one in ten Americans will be over the age of seventy-five, as against only one in twenty today.[49]

In what sense will elderly baby boomers be alone? Well, in the present decade, while the boomers are caring for their parents, there will be 2.2 Americans aged 35–54 for every American aged 65 and older. In the 2030s, there will be only 1.2 Americans aged 35–54 for every old boomer.[50] The baby boom generation will be the first generation in modern times to experience old age with so few children on whom to rely.

They will also be one of the first generations to hit old age having experienced such a high incidence of divorce. Today 12.7 percent of Americans 35 to 44 are divorced, as against only 2.9 percent in 1960.[51] Half of the marriages begun in recent decades will not last. And two children in five now grow up in divorced families.[52] One wonders whether the high rate of divorce will influence the degree of support that baby boomers will receive from their children! Indeed, a recent survey by Dr. Frank F. Furstenberg, Jr., and colleagues at the University of Pennsylvania indicated that almost one-fourth of divorced fathers had had no contact with their children in the last five years, and 20 percent more had not seen their children during the preceding year.[53]

Reliance on children is dicey even for today's elderly. Most of those (60 percent) currently over seventy-five live alone; only one-fourth live with their children, and only a trivial fraction receive significant financial assistance from their children. A substantial fraction of the very old—about one-fifth—have no children, either because they never had children or because they have outlived their children. While many of today's elderly have close contact with their children, many others do not. In a typical month over a quarter of the older elderly who have children do not physically spend time with them.[54] Daughters are more important caregivers to the elderly, but today fewer than half of the older elderly have a daughter who lives within an hour of them.

THE BOOMERS' ECONOMIC DILEMMA

Facing old age with less support from children is scary enough even if one is financially flush, but the baby boom generation is looking at a very long period of retirement, reduced Social Security benefits, rising health care costs, decreased health care benefits, and the likelihood of spending a good deal of time in a nursing home.

Labor force participation by those over sixty-five is currently only 12 percent. Even males 55–64 years old are dropping out of work; today only 68 percent of males in this age bracket even participate in the labor force. Twenty years ago the figure was 83 percent.[55] If this trend continues, retirement as early as age fifty will become commonplace. The postwar trend toward early retirement continues, notwithstanding the fact that people are living longer and saving less.[56] Today's thirty-year-old male can expect to live to age seventy-four, 3.5 years longer than the typical thirty-year-old in 1960.[57] For thirty-year-old females the expected end of life is at the age of eighty, which is 3.1 years more than it was in 1960.

Let's consider a current thirty-year-old male named Randy. Randy plans to retire at age fifty-five, which is certainly a popular retirement age at the present time. Given his life expectancy, Randy can expect to spend almost half of his remaining life in retirement. How will Randy finance his projected nineteen-year-long retirement? Well, Randy can start collecting Social Security early retirement benefits at age sixty-two. But thanks to the 1983 Social Security Amendments, those benefits will be only 70 percent of his Social Security normal retirement benefits.[58] Had the 1983 legislation not occurred, Randy would have been able to collect 80 percent of his normal retirement benefits starting at age sixty-two.[59] In addition to getting a 14.3 percent smaller Social Security check, Randy will immediately have to hand back to the government another 5 or so percent of his Social Security check, because, again thanks to the 1983 Amendments, certain Social Security benefits are subject to income taxation. Because, as previously mentioned, the extent of this taxation is not indexed against inflation, roughly three-fifths of Randy's Social Security benefits and those of his generation will be subject to income taxation, as against only a quarter today.[60]

"Well," Randy might say, "who needs Social Security? I'll have my pension from my job and my own savings to rely on." That is easy to say, but Randy should know that a good chunk—over 40 percent—of his old age income had been slated to come from Social Security.[61] He should also know that although private pension plans have become somewhat more generous over time, most private pension benefits— those arising from defined-benefit plans—are not generally protected against inflation; if Randy starts collecting his private pension benefit at age fifty-five, and if inflation is running at only 5 percent per year, Randy's real pension benefit at age sixty-five will be 40 percent smaller in real dollars than its initial value at age fifty-five.

It's doubtful that Randy and his fellow baby boomers will begin to save enough to cover their longer length of retirement, to offset their Social Security benefit cuts, and to hedge against inflationary erosion of their private pensions. For the past ten years baby boomers have been moving into what should be for them and the nation a prime period of saving, but, for reasons that aren't altogether clear, their saving as well as that of older generations has plummeted.[62]

Yet another rationalization around the baby boomers' long-term financial problem is the argument presented in *U.S. News & World Report,* May 7, 1990, that baby boomers can look forward to sizable inheritances from their parents.[63] This is off the mark for several reasons. First, the right question is not whether inheritances will be larger in absolute terms than they were in the past, but whether they will be larger relative to the incomes of the recipients than was the case in the past. Yes, young and middle-aged Americans in the past had poorer parents and grandparents, and the absolute amount of inheritances received in the past by young and middle-aged Americans were smaller. But those inheritors in the past also had smaller incomes, meaning that the ratio of their inheritances to their incomes could have been larger than is the case for today's boomers.

Second, inheritances relative to income will be smaller for baby boomers than for prior generations because they have more siblings with whom they must share their parents' and grandparents' bequests. Third, the boomers' parents are retiring earlier and living longer, and, therefore, consuming more of their bequeathable wealth. As the common bumper sticker says, "We're spending our children's inheritance." And fourth, more of the financial assets of the boomers' parents are in the form of pension and Social Security annuities that can not be bequeathed. Today almost 17 percent of household net worth consists of private pension fund reserves. The figure in 1960 was only 5 percent. And today's ratio of household net worth exclusive of pension fund reserves to national income is down 14 percent from 1960 (3.0 now compared with 3.5 in 1960). That means bequeathable wealth relative to income is 14 percent smaller than it was when the boomer's parents were in their middle ages.[64]

In addition to having smaller financial means relative to their pre-retirement incomes than is currently the case, retired baby boomers will surely face greater expenses, particularly in the area of health care. As is widely known, health care costs have been exploding for over two decades. A total of 12 of every 100 dollars of U.S. output now consists of health care, compared with only 3 in every 100 dollars in 1950. Much of this expenditure is on the elderly (those sixty-five and older); today's elderly account for more than one-third of all health care spending, although they constitute only 12 percent of the population. Health care spending among those eighty-five and older is the highest of any age group, and the population in this age group will have *quadrupled* when the boomers reach these ages.

The government's ability to cover the health care costs of the elderly has already been stretched to the limit. Since 1967, real Medicare expenditures have grown at a 9 percent annual rate, far faster than the increase in Medicare enrollees.[65] Even given what the Social Security actuaries term "intermediate" projections of future health care costs, as will be described in Chapter 8, the task of paying for Medicare in the near and longer term poses a huge problem that we have yet to face.[66]

Today about a quarter of the elderly (those over sixty-five) can expect to live in a nursing home for some period of time.[67] With fewer children to house them, an even larger fraction of boomers are likely to reside in nursing homes. The high costs of nursing home care—typically more than $30,000 a year—will be hard to cover even for the most thrifty of boomers.[68] A number of today's elderly, who, as a group, appear to have saved more when young than the current boomers, have found their savings wiped out by nursing homes. Indeed, 40 percent of current nursing home patients are on government relief, that is, they are enrolled in Medicaid.[69] Medicaid confiscates virtually all of its enrollees' assets to help pay for its costs. While there are ways effectively to evade Medicaid's asset tax, at least some boomers may be saving less given the prospect of having to surrender the bulk of their carefully accumulated lifetime savings to Medicaid.[70]

CAN THE GOVERNMENT BAIL OUT THE BOOMERS?

If the baby boomers can't count on their children, if their Social Security benefits have been cut, if their retirement will last longer, if their medical needs will be greater, if their relative inheritances will be smaller, and if their saving is deficient, will they have economically miserable old ages, or will the government bail them out? The answer will depend on the government's interests and capacities in the early part of the twenty-first century. When the boomers retire, government policy is likely to be boomer-oriented policy; the boomers and those slightly younger and older will constitute about 40 percent of the adult population and an even larger fraction of the voting population.[71]

So the boomers will probably try to use the government to bail themselves out of the costs of their old age. But as the "no free lunch" proposition tells us, unless the government wants to cut its own spending on goods and services, any redistribution to the boomers will have to be paid by subsequent generations, including the boomers' children. Will the children of the boomers have sufficient means to help out their older parents? Not if U.S. productivity growth remains paltry, and not if the boomers' children have already been saddled with large net payments to the government.

CAN THE BABY BOOMERS TRUST THE SOCIAL SECURITY TRUST FUND?

The concern that the boomers' children, who will be small in number relative to the boomers, will not have the funds to finance their parents' retirements was the central reason why the Greenspan Commission in 1983 sought to force the boomers, in effect, to save for themselves by squirreling away large sums of money in the Social Security Trust Fund.[72] While the Social Security Trust Fund now has roughly $300 billion, in 2020 it is slated to have almost $3 trillion, measured in today's dollars.[73]

But what the government does with its right hand, it can and often does undo with its left. Many members of Congress rightly worry that the government will effectively dissipate the baby boomers' forced saving by relaxing other fiscal measures. They realize how hard it is to keep themselves and their colleagues from spending additional funds coming into the government's coffers. As mentioned in Chapter 1, in this decade the Social Security surplus is shrinking the traditional unified budget deficit (which includes Social Security receipts and payments), and will even turn it into a surplus. When those unified budget surpluses materialize, the government is likely to eliminate them in its adherence to the Golden Rule (make the deficit zero if you're running a deficit, and make the surplus zero if you're running a surplus). How? By spending more, making larger transfer payments, or cutting taxes. If that happens, the money needed for the trust fund will ultimately have to be borrowed, and the money the baby boomers ultimately receive from the Social Security Trust Fund may have to be used to pay off this borrowing; in effect, the baby boomers will face retirement with a stash of government assets (the Social Security Trust Fund), but with encumbrances on the stash of assets.[74]

As with the S&L bailout, one can, on this issue, easily miss the fundamental problem because of the complexity of the government's financial transactions. In the scenario being discussed, the potential paper trail convolutions are so exquisite as to beg presentation:

Suppose the government cuts income taxes later this decade to avoid running a surplus in its unified budget. In this case, since Social Security receipts go, under law, automatically into the Social Security Trust Fund, the Treasury would have to borrow money from the public (sell IOUs to the public) equal in amount to the Social Security surplus. While the unified budget deficit would be zero, there would be a deficit in the non–Social Security part of the budget to make up for the surplus in the Social Security part of the budget. What would the Social Security Trust Fund do with its funds? By law it must hold its funds in U.S. Treasury bonds. Hence, the Social Security Trust Fund would turn around and purchase back from the public the IOUs the public had just purchased from the Treasury.[75]

A Martian watching this would think he was seeing a game of "hot potato," with the private sector giving the Treasury X (the Social Security surplus), the Treasury giving X to the Trust Fund, the Trust Fund giving X to the private sector (in exchange for Treasury bonds), and the private sector giving X back to the Treasury (in exchange for the same amount of Treasury bonds). The only difference in outcomes from what would happen if the Treasury had just kept X initially and hadn't made the first passoff is that the Trust Fund ends up holding some government IOUs. In effect, one government entity, the Treasury, ends up handing another government entity, the Trust Fund, pieces of paper saying the government owes it money.

"Hot potato" will be played in a different order when the boomers retire and the Trust Fund cashes in its bonds to pay benefits to the boomers. When the baby boomers retire, the Trust Fund's claims of X will have grown to Y through the accumulation of interest. The Trust Fund will sell its bonds worth Y to the private sector and then hand Y to the private sector as benefit payments. But the Treasury will have to make good on the Y worth of bonds held by the private sector. They will, in our scenario, tax Y from the private sector to come up with the amount needed to buy back (pay off) the private sector's holdings of Y worth of bonds. Our Martian will see the Treasury giving Y to the private sector (to pay off the bonds the public purchased from the Trust Fund), the private sector giving Y to the Trust Fund (to purchase the bonds initially held by the Trust Fund), the Trust Fund giving Y back to the private sector (as Social Security benefit payments), and the private sector giving Y back to the Treasury (as tax payments). In the process the government IOUs that one government agency (the Treasury) had given to another (the Trust Fund) will be returned from the latter (the Trust Fund) back to the former (the Treasury).

If you are not an economist or accountant and you have been able to follow this, congratulations. The bottom line is that blind allegiance to the Golden Rule and the focus on the traditional and traditionally misleading deficit can easily leave baby boomers in the same situation they would have faced in the absence of any buildup of a Social Security Trust Fund. Thus the continued use of the deficit in setting fiscal policy holds some special dangers for baby boomers. It also diverts their attention from the point they need to keep straight, namely, that their children and grandchildren are already scheduled to face a considerable fiscal burden and that there is little more that can be extracted through the government from these relatives in the early part of the next century.

DEFICIT ANGST

Beyond the recession, beyond our saving and growth problems, beyond the baby boomers' demographic and economic dilemmas, there is a deeper anxiety associated with the deficit, namely the sense that the ship of state has torn away from its mooring and is adrift without a rudder. Eisenhower, Kennedy, Johnson—all would be thunderstruck to think of the United States running peacetime official deficits the size of our current deficits. Yet we have run (reported) huge deficits for more than a decade, and the public has come to expect them. What do these deficits mean? Do they mean the government is as spendthrift as its "me generation" constituents? Do they mean hyperinflation and Argentina are around the corner? And what do we make of the smoke and mirrors game? Does it mean the deficit's definition is up for grabs? Does it mean we don't know in what direction we're sailing? Finally, have we drifted too far? Is the ship of state so laden with past debts that even with a meaningful fiscal compass we'd drown in a sea of red ink before making it to port?

As will be argued in the next chapter, whatever we think we're measuring with the official deficit, its value is uncorrelated with indices of our economic problems, including our saving, investment, and growth rates and our trade deficits. The lack of association of our problems with the official deficit does not mean our fiscal policy hasn't worsened our economic problems, only that a nonmeasure of our fiscal policy bears no relationship to our economic malaise. In contrast to deficit accounting, the postward generational accounting presented in Chapter 7 shows how we've spent almost half a century pursuing policies that were destined to lower our nation's saving, investment, and growth.

3

BLAME IT
ON THE DEFICIT

■

Every great musical has a recurring number which the audience ends up singing on its way home. In the U.S. musical "Blame It on the Deficit," the hit song is "The Deficit Made Me Do It." It's a richly choreographed piece in which a corpulent Uncle Sam overbuys, undersaves, borrows shamelessly, goes bankrupt, and ends up slinging sushi at MacFumio's. As Sam alternates between stuffing his mouth and selling off pieces of America, the chorus—with pleading arms outstretched—sings the refrain, "The Deficit Made Me Do It."

"Blame It on the Deficit" is playing to standing-room-only crowds at home and abroad. The British version has Uncle Sam selling back the London Bridge and the Queen Mary. The French have Sam do a sale-leaseback of Louisiana. And the Germans let a retired Field Marshal named Marshall come to the rescue. The show's a smash everywhere but Japan. The Japanese don't go in much for musicals, so they've had their movie industry—Hollywood—do a film version with the title: "It's a Miserable Life."

Kidding aside, is the federal deficit responsible for lowering U.S. saving, investment, and growth, increasing the trade deficit, raising world interest rates, and depressing the dollar? The standard refrain that implicates the deficit in these and related economic ills runs like this:

> Deficits let current generations off the hook for paying for the government's bills. As a result current generations consume more. This reduces national saving and means less investment in the United States. A reduced rate of U.S. investment means smaller additions to the U.S. capital stock and slower growth in real wages.

The refrain's second verse relates deficits to interest rates:

> U.S. interest rates reflect, in part, the expected return to U.S. capital.[1] In reducing investment, deficits make capital scarce, which raises the return to the U.S. capital and, thus, interest rates. Interest rates also rise because of concern about inflation. Investors know that the United States might try to inflate away (monetize) its debts and, as a result, require higher interest rates to compensate them for the risk of holding nominal dollar-denominated bonds, be they U.S. Treasury bonds or General Motors bonds, all of which promise to pay, through time, fixed (not inflation protected) amounts of dollars.

The third verse connects the fiscal deficit to the trade deficit and to the value of the dollar:

> The scarcity of U.S. capital makes the profitability of investing in the United States greater. However, increased foreign investment translates into a larger trade deficit. In addition, increased demand for dollars to be used in investing in the United States raises the value of the dollar on world currency markets.

A chorus of prominent economists has been singing this tune since 1981. One of them is MIT's Paul Krugman, whom Nobel Laureate Paul Samuelson calls "the rising star of this century and the next."[2] It is instructive to recite some verses from Krugman's recent book, *The Age of Diminished Expec-*

tations, connecting the federal deficit to U.S. saving and trade deficits:

> [T]he huge federal budget deficit meant that the federal government was engaged in massive dissaving . . . that accounts for about half of the decline in saving since the late 1970s.[3]

> The only *reliable* way to raise national savings is to eliminate the budget deficit.[4]

> [A] revised version of the "twin deficit" theory [the budget deficit causes the trade deficit] is still the best explanation for the emergence of unprecedented trade deficits in the 1980's.[5]

> [T]here is only one reliable way to do it [reduce the trade deficit]: balance the federal budget.[6]

Another prominent economist drawing connections between the deficit and our economic ills is Harvard's Benjamin Friedman. In his *Day of Reckoning*, which was acclaimed by *Business Week* as "one of the ten best books of the year," Friedman draws connections between the deficit, interest rates, investment, the dollar, and what he sees as our troubled economic future:

> Our new (since 1981) fiscal policy, generating ever larger deficits even in a fully employed economy, had long since replaced tight monetary policy as the reason for high real interest rates.[7]

> And with these high real interest rates, our net investment has been smaller compared to our income than at any time since World War II.[8]

> Earlier on [between 1981 and 1987], the dollar had risen because interest rate differentials made investing in our markets more attractive, yet there was only a limited amount of dollars for foreigners to hold. . . . But with our trade in deficit, in the aggregate foreigners had to keep accumulating dollars. Their efforts to sell this continuing accumulation now began to push the dollar lower.[9]

[I]t is fair to say that the deficit has been the greatest single force underlying the most severe failures of our economic performance in the 1980's, especially those with the most troubling implications for the future.

Government economists are as exercised about the deficits as university economists. Alan Greenspan, Chairman of the Board of Governors of the Federal Reserve and, arguably, the government's most powerful, if not its most influential, economist, writes that

... large and persistent deficits are slowly but inexorably damaging the economy. The damage occurs because deficits tend to pull resources away from net private investment. And a reduction in net investment has reduced the rate of growth of the nation's capital stock. This, in turn, has meant less capital per worker ... and this will surely engender a shortfall in labor productivity growth and, with it, a shortfall in growth of the standard of living.[10]

IS DEFICIT ANGST SUPPORTED BY THE FACTS?

Krugman, Friedman, and Greenspan are, without question, outstanding economists. Their books and articles provide a wealth of information and insight about the U.S. economy, and their concern with U.S. saving, investment, and growth is very well-founded. But their connection of these problems to a mismeasure of our fiscal policy, namely the federal deficit, can and should be questioned.

Large official federal deficits and low saving, investment, and growth have coincided in certain years in the past, including the 1980s. On the other hand, there are other years, including some in the 1980s, in which they have not. To know if there is a systematic relationship between deficits and our economic problems one must consider how the deficit relates to the economy's track record over a longer period of time.

Different economists, looking at the same set of facts,

often reach different conclusions. One should therefore examine at least some of the facts for oneself. Figure 3–1 plots, for the years 1950 through 1990, the NIPA federal deficit as a share of NNP, the full employment deficit (the NIPA deficit adjusted for the business cycle) as a share of NNP, and the national saving rate. Since Americans try to maintain their consumption levels during temporary recessions by spending their past savings, the national saving rate is quite sensitive to the economy's performance. So too is the federal deficit, because tax revenues and some spending programs depend on the economy's performance. Hence, it is not surprising that the national saving rate is correlated with the ratio of the federal deficit to NNP. The real question is whether that correlation is due to the state of the economy. If we consider the full employment deficit, which corrects

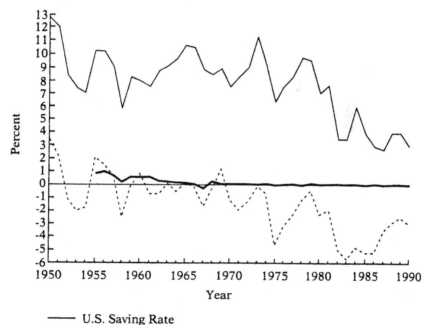

— U.S. Saving Rate

- - - - Federal Deficit as a Percent of NNP

━━ Full Employment Deficit as a Percent of NNP

Figure 3–1 *U.S. Deficits and Saving as a Percent of NNP, 1950–1990*

for the state of the economy, there is no correlation between U.S. saving and the federal deficit.

Figure 3–2 plots the full employment deficit relative to NNP against the U.S. rate of productivity growth (output per hour in the nonfarm business sector). Certainly there is no close annual relationship between the two curves. There are years, like the early 1950s, when the deficit increases and productivity falls, and there are other years, such as 1975–80, when the deficit declines and productivity falls. It's obvious from the diagram that productivity growth is desultory. Productivity growth in the 1980s averaged 1.09 percent per year, as against 1.24 percent in the 1970s, 2.50 percent per year in the 1960s, and 2.64 percent in the 1950s. But it's certainly not apparent from the graph that U.S. productivity growth has been permanently reduced either by the huge deficits of the 1980s or by the smaller ones of the past.

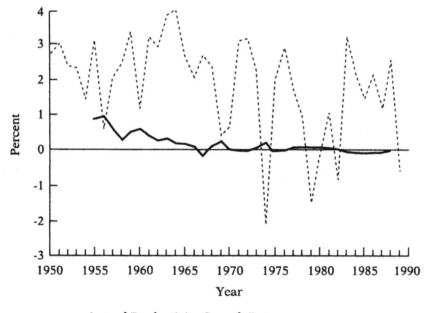

- - - - Annual Productivity Growth Rate
—— Full Employment Deficit as a Percent of NNP
Figure 3–2 *Labor Productivity and Full Employment Deficit, 1950–1990*

Figure 3–3 repeats the analysis for the U.S. trade deficit measured relative to NNP. At least to your author's naked eye, it is hard to see a clear relationship between the business-cycle adjusted deficit and the national saving rate, the productivity growth rate, or the trade deficit measured relative to net national product. Clearly, other variables that influence saving, productivity growth, and trade deficits aren't being taken into account in these charts, and these so-called external influences may be masking a strong relationship between these variables and the deficit. One needs to "control" for these additional influences. This type of analysis is called multivariate or multivariable.

MULTIVARIATE ANALYSES OF THE IMPACT OF THE DEFICIT

Such multivariate studies have been conducted. A range of very careful analyses indicate no close connection between

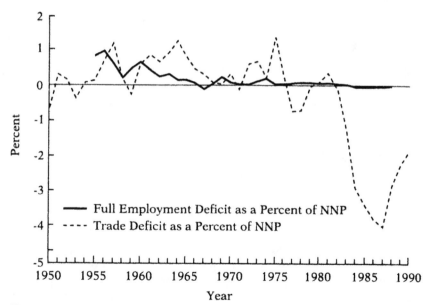

Figure 3–3 *Trade and Full Employment Deficits as a Percent of NNP, 1950–1990*

the official deficits and such fundamental economic variables as saving rates, interest rates, trade deficits, and inflation. These studies are not the writings of extreme supply-siders with ideologic-political agendas. Far from it. They have been conducted by an array of distinguished academic economists and have appeared, for the most part, in *The American Economic Review* and the *Journal of Political Economy*, the top two general interest scholarly journals in economics, as well as *The Journal of Monetary Economics*, the top journal specializing in macroeconomics.

Three of the most recent and comprehensive studies of the impact of deficits on U.S. consumption and saving are those by Professor Roger Kormendi of the University of Michigan, Professor David Aschauer of Bates College, and Professors John Seater and Roberto Mariano of North Carolina State University and the University of Pennsylvania, respectively.[11] Each of these studies indicates that, controlling for variables that economic theory says should affect consumption and saving, the government's deficit has no effect on U.S. consumption and saving. Another economist, Gerald Dwyer of Clemson University, has studied the relationship of deficits to inflation and reports: "No evidence is found that larger government deficits increase prices, spending, interest rates, or the money stock."[12]

Paul Evans, Professor of Economics at Ohio State University, has almost single-handedly debunked other assorted myths about the deficit's negative effects. He began his examination of the deficit's impact with two detailed studies of the relationship between the federal deficit and interest rates. The first study used data going as far back as the Civil War.[13] To quote Evans, his research considers

... three periods [the Civil War, World War I, and World War II] in which the federal deficit has exceeded 10 percent of national income. In none of these periods did interest rates rise appreciably. Regression analysis applied to data from these three periods has not uncovered a positive association between deficits and interest rates. There also appears to be no evidence for a positive association between deficits and interest rates during the postwar period.

Evans's second article goes farther, to ask whether future expected budget deficits affect interest rates. This exhaustive study, which uses data from 1908 through 1984, finds no evidence that interest rates are related to current, past, and expected future budget deficits as conventional Keynesian macroeconomics presumes. Professor Evans has also examined the relationship of deficits to interest rates for Canada, France, Germany, Japan, and the United Kingdom.[14] In this third analysis he reports "no statistically significant positive association between budget deficits and nominal interest rates in these six countries."

Finally, Professor Evans has examined the relationships between the federal deficit and the dollar's exchange rate, and the federal deficit and the trade deficit. Evans finds "no evidence that the dollar appreciates when the federal budget deficit increases,"[15] and "virtually no evidence that government budget deficits affect the current accounts [trade deficits] of Canada, France, Germany, Italy, Japan, the United Kingdom, and the United States."[16]

While Evans's work may well be the most detailed examination to date of the relationship of deficits to interest rates and trade deficits, his conclusions are shared by virtually all economists who have looked at the data. For example, Peter Bernstein and Robert Heilbroner, authors of *The Debt and the Deficit*, present evidence that "has failed to show any consistent relationship between budget deficits and current accounts or between budget deficits and real interest rates."[17]

Do the findings just described mean, as supply-siders claim, that the deficit doesn't matter to national saving, growth, current accounts, interest rates, and the rest? Yes, but not for the reasons the supply-siders have in mind. *The deficit isn't empirically related to the fundamental economic variables because the deficit isn't measuring anything that should be empirically related to such variables.* The supply-siders incorrectly view the above-cited results as saying that the government's generational policy doesn't matter. What the results are really telling us is that a *mismeasure* of the government's generational policy doesn't matter.

DON'T THE FACTS IN THE 1980S SPEAK FOR THEMSELVES ABOUT U.S. DEFICITS LOWERING U.S. SAVING?

Given the association of low U.S. saving and large official federal deficits since 1981, it's worth focusing on saving in the 1980s to see why this association is, in fact, purely coincidental. To give these facts their best day in court, let's consider them from the Keynesian perspective. Recall that, according to the Keynesians, the great bulk of American households are either so myopic or so cash-constrained that they make each year's consumption decision based on that year's disposable income, which means their pretax incomes minus "taxes" (to the government) plus "transfers" (from the government). Accordingly, if the government "taxes" you a dollar more this year, you'll consume a dollar (or close to a dollar) less this year, even if the government is going to return that dollar plus interest to you in the future in the form of a "transfer." Alternatively, if the government "transfers" you a dollar more this year, but tells you it will "tax" you that dollar plus interest in the future, you will, according to the Keynesians, ignore the future taxes and consume a dollar (or close to a dollar) more this year. Despite considerable evidence that American households don't act this way—that they don't immediately spend every dollar they get their hands on—the Keynesians have adopted this as their norm image of household economic behavior.

To the Keynesians a dollar taken by the government with the word "tax" is different from a dollar taken with the word "borrowing," because when the word "tax" is used, the household handing over the dollar has no real option. It must surrender the dollar on pain of penalty. Since the households Keynesians envision would never voluntarily fork over their money to the government, even if they knew they were going to get it back with interest, the voluntary-involuntary nature of the transaction makes a big difference to the Keynesians.[18] Thus it's not surprising that the Keynesians take labels such as "taxes," "transfers," and "deficit" seriously.

The large federal deficits reported in the 1980s do not, however, simply reflect the difference between taxes and transfers. Interest payments were a large component of these deficits. For example, in 1985 interest payments amounted to nearly two-thirds of the total deficit. From a Keynesian perspective the key components of deficits that are supposed to influence household consumption are taxes and transfers (cash payments to individuals), not interest payments.[19] So the key variable for Keynesians is how the difference between taxes and transfers changed in the 1980s when compared to earlier periods.

In addition, one should consider not simply how federal taxes less transfers have changed, but how this difference has changed at all government levels—federal, state, and local—combined. While one wouldn't know it from all the attention it receives, the federal government is no colossus relative to state and local governments.[20] During the 1980s, when the federal government was running (reporting) large deficits, state and local governments were, as a group, running (reporting) large surpluses due to sizable excesses of their taxes over their transfers.

The increased state and local government net taxation in the 1980s offset, almost entirely, the reduction in federal government net taxation, leaving Americans with roughly the same disposable income (net national product less taxes plus transfers) relative to net national product (NNP) as they had from 1950 through 1979. For all levels of government combined, the ratio of disposable (after taxes paid and transfers received) income to NNP averaged .778 between 1980 and 1989. It averaged .774 for the 1970s, .761 for the 1960s, and .776 for the 1950s.[21] Hence, net disposable income as a share of net national product was just about the same in the 1980s as in the 1970s and 1950s, and it was only slightly higher in the 1980s than in the 1960s.

To see just how poorly the Keynesian assumption fits the facts, compare the 1980s with the 1950s. In the 1980s disposable income relative to NNP was trivially larger—only 0.2 percent of NNP. In contrast, Americans' consumption expenditures were 4.0 percent larger as a share of NNP in the 1980s than in the 1950s.[22] If the Keynesians were right, the ratio of Americans' consumption to their net national product should have risen by only 0.2 percentage points, not the actual twenty times larger 4.0 percentage points actually observed. *Thus, while the U.S. saving rate in the 1980s was less than half that of the 1950s, this saving decline cannot be ascribed to Americans spending like mad because their net taxes were reduced, because in point of fact Americans' net taxes were not reduced in the 1980s.*[23]

DON'T DEFICITS DIRECTLY REDUCE GOVERNMENT SAVING, AND THEREBY NATIONAL SAVING?

Those readers who paid perhaps too much attention to national income accounting in their undergraduate macroeconomic classes might recall that the budget margin (surplus or deficit) is referred to in national income accounting as government saving or dissaving, as the case may be. Most commentators discussing recent U.S. saving behavior point to our pitiful rate of saving in the 1980s and, in the same breath, discuss the enormous government dissaving during that decade. They usually don't bother to state explicitly their implied contention that government dissaving is responsible for national dissaving.

Now total national saving (call it C) equals the sum of government saving (call it A) plus private saving (call it B), or $A + B = C$. If A plus B equals C, does a decrease in A (reflecting a larger government deficit) necessarily mean a decrease in C, national saving? Not if B, private saving, changes as well. This is just what those careful studies by Kormendi,

Aschauer, and Seater and Mariano find—no close association between changes in A and changes in C, meaning that when A goes down, B typically goes up, generally leaving C unchanged.

The fact that increases in officially measured government dissaving are not associated with reduced national saving should not be surprising. As already discussed and as will be demonstrated in detail in Chapter 6, budget surpluses and deficits are economically arbitrary and simply reflect the government's vocabulary. Government dissaving (the deficit) and private saving (total national saving minus the deficit) are no less arbitrary.

To see why the words "government saving" are loaded, take the question raised in Chapter 1: how to label our contributions to and benefits from Social Security. Suppose the government used the words "loans" and "repayment of principal plus interest" to characterize our Social Security contributions and at least a component of our Social Security benefits. In that case official private saving would be substantially larger than the amount currently reported, because we, the public, would hold explicit government IOUs which the national accounting would count as a private asset.

The idea of thinking of Social Security contributions as private saving is just as reasonable as thinking of it as government saving. After all, roughly half of Americans—workers and retirees alike—have the bulk of their retirement savings tied up in Social Security, counting in the employers' matching contributions. Today's workers contribute 15.3 percent of their earnings to Social Security. True, current workers will not get everything back with interest that they contribute to Social Security, and will get even less because of the 1983 Social Security legislation, but they will get back much of what they contribute.[24] Hence, from the point of view of today's workers that portion of their Social Security contributions that they will get back with interest works much like a private saving account. They put money in now, and they get the money back with interest.

77

The ambiguity in classifying a significant portion of the nation's saving as government and the rest as private is not limited to Social Security contributions. It's ubiquitous. Take, for example, the income "taxes" workers pay today. Some of these "taxes" can be thought of as paying for the workers' future unemployment benefits. Others can be thought of as paying for the workers' future Medicaid benefits, which many of today's workers will, unfortunately, ultimately receive in the form of nursing home care. Obviously, one could play this game ad infinitum; one could call some other component of our incomes taxes "implicit private sector saving for the future payment for protection by the U.S. military;" one could classify current gasoline tax payments as "implicit private sector saving to finance future government payments on the education of our children," and on and on.

Some readers may be uneasy, if not irritated, by these suggested reclassifications of government receipts and payments. Some might say: "When I put money in my IRA or savings account, it's my money, with my name on it. I get pieces of paper in the mail that show exactly how much money I have through time. I am sure to get back what I put in. That's why it's private saving. Giving the government money that it may or may not return in the future is not the same; it's not private saving!"

Don't be so sure. How important is getting back a piece of paper from the government in exchange for your handing the government money today? Isn't there a range of implicit commitments on which the government is very likely to make good? By the way, the Social Security Administration will send you, upon request, a piece of paper indicating your claim to future benefits. True, it's not a legal claim in the sense that the law determining benefits may change, but it is a likely claim. Your IRA claim may be a stronger *legal* document, but the real return on your IRA contributions, like the return on your Social Security contributions, is no more certain. If, for example, your IRA is invested in bonds, bond prices may fall, or your coupon payments may get eaten up by inflation.

The purpose of this argument is not to engage in sophistry, but to point out that with somewhat different words we could be doing essentially the same national saving, but reporting quite different decompositions of that saving as between government and private saving. Stating the point differently, the fact that the government plays such an important role in determining our future consumption opportunities should give one pause in taking seriously anyone's, including the government's, division of total saving into strictly private and strictly government components. Yes, under one definition of government dissaving, this dissaving increased during the 1980s, but under other definitions it has declined.[25]

If the definition of government saving is up for grabs, is there no meaningful way to understand private-sector saving behavior? On the contrary, there is a way. As discussed in the next chapter, there is a straightforward way of analyzing private-sector saving behavior that doesn't require the use of the ill-defined words "taxes," "transfers," and "deficits." This analysis indicates that it is the private sector's consumption behavior, not the government's, that is responsible for the dramatic decline in U.S. saving since 1980. Of course, as previously mentioned, the government's generational policy can influence the level of private-sector consumption. Hence, to understand fully the government's role in altering saving behavior one needs to relate the rate of private-sector consumption to changes in generational accounts as well as other key components of government policy.

DOESN'T THE GOVERNMENT DIRECTLY RAISE INTEREST RATES WHEN IT BORROWS IN CREDIT MARKETS?

A second reflexive, rather than reflective, connection that is often drawn between the (reported) deficit and economic variables involves the deficit's alleged raising of interest rates through the process of "financial crowding out." "Financial crowding out" refers to the U.S. Treasury's sale of bonds. Alan Greenspan explains:

> The Treasury has been a large and growing customer in financial markets in recent years. It has acquired, on average, roughly 25 percent of the total funds borrowed in domestic credit markets over the last four years [1985–89], up from less than 15 percent in the 1970s. For the Treasury to raise its share of total credit flows in this fashion, it must push other borrowers aside. [And] private investment is crowded out by higher real interest rates.[26]

This is another example of guilt by association. To begin with, it's not clear that any crime has been committed; Professor Evans's research clearly demonstrates that federal government borrowing in financial markets has not systematically influenced interest rates. Certainly there are periods in which the feds sell a lot of bonds (swaps IOUs for dollars) and interest rates rise, but there are other periods in which the feds sell a lot of bonds and interest rates fall. Figure 3–4 graphs the annual average value of the six-month U.S. Treasury bill interest rate against the deficit-to-NNP ratio. In the years after 1970 the two curves have a roughly similar shape—when the deficit increases, the interest rate falls, and when the deficit falls the interest rate tends to rise. This is precisely the *opposite* correlation predicted by those claiming the deficit is responsible for raising interest rates.

To be sure, the U.S. government is a big participant in the U.S. market for government (federal, state, and local) securities, but the government securities market is only one component of the entire U.S. bond market, which includes bonds issued by private business and corporations. Moreover, the U.S. bond market is only a component of the larger U.S. credit market, which includes commercial and residential mortgages, consumer loans, business trade credit, and credit extended between friends and relatives. And the U.S.

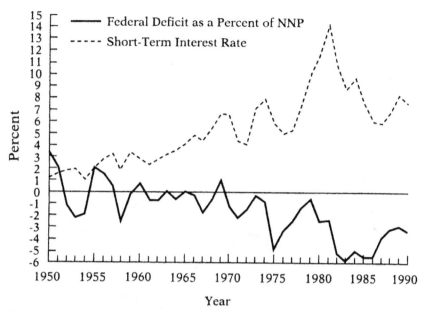

Figure 3-4 *Federal Deficit and Short-Term Interest Rate, 1950–1990*

credit market is only a component of the world credit market.

More fundamentally, world capital markets are now fully integrated, and real (after inflation) U.S. interest rates are world interest rates. They reflect the profitability of U.S. and foreign-owed firms operating not only in the United States but also in Europe, Japan, and the rest of the world.[27] If firms operating outside the United States become more profitable, they will be able to offer higher interest rates to American investors as well as non-Americans in borrowing (in selling their bonds/IOUs to raise capital). This will drive U.S. interest rates up as well, because U.S. borrowers (firms in the United States, private U.S. citizens, and the U.S. Treasury) will have to offer competitive interest rates if they want to borrow.

The same is true if firms operating inside the United States become more profitable. Given the size of the world capital market, which includes all the borrowing of all the

81

governments, all the firms, and all the households of the United States, Western Europe, Japan, the NICs (newly industrialized countries such as Korea, Malaysia, and Taiwan), and so on, the notion that the U.S. federal government is the pivotal player in determining world interest rates is simply casual empiricism informed by presumption.

There is a deeper problem with the financial crowding-out story that would invalidate its premise even if U.S. interest rates were not determined in the world financial market. If, as argued above, the receipts the government takes in and the monies it pays out both today and in the future could be relabeled with no fundamental change in the economic position of American households, then large chunks of today's federal "taxes" could equally well be labeled federal "borrowing." With such a verbal description of U.S. policy, the role of the federal government in the bond market would appear many, many times larger than it currently appears. Thus if one wants to tell a financial crowding-out story, one can make the federal government's role in financial markets as large as one likes. It will be shown in Chapter 6 that with the right words one can also make the government's role in financial markets as small as one likes.

The point is that Uncle Sam takes in money from a lot of different people in this country. Sometimes when he takes in money he hands back a fancy IOU engraved with the words "U.S. Treasury Bond" or "U.S. Treasury Bill." At other times he hands back an invisible IOU. Uncle Sam also hands out a lot of money. Sometimes, when he hands out money, he takes back his fancy, engraved IOUs; at other times he takes back his invisible IOUs. The fundamental economic issue is not the exchange of engraved pieces of paper. Rather, it is how much money particular individuals and households give up now and later versus how much they get back now and later. This treatment of different generations over the remainder of their lives helps determine U.S. household consumption, the nation's saving, the nation's investment, the nation's capital intensity (the size of its capital stock relative to its labor force), and, in conjunction with capital intensities abroad, U.S. real interest rates. U.S. real interest rates reflect real economic policy; they are not the simple reflection of the fraction of the total monies the federal government takes from the public this minute or this hour or even this year using a select set of words and handing out stacks of engraved paper.

BLAME IT ON THE DEFICIT—BUT WHICH DEFICIT?

The response of some Keynesians to the evidence that the official deficit is not statistically related to U.S. saving rates, investment rates, productivity growth rates, money supply growth rates, interest rates, exchange rates, or trade deficits is: "Well, maybe these statistical analyses just didn't use the right deficit." but, as discussed in Chapter 1, correcting the official federal deficit opens up a Pandora's box. The possible corrections have a beginning but no clear end. They include corrections for government assets, inflation, economic growth, state and local government surpluses, the business cycle, demographic change, changes in the market value of existing debt, unfunded Social Security liabilities, unfunded civil service pensions, unfunded military retirement benefits, FSLIC liabilities, FDIC liabilities, liabilities on federally guaranteed loans, implicit commitments to future welfare recipients, implicit commitments to preserving the national parks, implicit commitments to continued foreign aid, and on and on.

While a few of these potential corrections simply change the level of government debt but don't greatly alter the pattern of deficits (changes in the debt) over time, most of the corrections change both the level of debt and the time-pattern of the deficit. Consider, for example, Figure 3–5, which plots, for 1955 through 1988, the official federal deficit as a fraction of NNP and Professor Robert Eisner's cyclically adjusted "high-employment deficit," with his corrections for inflation and market revaluation.[28] According to the official numbers, the federal government ran deficits in

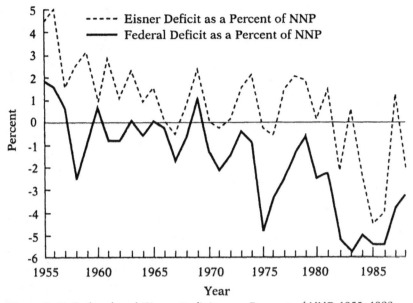

Figure 3–5 *Federal and Eisner Deficits as a Percent of NNP, 1955–1988*

ten out of ten years in the 1970s. According to Eisner's corrected series, the federal government ran *surpluses* for six
out of those ten years!

The year 1983 features the largest discrepancy for the period 1955–88 between the official deficit and Eisner's corrected deficit. In that year the National Income and Product
Accounts (NIPA) report a federal deficit equal to 6.1 percent
of GNP, while Eisner reports a surplus equal to 0.6 percent
of GNP. Hence, the two deficits differ by 6.7 percent of NNP,
or about $240 billion in 1983 dollars. A 6.7 percent of NNP
correction to the deficit is huge; since 1950 the NIPA deficit
has never exceeded 6.7 percent of NNP.

A comparison of the way the NIPA and Eisner deficits
vary through time is also instructive. In twelve of the thirty-
five years considered in Figure 3–5 the two deficits move in
opposite directions; in those twelve years when the NIPA
deficit indicates policy is tightening (loosening), Eisner's
deficit indicates policy is loosening (tightening). For exam-

ple, from 1982 to 1983 the NIPA numbers show the deficit increasing by 0.7 percent of NNP, while Eisner's numbers show the deficit decreasing by 2.7 percent of NNP.

At the risk of overkill, let's consider another proposed correction to the NIPA debt, namely the inclusion of unfunded Social Security liabilities. Figure 3–6 displays two sets of hills, whose sizes vary through time. The lower hills show the NIPA federal debt exclusive of Social Security liabilities, while the upper hills include those liabilities.[29] The first thing to notice is how high the latter set of hills is relative to the former. Including Social Security liabilities more than triples federal debt during almost all the years for which data on these liabilities are available.[30]

Next, look at the slopes of the hills. These slopes indicate how the debt changes over time. A rising slope means the debt is rising and the government is running deficits. A falling slope means the government is running surpluses. The slopes of the lower and upper hills differ substantially in

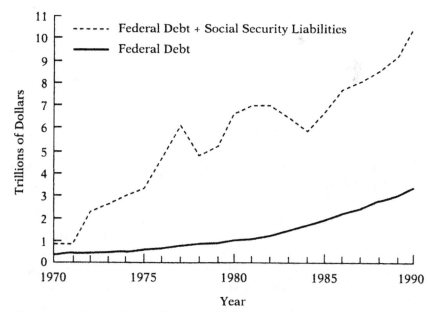

Figure 3–6 *Federal Debt With and Without Social Security Liabilities*

85

most of the years considered. Take 1973 for example. The slope of the lower hills for 1972 is rising, but not very rapidly, because the official federal deficit was only $16.8 billion. The 1973 slope of the upper hills is, in contrast, very steep, reflecting the fact that unfunded Social Security liabilities increased between 1972 and 1973, according to Social Security's actuaries, by $1.430 trillion. By the way, after factoring in inflation, $16.8 billion in today's dollars is $49.5 billion, while $1.430 trillion in today's dollars is $4.213 trillion. Hence, those arguing that the government should measure its debt by using the upper hills rather than the lower hills are saying that, counting in 1991 dollars, the government ran in 1973 a $4.213 *trillion* deficit, but reported only a $49.5 *billion* deficit. Of course, $4.213 trillion is a long way away from $49.5 billion. Did the feds in 1973 underreport the deficit by a factor of 85? Well, since each of us is free to roll his own deficit, the upper hills have as much claim to describing the government's debt as do the lower hills.

LOST IN THE NUMBERS?

What should we conclude from the plethora of unrelated alternative federal deficits? Clearly, they can't each be telling us whether or not fiscal policy is stimulating the economy, because that question has a single answer, not 40 or 4,000 different answers depending on which deficit series we want to consider. Nor can they each be telling us the fiscal burden being imposed on future generations, because that burden is either larger or smaller than our own burden, but not both. Nor can they each be explaining past or present saving, investment, growth, interest rates, or inflation, because each of these economic variables has a single economic history, not a multitude of economic histories to be explained. In sum, whatever were and are the true economic policies of the past and present, the grab-bag of alternative, and completely unrelated, deficit time-series cannot each be measuring that policy.

The government's official reaction to the embarrassing

problem of too many deficits is to choose the one it likes, anoint it as the "on-budget deficit," and effectively proclaim that it and only it should be discussed.[31] But here the government has a problem. It's the same problem Hans Christian Andersen's naked Emperor has when switching from his resplendent emerald gown to his magnificent crimson robe with its ermine-trimmed train. No matter how many attendants the Emperor has holding up his train, everyone keeps seeing and talking about the gown. This is particularly vexing for the King's council of ministers, who must decide the color of the courtiers' attire. Every time they think they've reached a decision on a matching color, one of the ministers lapses and exclaims, "But it's going to clash!"

Will our economic policies match, or are they destined to clash? We'll never know if we keep looking at the deficit (psst, don't forget, Social Security's out this week, but the S&L bailout's in). In contrast, generational accounting and the three other indicators discussed in the next chapter can really help illuminate the fundamental nature of our public policies.

4

FIGURES LIE
AND LIARS FIGURE

———— ∎ ————

"Figures lie and liars figure" was a pet phrase of President Richard Nixon's Attorney General, John N. Mitchell, who spoke, no doubt, with knowledge born of experience. A tonier version of Mitchell's dictum applies to the use of government statistics to understand public policy: *There are lots of figures and lots of ways to cook the figures.* Sorting through the figures and keeping tabs on the cooks requires a clear sense of what policies should be measured. From the perspective of intertemporal (across-time) economic theory, four features of economic policy ought to be measured. Unfortunately, our government measures none of the four.

This chapter discusses the four fundamentals of fiscal policy. In so doing it places generational accounting into perspective. Generational accounting tells us about only one of the four types of policy, namely the treatment of different generations. The three other policy types can also have powerful effects on the economy, some of which can offset or enhance the effects of generational policy. Hence, in considering the impact of generational policy, one needs to factor in changes in the other three policies as well.

The chapter also discusses how particular real-world policies translate into changes in the fiscal fundamentals. One focus, in this regard, is exposing the wide variety of ways, some quite subtle, in which governments redistribute income, broadly defined, across generations. Because of our choice of accounting labels, many policies that shift generational burdens significantly have no effect on federal, state, or local deficits but, rather, are described in benign terms like "balanced budget" or "pay-as-you-go" policies.

Finally, in identifying the basic elements of fiscal policies and pointing out that each has gone unmeasured, this chapter argues for radically changing the nature and language of our policy debate. This debate, for too long, has been held captive by fiscal indicators that systematically ignore the future and compartmentalize our thinking about policy options. In addition, the indicators we have been using have been, for the most part, grossly misleading. Here are a few examples, each of which is discussed in the chapter:

- Government investment has been counted, in effect, as government consumption.

- The deficit has missed massive redistribution across generations, including that arising from changes in the tax and transfer structure, changes in asset market valuations, and increases in pay-as-you-go tax-transfer schemes.

- Exclusive focus on federal income tax rates has missed the fact that the poorest members of U.S. society are in the highest effective marginal tax brackets.

- Analysis of our tax system's progressivity based on annual income has misclassified as regressive some of the most progressive features of our fiscal system.

Whether the question be our treatment of different generations, the treatment of the rich versus the poor, the level of government spending, or the distortion of economic incentives, there is a critical need to develop long-term, comprehensive, and accurate measures of our public policies.

THE FOUR POLICY FUNDAMENTALS

The four fundamental types of policy are spending policy, generational policy, distribution policy, and distortionary policy. They address, respectively, the following four questions:

- How much is the government consuming over time? (spending policy)
- Which generations will pay for this consumption? (generational policy)
- How are each generation's projected lifetime payments spread over its richer and poorer members? (distribution policy)
- How does the government's extraction of these payments distort economic choices? (distortionary policy)

Government consumption spending ranges from paying the salaries of the military to buying lunch for the President. Spending policy tells us how much of the economy's resources the government directly absorbs ("eats" is a good metaphor); the other three policies consider who gets stuck with the spending bill and which economic choices are distorted as those being stuck try to avoid paying.

The four policies are conceptually distinct. Suppose, for example, U.S. politicians decide to spend a bundle on a party to celebrate the "new world order." Suppose further that they want to spread the burden of paying for the party evenly across all current and future Americans and to raise the required funds in a nondistorting fashion. In principle, they can do this by increasing the net payments of all the members of current and future generations by an equal percentage and by extracting these additional payments in ways that don't further distort economic choices.[1]

In practice, when one of the four policies is changed, one or more of the others is changed as well. The 1990 budget agreement is a good example. This law, if it is not circumvented, will substantially cut the time-path of real spending, raise lifetime net payments of current generations, reduce the fiscal burden on future generations, redistribute away from the lifetime rich toward the lifetime poor (those with low present values of current plus future income), and reduce incentives of upper-income groups to work and save.

Translating the 1990 budget agreement or similar legislation into a clear statement of how it alters the four policy fundamentals requires some effort. But such an effort is necessary if we are to see through to the real actions being taken. The examination of actual or proposed legislation in terms of the four fundamentals would also greatly focus policy discussions. One of the biggest problems with using the deficit to discuss policy is that the word connotes different things to different people. For some a deficit means government spending is too high; for some it means the government is burdening the next generation; for some it suggests the rich are getting off too easy; and for some it means marginal tax rates (the tax rates paid on the last dollar earned, in the case of income taxes, or spent, in the case of excise taxes) are lowering total tax collections. Because "deficit" is such a catchall term, deficit discussions can easily wind up with our talking past one another.

Knowing how proposed policies change the four fundamentals will improve the quality of our fiscal policy debate, but it will not eliminate the need for that debate. Virtually all fiscal actions come at a cost to some segment of current or future society. We can't avoid that. What we can avoid is (1) mistaking winners for losers, (2) choosing policies that are fundamentally at cross-purposes, and (3) missing the long-term costs of policies for their short-term benefits.

MEASURING, EVALUATING, AND DISCERNING FISCAL FUNDAMENTALS

Spending Policy

Understanding spending policy is important for two reasons. First, in assessing how much the government is consuming now and is likely to be consuming in the future, we can also project the total bill being foisted on current and future generations collectively. As we shall see in Chapter 5, the size of that total bill is a key ingredient in determining the likely burden to be imposed on future generations, that is, in doing generational accounting.

Second, the projected course of public spending indicates the government's direct effect over time on national saving. When the government consumes more, its additional consumption directly lowers national saving, since national saving equals national product less total consumption (private plus public). Of course, the bill for public consumption falls on the private sector, and the private sector could, in principal, reduce its own consumption dollar for dollar with the increase in public consumption, leaving national saving unchanged. Whether this happens depends on the allocation of the bill across and within generations, as well as the distortions associated with collecting the bill.

In point of fact, the annual rate of government spending—the ratio of total annual government expenditures on goods and services to annual net national product—has averaged between .22 and .23 in each of the last four decades.[2] So much for the argument that the recent collapse in U.S. saving is due to an increase in the rate of government consumption. To the contrary, the decline in the national saving rate very closely tracks the decline in what we may call the *people's* saving rate, which in the 1980s was less than half the average observed in the previous thirty years.

The people's saving rate may be contrasted with the familiar, but misleading, private saving rate. As pointed out in Chapter 3, private saving equals national saving plus total (federal, state, and local) government dissaving. And total government dissaving is measured by our national income accountants simply as the total government sector deficit. But, as argued, the government deficit is economically arbitrary. Hence, both total private saving and the rate of private saving out of national output are equally arbitrary. That is not the case for the people's saving rate, which considers how much the private sector saves of the nation's output left over after the public sector has consumed, that is, the denominator of the people's saving rate is defined as output (NNP) less government spending, and the numerator equals this difference (the denominator) less private consumption.[3] (See Figure 4–1.)

The fact that federal as well as state and local spending did not increase in the 1980s relative to the economy should also give pause to those who say that increased federal spending is responsible for the large federal budget deficits in the 1980s.[4] Of course, the deficit tells us nothing directly about government spending, since such spending can increase, fall, or remain constant at the same time the deficit increases, falls, or stays constant. Even when increased public spending is not deficit-financed, that is, when taxes are increased or transfers are cut to pay for the additional spending, the fact that the deficit has not changed tells us

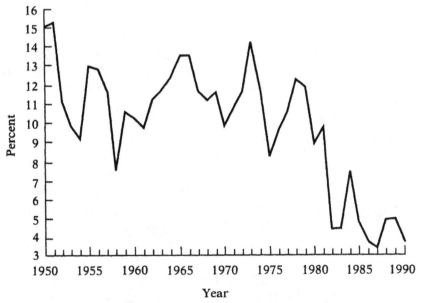

Figure 4–1 *U.S. People's Saving Rate, 1950–1990*

nothing about how the true burden of paying for the increased public purchases of goods and services will be spread across different generations. Which tax (transfer) the politicians raise (reduce) will make all the difference in the world to which current and future generations actually end up bearing the ultimate burden.

In projecting government consumption expenditures through time, one needs to take into account the likely course of defense spending; spending on education, police, turnpikes, and the space program; Congressional salaries; and so forth. One should also consider how demographic change will alter expenditures on various age-specific items, such as elementary and secondary education.

Ideally, one would count here only true consumption spending; one would not repeat the mistake that drives crazy almost everyone who has thought seriously about Uncle Sam's accounting, namely, the confusion of government investment with government consumption.[5] When Uncle Sam and his counterparts at the state and local levels purchase durable goods, including buildings, bridges, and Patriot missiles, they're investing, not consuming. On the other hand, the annual value or benefit of using those durables—what economists call "implicit rent" or "rental equivalent"—should be counted as the true annual spending on durables.[6] *Misclassifying public investment as public consumption, which, in effect, is the government's practice in calculating its budget deficit, biases our political system against infrastructure investment.* This was particularly true in the 1980s, when every federal dollar spent on repairing bridges, building airports, renovating schools, purchasing trucks for the Post Office, and so forth was counted as a dollar that would increase the federal deficit. During the 1980s, when total national output was growing, on average, at 2.7 percent per year, public capital increased at only 0.9 percent per year.[7] *The annual growth rate of public capital in the 1980s was only 40 percent of the corresponding rate in the 1970s.*

Generational Policy

Recall that generational accounts indicate in present value the lifetime bills the government is sending, on average, to members of each generation, including future generations. As demonstrated in Chapter 5, generational accounts can be exhibited on a single sheet of paper. While we have to look at more than just one number to understand generational policy, that is a small price to pay for getting the right answer to this critically important policy question. The United States is facing nothing short of a crisis in national saving. Together with generation-specific information on consumption propensities, generational accounting can provide a useful and accurate guide for choosing policies that will truly raise national saving.

Generational accounting can provide correct guidance here, because it treats uniformly all mechanisms by which the government shifts its bills between different generations, including those mechanisms that leave the official deficit unchanged. The most familiar mechanism is tax cuts, which lead to larger official government deficits and thus a buildup of government IOUs to be paid in the future. Significant burdening of future generations can certainly be associated with an increase in the number of outstanding pieces of paper stamped "Government IOU," but not necessarily. As indicated in previous chapters, and discussed in detail in Chapter 6, announced tax cuts and increases in formal government IOUs may not fundamentally entail a shifting of generational burdens. Tax cuts and increases in formal IOUs may simply reflect a change in labeling of public-sector receipts and payments, without any fundamental change in generational policy.

But if increased deficits may simply represent labeling changes, how can one distinguish a real change in generational policy from a change in labels? The answer is by thinking through each generation's future as well as current payments. If a generation's burden has increased, its present value of net payments—its generational account—will

96

rise no matter what labels the government has decided to use. The following subsections discuss three policies that have been used, perhaps unwittingly, in the United States and other countries to redistribute across generations. None of these policies shows up in the official debt statistics because of the government's labeling of the receipts and payments associated with each of the policies. In each case, were the government to use just the right (if still arbitrary) set of labels, each of these policies would show up on the books as increasing government debt.

"Pay-As-You-Go" Financing of Government Transfers

"Pay-as-you-go" social security is the best known example of this type of policy. In the social security "Ponzi game" (named after Charles Ponzi, a Bostonian who initiated a chain letter), workers pay money to Social Security, which hands the money over to retirees in the form of "retirement benefits." Since the money workers pay is called "taxes," and the money retirees receive is called "transfers," and since "taxes" equal "transfers," true pay-as-you-go social security has zero impact on the deficit.

Despite the invariance of the deficit, this policy can redistribute massive sums across generations. To see why, note that under "pay-as-you-go" financing, every age cohort but one pays, when young, for the retirement benefits of the contemporaneous elderly; the one exception, of course, is the first set of elderly at the startup of the program. This first set of elderly receives benefits without having had to finance the retirement of its immediate predecessors.

If this first set of elderly gets a windfall, does this windfall come at the expense of younger startup generations as well as future generations? The answer, as most U.S. baby boomers know, is yes. Most baby boomers will receive a small positive, if not negative, rate of return on their Social Security contributions; put another way, using a market discount rate, the present value of their current and future contributions will exceed the present value of their projected future benefits. Not surprisingly, many, and perhaps most, boomers would love to opt out of the Social Security chain letter and invest their contributions in market securities, which yield a higher real rate of return. The boomers' children will get an even rawer deal from Social Security. They are projected to lose, on net, roughly $16,500 in present value from being forced to participate in this scheme, whose financing tagline should surely be changed from "pay-as-you-go" to "you-go-and-you-pay."[8]

"Revenue-neutral" Changes in the Tax Base

This "balanced budget" mechanism by which politicians redistribute across generations is less well known. The following are three illustrations of such policies:

Switching the tax base away from capital income toward labor income,[9] is good for the initial elderly (those who are old at the time of the switch), since most capital income is received by the elderly. It is bad for initial young and middle-aged generations, who are forced to pay higher taxes on their wages and salaries. This change in tax bases also makes future generations, on balance, worse off, because the additional labor income taxes they face in their youth and middle age have a higher present value than does the reduction in capital income taxes.

Switching from sales and excise taxes (consumption taxes) to wage taxation redistributes from initial younger and future generations to initial older generations, because the initial set of elderly are relieved of paying sales and excise taxes, but escape, via their retirement, the higher wage taxation.

Making the federal income tax more progressive shifts a larger share of the tax burden onto middle-aged and younger workers. The annual incomes of these workers are, on average, higher than those of the retired elderly, and given total income tax collections, greater progressivity means those with higher incomes pay more while those with lower incomes pay less.

Such changes in tax bases aren't simply hypothetical. Since 1960, sales and excise taxes have declined from almost one-third of total government tax collections to less than one-fourth. Capital income taxation has also changed. For example, in 1960 corporate income taxes accounted for 16 percent of tax collections; today's figure is 7 percent. In addition to shifting the tax base between labor income, capital income, and consumption, the government has, over the past thirty years, substantially reduced the progressivity of the federal income tax. In 1960 the tax rate in the highest bracket was 91 percent. By 1968 it had fallen to 70 percent, where it stayed through 1981, when it was reduced to 50 percent. The top rate today is 31 percent.[10]

Running Generational Policy Through Asset Markets

This is the government's most subtle mechanism of inter-generational redistribution. It consists of policies that lower the market value of the private sector's holdings of tangible and financial assets. Since older generations are the primary owners of assets, a reduction in asset values hurts the elderly but helps existing young and future generations, who purchase, through time, these assets from older generations at lower prices.[11]

An important example of policies that change asset prices is the government's periodic investment incentives, such as its acceleration of depreciation allowances in 1981. Investment incentives are basically public subsidies to businesses that engage in new investment. Attention here should be fixed on the word "new." The investment incentives are effectively restricted to new investment. "Old capital"—plant and equipment purchased in the past (really, written off for tax purposes in the past)—is not entitled to the subsidy.[12] Hence old capital must sell at a discount reflecting the preferential tax treatment available to new capital. An increase in investment incentives means a bigger discount on old capital, that is, a bigger capital loss to owners of old capital. That loss accrues to older generations, while young and

99

middle-aged generations are better off because they can now purchase old capital at a lower price.[13]

To see this in more concrete terms, assume you're sixty and are just about to put your dry cleaning business up for sale and retire. The business, by the way, represents your life's savings. You have previously written off for tax purposes your business's building and all its equipment. While the building and equipment have been written off, they are in excellent condition—indeed, physically they are as good as new. Now suppose our political leaders announce they are providing a 10 percent investment tax credit available to any business purchasing new structures or equipment. What will happen to the price at which you can sell your dry cleaning business? It will fall in value by 10 percent. The reason is that the thirty-year-old potential buyer with whom you have been talking now realizes that, instead of buying your dry cleaning business, he can, for the same price, buy a new building and new dry cleaning equipment, and get a 10 percent subsidy from the government on those purchases.[14] What's more, your other potential buyers will realize the same thing. As a result, you will be forced to sell your business to the thirty-year-old for 10 percent less than you had previously intended. The government has, in effect, taxed away 10 percent of the value of your business, collected the proceeds, and handed them to the thirty-year-old. Notice that this effective imposition of a new cost on you and the effective removal of a net payment on the thirty-year-old would leave not only the reported deficit unchanged, but reported taxes and transfers as well.

Another example of redistributing across generations through changes in real asset values involves the government's printing of money. When the government prints more money, prices go up. But the government's official IOUs (its outstanding bonds) are nominal liabilities, which means they are promises by the government to pay fixed numbers of dollars in the future, regardless of the ensuing inflation. But in printing money and thereby raising prices, the government lowers the real value of these nominal IOUs. Since the IOUs are, by and large, held by older generations, this policy hurts older generations and helps younger and future generations, who now have to make smaller real net payments to help pay off these watered-down pieces of paper. A closely related devaluation of government IOUs occurs if the government simply announces it will print more money in the future. That will raise nominal interest rates and, since bond prices are inversely related to nominal interest rates, will lower the real value of outstanding government bonds.

To summarize, the government has a lot of ways in which it unburdens some generations and burdens other generations. Some of these are so sneaky that even the government doesn't understand them. If those sneaky redistributions across generations occurred rather infrequently and were small in magnitude, they wouldn't be worth talking about. But they occur quite frequently and are often huge, so they definitely need to be taken very seriously.

Distribution Policy

Generational accounts reveal how much we and our contemporaries are likely, on average, to pay, due to sneaky as well as unsneaky policies. But we also want to know how our own bill differs from the average in our age group. If we think our lifetime incomes will be rather low, can we expect to pay much less than others our age whose lifetime incomes will be quite high? And how much less? Proper description of distribution policy entails a comparison of the lifetime bills of poor members of a generation with the lifetime bills of rich members of the generation, where poor and rich refers to those whose projected lifetime incomes are low and high, respectively. This is a question of *progressivity*. One determines the progressivity of our fiscal system by asking whether the lifetime bills of the rich are a larger fraction of their lifetime incomes than is the case for the poor.

In addition to equity considerations, knowing about lifetime progressivity can also help us formulate policy toward saving. The lifetime rich of all generations appear to have higher propensities to save than do the lifetime poor of the same age (that is, their propensity to immediately consume an additional dollar of lifetime income is lower).[15] Hence, making our fiscal policy more progressive on a lifetime basis may come at the cost of further reductions in national saving, because increased progressivity takes from high marginal savers and gives to low marginal savers.

While one might think that progressivity in the distribution of lifetime net payments would be very similar to the annual progressivity of the U.S. federal income tax, that is far from obvious. Take a retired millionaire who reports very little current income because he's invested his wealth in growth stocks, which pay small dividends. If one looked only at the millionaire's current federal income tax payments, he'd look as though he was getting a great deal.[16] If, on the other hand, one takes into account the future capital gains taxes he'll pay when he sells the stocks, as well as the future sales and luxury taxes he'll pay when he spends down his wealth, the millionaire may end up ultimately handing a reasonable share of his economic resources to Uncle Sam.

Since the proper base for measuring progressivity in the analysis of distribution policy is lifetime income, not current income, and since such an analysis would consider all taxes paid (as well as all benefits received), not just federal income taxes, a proper distribution analysis may well yield a view of the fairness of the U.S. fiscal system dramatically different from that based on current annual income. Unfortunately, examining actual distribution policy goes beyond the scope of this book, primarily because the calculations required necessitate much more detailed information than is needed to do generational accounting. If generational accounting becomes a mainstay of policy-making, distributional analysis will surely occur as well.[17]

Distortionary Policy

The big incentive problems created by the government involve motives to work and save. Obviously taxes on labor earnings give people less reason to work. But so too do sales and other excise taxes, since paying taxes when we spend our hard-earned money is not really different from getting paid less to begin with. If labor, sales, and excise taxes lessen our incentives to work, which taxes give us less reason to save? The answer is taxes on interest, dividends, profits, rents, and other asset income (capital income in econ-jargon).[18] We pay some of these taxes directly in personal income taxes, and some indirectly in corporate income taxes.

Economists view government disincentives to work and save as altering the prices people face for consuming certain commodities relative to consuming other commodities. In the case of work incentives, the commodities involved are standard goods and services on the one hand, and leisure on the other. Direct and indirect taxation of labor income lowers the price of consuming leisure (not working) relative to consuming hot dogs, trips to Hawaii, TV sets, motorcycles, and all other standard goods and services.

When it comes to saving incentives, relative prices of current and future consumption are distorted. Direct and indirect taxation of our capital income lowers the price of consuming today compared with consuming tomorrow. The logic behind this is simple: When our income from savings is taxed at a higher rate, we need to put more aside today (forego more consumption today) in order to consume tomorrow the same amount we would otherwise have consumed. Hence, taxes on asset income make consuming tomorrow relatively more costly than consuming today. The upshot is this: Faced with this intertemporal distortion, people will consume more now than they otherwise would.

A proper description of distortionary policy requires specifying how the government has mucked up the relative prices people face over their lifetimes. Ideally one would do this separately for rich, middle-income, and poor members of each generation. *If the government were forced to reveal its distortionary policy in this manner, we'd see that for most Americans disincentives to work and save are as high today as when the Republicans took office in 1981.*

How can that be? After all, weren't marginal taxes reduced with the Reagan tax cuts and the Tax Reform Act of 1986? Yes, but primarily for high-income Americans. Middle-income baby boomers have seen their effective (total) marginal labor income tax rates *rise* through increases in federal sales and excise taxes, state and local sales and excise taxes, state income taxes, and federal payroll taxes, as well as limitations on federal income tax deductions of various types.[19] Boomers also had their effective marginal labor income tax rates raised when the government decided in 1983 to reduce the boomers' future Social Security benefits and to tax them under the federal income tax. This means that every dollar boomers contribute now to Social Security returns less in future Social Security benefits (measured in present value) than previously.[20] Social Security is, by the way, not small potatoes; most Americans now pay more to Uncle Sam in Social Security taxes than they do in income taxes.

Assessing work disincentives based solely on the federal income tax is particularly misleading when it comes to the poorest members of society, those on welfare. Since they pay no federal income tax, one might think the work disincentives facing welfare recipients would be rather small. Not so. *In fact, U.S. welfare recipients face the highest effective marginal tax rates (the lowest relative price of leisure) of all Americans, and their marginal tax rates have risen in the past decade.* This high marginal taxation is embedded in our various "transfer" programs (e.g. Food Stamps, AFDC, WIC, SSI, Medicaid), which reduce welfare recipients' benefits by a large fraction of a dollar for every dollar the welfare recipients earn through work. In Massachusetts, for example, the tax brackets of welfare recipients can easily exceed 90 percent.[21]

To summarize, while the nation, since 1980, has dwelt on federal marginal income tax rates, whatever "reform" of work disincentives arose from changes in federal income taxation were quietly subverted. This is precisely what one might expect from a political process that faces no requirement to report its true distortionary policy in a systematic manner for the rich and poor alike.

Effective marginal taxes on capital income are also noticeably higher now than they were a decade ago—32 percent now versus 23 percent in 1981.[22] As economists would say, the relative price of consuming today as against tomorrow is lower today than in 1981. What happened to Reagan's vaunted saving incentives? The answer is three pieces of legislation with three overblown titles: The Tax Equity and Fiscal Responsibility Act of 1982, The Deficit Reduction Act of 1984, and the "revenue-neutral" Tax Reform Act of 1986. The first two undid the substantial progress achieved in 1981 in reducing saving disincentives. These "reforms" raised effective capital income taxes by reducing the speed at which corporations could write off depreciation, thereby reversing the "reforms" of the 1981 Economic Recovery Tax Act. How can different pieces of legislation that do exactly opposite things all be called reforms? Don't ask.

In 1981 the cry of the times was "Americans need incentives to save!" But after a few years, when Americans needed, if anything, more incentives to save, the cry switched to "Let corporations pay their fair share!" This anthropomorphizing of corporations continues, by the way, to mystify economists. Corporations do not, of course, pay taxes; their owners do. And their owners, by and large, are you and I. Indeed, one of the largest collective holders of U.S. corporate stock are past and present American workers who own companies, like Exxon, AT&T, and Raytheon, through their employers' pension funds. As of 1988 U.S. pension funds owned 23 percent of all U.S. corporate stock.[23]

In calculating saving disincentives, whether it be those in the 1980s or those in some other period, it is essential to factor in not only capital income taxes individuals and business pay in the short run, but also what they will pay in the long run. Depreciation allowances provide a good illustration of the need to think about future as well as current taxes. Depreciation allowances are often provided as "accelerated" up-front deductions, letting businesses pay less taxes on their investments in the present in exchange for more taxes on their investments in the future. Assessing the total marginal tax on the capital invested in businesses requires comparing, on a present value footing, the future higher taxes with the current lower taxes. Economists inside and outside Washington have routinely been doing such calculations since 1979.[24] These present value calculations are now well understood by members of Congress as well as the Administration. Today, no one in Washington would contest the need to think carefully about future as well as current capital income taxes. On the contrary, with respect to capital income taxation such future-think has become absolutely routine.

TOWARD A NEW FISCAL LANGUAGE

The Intertemporal Perspective

An important feature of each of the four fiscal fundamentals just discussed is that they are forward-looking; they consider not only what the government is doing now, but also what it is scheduled to do through time. The reason we need to talk today about what policy will be tomorrow is simple. All of us, whether we choose to admit it or not, are forward-looking and are forced to consider how we will be treated by the government over time. Each of us has some time left to live. Most of us, fortunately, have a lot of time left to live. None of us makes economic decisions solely for the next second, or the next minute, or the next week. On the contrary, virtually all of us routinely make economic choices that will affect us many years into the future. Those decisions range from the purchase of a car (the services of which will last for many years), to choosing when to retire, to contributing to an IRA, to getting a divorce (obviously, not primarily an economic decision, but nevertheless one with profound long-term economic implications), to relocating, to going back to school, to . . . Even going to dinner at an expensive restaurant raises the question of the future, since spending money on a terrific meal now means having less to spend on something else later.

Since essentially all our economic decisions today are made in light of what we expect to happen in the future, including the government's future actions, a proper description of current economic policy comprises more than a statement of what taxes the public sector is levying this minute or even this year. It must lay out what we think taxes, among other things, will be in the future. It makes no sense to discuss economic policy while wearing blinders.

To be fair, the government is increasingly adopting a longer planning horizon in formulating its policy. Examples here include the 1977 and 1983 Social Security amendments that considered the long-term integrity of Social Security, the 1985 multiyear Gramm–Rudman targets, and the 1990 budget act's five-year time horizon. In addition, a variety of excellent studies by government economists have examined the long-term implications of actual or proposed pieces of legislation.[25] Unfortunately, such thinking about the future has gone on in a sporadic and piecemeal fashion.

Why Distinguish People
on the Basis of Their Generation?

People differ along a number of dimensions, so why is the treatment of different generations such a big deal? The answer is immediate once one sets aside the static mindset of conventional Keynesian macroeconomics and thinks about the dynamic nature of economies. Economies are continually evolving; there are always new technologies, new firms, and new commodities coming onto the scene. But most important, there are always new people with new ideas and fresh energy showing up to replace and supplement those who came before.

Even were the new generations equal in number to and precise clones of their fathers and mothers, their saving and other types of economic behavior might differ dramatically from that of their forebears if they experience different treatment at the hands of the government. For this reason alone, then, understanding the public sector's impact through time on national saving, real wage growth, and so on, necessarily requires knowing how the government will treat successive generations. Viewed in this light, it is not surprising that generational policy is central to modern dynamic "overlapping generations" models of the economy.[26] Such models now dominate curricula in graduate economics programs.

Why Focus on Within-Generation Distribution Policy?

Determining an equitable answer to the question, "Who will pay?" requires thinking about not only which *generations* will pay but also which *members of any particular generation* will pay. Generational accounting forces us to confront our views about intergenerational (across-generation) equity; measuring our distribution policy forces us to consider intragenerational (within-generation) equity. In combination, generational and distribution policies can be adjusted to achieve the desired distribution of welfare across and within generations. For example, if we believe that the rich elderly are being favored over the poor middle-aged, this can be corrected by redistributing (1) from the rich elderly to the poor elderly, (2) from the rich middle-aged to the poor middle-aged, and (3) from the elderly in general to the middle-aged in general. Clearly, in practice, the government would probably just take money directly from the rich elderly and give it to the poor middle-aged, but conceptually, at least, it would be choosing both its desired generational policy and its desired within-generation distribution policy.

Why Consider Lifetime Rather than Annual Fiscal Burdens?

As mentioned in Chapter 1, there are very few Americans living hand-to-mouth, that is, whose current well-being depends solely on their current income. For the great majority of Americans, rich and poor alike, expected future income is a critical determinant of current consumption and welfare. Hence, when the government changes its policies, the welfare impact for the bulk of Americans depends on the change in their projected lifetime net payments (measured in present value) to the government. This point notwithstanding, conventional policy analysis ignores the lifetime positions of Americans and instead measures policy impacts on households by comparing, for rich and poor households, the changes in current-year net taxes (usually expressed as a fraction of current-year income).

To see the problem caused by this practice, consider how conventional analysts would react if one suggested evaluating the progressivity of the recently enacted 10 percent luxury tax by taking each American's average daily luxury tax payments in 1991 and dividing by the income the American received on the first Thursday in 1991. People get paid on different days. Hence, this ratio of taxes to income would make a millionaire baseball player, who didn't get paid on that Thursday, but paid a lot in luxury taxes over the year, look like a pauper forced to pay big bucks to Uncle Sam; that is, this method of exhibiting relative tax burdens could make a highly progressive policy seem highly regressive. How would conventional analysts react? They would cry foul.

But were policy analysts in the habit of evaluating progressivity by comparing projected lifetime fiscal burdens with projected lifetime incomes, they would also cry foul if someone suggested dividing annual tax payments by annual incomes. While annual income is not as poor a measure of an individual's lifetime living standard as is income received on the first Thursday in January, there are very considerable fluctuations in people's annual incomes over time. Take the case of a highly paid executive who spends a year between jobs, during which time he lives off the "golden parachute" from his previous job. If one looks at the executive's current income he'll look rather poor; if one looks at his expected lifetime income, including the value of his assets, however, he'll look rich.

109

Economists have begun to show just how poor annual income is as a reference point for considering tax burdens. Professor James Poterba, a public finance expert at MIT, recently examined the alleged regressivity of the gasoline tax.[27] Poterba ranked individuals not on the basis of their annual incomes but on the basis of their annual consumption expenditures. Since people base their consumption on their estimate of their lifetime incomes, annual consumption expenditures is a fairly good proxy for expected lifetime income. Poterba showed that the gasoline tax is roughly proportional to annual consumption expenditures. That means a tax that virtually everyone has been conditioned to believe is regressive is not regressive when properly measured relative to people's true standards of living.[28]

Other economists have examined the lifetime progressivity of the Social Security system and found it to be highly progressive. Why? Because those who contribute the least receive the highest rates of return on their contributions. One such study showed that lifetime-rich baby boomers who make the maximum contributions to Social Security will *lose*, over the course of their lifetimes, almost *$100,000* in present value because of their forced participation in Social Security.[29] In contrast, lifetime-poor boomers will roughly break even; they will pay close to zero in net present value over their lifetimes. This huge and highly progressive within-generation redistribution is, roughly speaking, of the same order of magnitude as the within-generation redistribution arising from our progressive federal income tax coupled with our welfare system. Despite this fact, some U.S. Senators claim that the increase in the size of the Social Security system relative to the economy has made our fiscal policy much more regressive. For example, in his 1991 Social Security tax cut proposal Senator Daniel Patrick Moynihan states:

> The tax structure of the United States is fast becoming one of the most regressive of any Western nation. In the 1980s we cut income taxes for the better off and raised payroll taxes

110

for low and middle income workers. Social security revenue as a percent of total federal revenue rose by 23 percent from 1980 to 1988, while personal and corporate income tax revenue as a percent of total federal revenue declined by 6 percent and 23 percent respectively.[30]

Is Senator Moynihan right? Is Social Security highly progressive or highly regressive? The answer depends on your frame of reference. If you take the lifetime frame of reference, which is surely the more appropriate one for the vast majority of Americans based on how they actually act, the Social Security system as a whole is one of the most progressive elements of U.S. distribution policy.[31]

THE NEED TO THINK COMPREHENSIVELY

One of the features of the generational accounting exhibited in the next chapter and the measurement of the other fiscal fundamentals recommended in this chapter is that they deal in a comprehensive manner with the various taxes, transfers, credits, subsidies, excises, fees, deductions, exemptions, and so on of all different public sector entities.[32] The lifetime perspective—by including future as well as current net payments—is itself one of three important ways in which generational accounting and proper analysis of distributional policy and distortionary policy are comprehensive.

The second way has to do with the word "net" in net payment. When Senator Mitchell at the end of 1987 observed in the *Wall Street Journal* that "there has been a shift of about $80 billion in annual revenue collections from the progressive income tax to the regressive payroll tax," he was playing Senator Moynihan's game of focusing on the "regressive" payroll "taxes" that people pay when young and ignoring the "progressive" benefit payments people receive when old. In effect, he was not netting the future benefits against current taxes. Discussing Social Security by looking only at its taxes is not far afield from claiming that welfare

111

recipients are bearing the largest tax burden of everyone in the United States because they pay sales taxes like everyone else, but their incomes (ignoring their welfare benefits) are zero. If we want to discuss distribution policy in a meaningful way, we need to look at the total net treatment of all Americans, be they workers or welfare recipients.

The third comprehensive feature of the proposed new fiscal approach is the combined treatment of state and local as well as federal government policies. As mentioned, state and local government finance has loomed as large as the federal government's throughout the postwar period and, in some respects, has grown in relative terms in the last two decades. State and local governments now spend $1.60 on goods and services for every dollar spent by the federal government, up from $1.20 in 1970.[33] Some of the growth in state and local government relative to the central government reflects a conscious policy to enhance local control of public finances. "Revenue sharing," in which the federal government collects money from people living in the various states and then hands it back to them through their state governments, is the concrete expression of this policy. A total of 13 percent of total federal revenues is currently being shared with the states.[34]

Even without revenue sharing it would be tricky to tell state and local governments and the federal government apart. Federal and state governments jointly finance a number of welfare programs, including Aid to Families with Dependent Children (AFDC) and Medicaid. They also share in the costs of building highways. An example is Massachusetts's plan to renovate the North–South Freeway as it runs through Boston—the so-called Artery Project. The feds are paying for the portions of the freeway just before one enters and just after one leaves downtown Boston. But renovating the freeway in between will be solely the state's responsibility. And how will the Massachusetts government pay for its stretch of the freeway? In part, by charging the federal government. How? By raising state income taxes, which are deductible from the federal income tax.

112

THE POTENTIAL BENEFITS OF THE NEW FISCAL INDICATORS

The adoption of the proposed fiscal indicators can have real benefits. First, since the indicators deal in a consistent manner with all public policies affecting the fiscal fundamentals, they can reveal whether the various policies reinforce or offset one another. This is particularly important in the area of U.S. generational policy, where offsetting generational actions have often been the rule, rather than the exception. Second, they can point out the direction of true reform and can indicate the size of our generational, distributional, spending, and incentives problems. Third, they can reopen the discussion of a range of fiscal proposals that have been cursorily dismissed as regressive when, in fact, they are not regressive on a lifetime basis. Finally, by showing each generation that the government is fundamentally treating it as a distinct group, the new indicators open the door to generation-specific policies. Such policies range from reforming Social Security for baby boomers, to generation-specific catastrophic health insurance, to making federal income tax rates age-specific.[35]

5

GENERATIONAL ACCOUNTING

——— ∎ ———

F or many of you, especially those of you who are young or middle-aged, reading this chapter may be like opening your bills—rather depressing. This chapter shows how much, in present value, the average member of your generation owes or, as the case may be, is owed over the rest of his or her life based on current policy. For American newborns the news is particularly bad. They can expect to fork over almost two-fifths of their lifetime incomes to the government. Future Americans have it even worse. When they arrive on the scene their lifetime net tax bills will be at least a 21 percent larger share of their lifetime incomes than is the case for those just born.

The first tables you'll be considering do not incorporate the 1990 federal budget agreement.[1] A subsequent table shows how much you and your contempories were hurt, on average, by this piece of legislation. This is just one of nine policy stimulations considered in this chapter, each of which involves substantial changes in generational accounts for particular age cohorts.

Before reading further you may want to pour a stiff drink and get into a reclining position. Now, if you're ready, take a look at Tables 5–1 and 5–2 to see how much, on average and

Table 5-1
The Composition of Male Generational Accounts (r = .06, g = .0075): Present Values of Receipts and Payments
(thousands of dollars)

Generation's Age in 1989	Net Payment	Payments						Receipts					
		Labor Income Taxes	FICA Taxes	Excise Taxes	Capital Income Taxes	Seigno-rage[a]	Property Taxes	OASDI	HI	Welfare AFDC	Welfare General	UI	Food Stamps
0	73.7	24.8	26.5	22.9	9.5	0.0	1.6	4.5	1.1	0.3	4.4	1.0	0.3
5	93.2	31.8	34.0	26.3	12.2	0.1	2.0	5.5	1.5	0.4	4.3	1.2	0.4
10	116.8	40.8	43.6	29.8	15.6	0.1	2.6	6.7	1.9	0.5	4.6	1.6	0.5
15	145.3	52.2	55.8	32.8	20.0	0.1	3.3	8.1	2.4	0.6	5.1	2.0	0.7
20	169.1	61.9	66.2	33.9	24.8	0.1	4.1	9.5	2.9	0.7	5.3	2.4	0.8
25	193.0	70.3	75.1	35.8	32.4	0.1	5.3	12.0	3.8	0.9	5.6	2.6	0.9
30	194.5	69.6	74.4	34.2	38.4	0.1	6.1	14.3	4.6	0.8	5.4	2.3	0.9
35	186.0	65.2	69.7	32.0	43.8	0.0	6.9	17.2	5.7	0.6	5.2	2.0	0.8

40	176.2	60.9	65.1	30.5	49.8	0.0	7.6	21.9	7.4	0.5	5.3	1.8	0.7
45	155.4	54.4	58.1	28.7	54.2	0.0	7.8	29.8	10.0	0.4	5.5	1.5	0.6
50	114.1	42.1	45.0	24.4	52.1	0.0	7.1	37.1	12.4	0.3	5.4	1.1	0.5
55	69.7	31.0	33.2	20.8	48.7	0.0	6.6	47.9	16.0	0.2	5.4	0.7	0.4
60	18.9	20.2	21.5	17.9	44.1	0.0	6.1	62.6	22.0	0.1	5.6	0.3	0.3
65	−31.8	9.1	9.7	14.7	37.0	0.0	5.4	71.2	30.7	0.0	5.6	0.0	0.2
70	−42.7	4.0	4.3	11.9	29.3	0.0	4.5	61.9	29.6	0.0	4.9	0.0	0.2
75	−41.5	1.8	2.0	9.5	22.5	0.0	3.7	48.9	27.9	0.0	4.1	0.0	0.1
80	−35.6	0.6	0.6	7.5	17.2	0.0	3.0	36.9	24.4	0.0	3.0	0.0	0.1
85	−28.2	0.0	0.0	6.1	14.3	0.0	2.4	28.2	20.9	0.0	1.8	0.0	0.1
90	−1.5	0.0	0.0	1.2	6.7	0.0	0.5	5.4	4.2	0.0	0.2	0.0	0.0
Future generations	89.5												

a."Seignorage" is the revenues the government creates directly by printing money

Table 5-2
The Composition of Female Generational Accounts (r = .06, g = .0075): Present Values of Receipts and Payments
(thousands of dollars)

Generation's Age in 1989	Net Payment	Payments						Receipts					
		Labor Income Taxes	FICA Taxes	Excise Taxes	Capital Income Taxes	Seigno-rage	Property Taxes	OASDI	HI	Welfare AFDC	General	UI	Food Stamps
0	36.4	14.0	14.9	20.2	3.5	0.0	2.1	5.0	1.5	2.3	7.8	0.4	1.3
5	46.5	17.7	18.9	23.0	4.5	0.0	2.6	6.1	1.9	2.9	7.2	0.6	1.7
10	60.4	23.3	24.9	27.2	5.9	0.1	3.5	7.5	2.5	3.8	7.8	0.7	2.2
15	70.7	28.1	30.1	29.0	7.2	0.1	4.2	8.6	3.0	4.6	8.2	0.9	2.6
20	85.5	34.8	37.2	32.2	9.3	0.0	5.4	10.9	3.9	5.2	9.2	1.1	3.3
25	91.0	36.3	38.8	33.2	11.7	0.0	6.5	13.1	4.8	4.5	9.0	1.1	3.0
30	90.9	35.1	37.5	33.1	14.9	0.0	7.4	15.7	6.1	3.5	8.5	1.0	2.4
35	86.9	32.9	35.2	32.1	18.3	0.0	8.1	18.6	7.7	2.5	8.2	0.9	1.9

40	78.2	29.7	31.7	30.1	21.4	0.0	8.6	21.9	9.8	1.7	7.8	0.7	1.4
45	62.9	25.4	27.2	27.4	23.8	0.0	8.9	27.0	12.6	1.0	7.6	0.6	1.0
50	41.0	20.4	21.8	24.2	25.0	0.0	8.9	34.0	16.3	0.6	7.3	0.4	0.7
55	11.7	14.9	15.9	20.8	24.9	0.0	8.7	43.9	21.3	0.2	7.2	0.3	0.5
60	−22.5	9.3	9.9	17.4	23.4	0.0	8.2	55.1	27.8	0.0	7.2	0.2	0.4
65	−53.7	4.8	5.1	14.2	20.8	0.0	7.6	61.2	37.4	0.0	7.2	0.1	0.4
70	−60.2	2.0	2.2	11.5	17.3	0.0	6.9	56.5	36.8	0.0	6.5	0.0	0.3
75	−57.9	0.7	0.7	9.1	13.2	0.0	6.0	47.4	34.5	0.0	5.5	0.0	0.3
80	−50.8	0.0	0.0	7.2	8.8	0.0	5.1	37.4	29.9	0.0	4.5	0.0	0.2
85	−42.7	0.0	0.0	5.8	4.5	0.0	4.2	28.7	24.7	0.0	3.6	0.0	0.2
90	−7.4	0.0	0.0	1.0	0.4	0.0	0.7	4.7	4.2	0.0	0.6	0.0	0.0
Future generations	44.2												

in present value, members of your generation will pay, on net (in taxes paid less transfers received), over their remaining lives. Table 5–1 displays the accounts for males, and Table 5–2 the accounts for females. To save space, the tables include only every fifth age. Note that the numbers are in *thousands* of dollars. The calculations assume a 6 percent real (inflation-adjusted) discount rate (r) and an 0.75 growth rage (g), both of which are reasonable values for the U.S. economy.[2] Plausible alternative discount and growth rates lead to larger or smaller generational accounts but leave unchanged the assessment of the relative burden being foisted by current generations upon future generations as well as the generational implications of alternative policies.[3] As you look for the entry closest to your age, you'll see not only the lifetime average bills for members of the different generations, but also the breakdown of these bills between the different types of taxes and transfer payments.

If you haven't passed out yet, also take a look at the bottom of each table, where you'll see the burden on future generations. This burden is calculated under two assumptions: first, that policy toward existing generations will remain unchanged and, second, that the lifetime bill facing each new generation after 1989 is identical except for an adjustment for growth. As will be discussed shortly, there are other assumptions one can make to document the imbalance in generational policy. What is being done at the bottom of these tables is to assess the burden on future generations if current generations are treated, over time, neither better nor worse than can be extrapolated based on existing policy.

In looking at the accounts, keep in mind that they are forward-looking. They ignore what net payments particular generations made in the past. The generational accounts are not total lifetime bills, but, rather, remaining lifetime bills. That's why the accounts are positive for young and middle-aged generations, but negative for older generations. Through the rest of their lives young and middle-aged gener-

120

ations can expect, on balance, and on a present value basis, to pay more money to the government than they receive, whereas older generations can expect, on balance, to receive more money from the government than they will pay.

Compare, for example, the $176,200 average bill of forty-year-old males with the negative $42,700 average bill of seventy-year-old males. Males aged forty can anticipate spending many more years working and paying income and payroll taxes on their labor earnings as well as other taxes. While those males will receive some welfare and unemployment benefits in the short run, most of their transfers will come much later from Social Security (including Medicare). The substantial taxes forty-year-olds will pay over the next twenty or so years have a larger present value than do the substantial transfers they'll receive in the following twenty or so years. This reflects the fact that dollars paid (received) farther in the future have lower present values than dollars paid (received) today.[4] For seventy-year-old males the story is quite different. These males are generally retired and are already receiving sizable Social Security retirement and Medicare benefits. On average, the present value of the ongoing benefits of the males exceeds the present value of their remaining tax payments.

Another perhaps surprising, but easily explained, feature of the accounts is that they are largest for those around age thirty. Why will thirty-year-olds, who have already paid in lots of taxes, pay more in present value than, say, ten-year-olds, who have virtually all their taxpaying years still in front of them. The answer is that thirty-year-olds are just about to reach their peak taxpaying years, whereas ten-year-olds are over more than twenty years away from their peak taxpaying years and still farther away from when they will receive most of their benefits/transfers from the government. Again, because money paid off in the future has a smaller present value than money paid today, being close to the peak taxpaying years makes a big difference in the calculation.

MALES VERSUS FEMALES

If you compare Tables 5–1 and 5–2, you'll see that the life-time net tax payments males can expect to make are much larger at each age than are the corresponding amounts for females. Part of the explanation here is that males account for two-thirds of total U.S. labor income and pay most of the taxes collected on this income.[5] Part is that females receive more transfer payments. And part is that females live longer.

The differences in the male and female accounts are siz-able. According to the tables, the average lifetime bill handed to males born in 1989 was $73,700, whereas the bill handed to newborn females was $36,400. Most (82 percent) of the difference between these numbers reflects the $22,400 larger present value of taxes on labor earnings that newborn males will pay relative to newborn females.

What should one make of these differences? Is the govern-ment treating females better than males? Not necessarily. Females are paying less because their lifetime incomes are lower. The lower relative incomes of females also means that a larger fraction of females than males are eligible for various government assistance programs.

A WORD OF CAUTION ABOUT INTERPRETING GENERATIONAL ACCOUNTS

As illustrated by the male–female differences, one cannot necessarily make equity judgments about the treatment of different members of society simply by comparing their gen-erational accounts. This is particularly important to bear in mind when considering the accounts of the elderly as com-pared with those of the middled-aged and young genera-tions. The remaining lifetime bills of the elderly are smaller than those of the middle-aged and young because the elderly made most of their tax payments in earlier years.

To answer the normative question of whether the elderly are being treated too well or too poorly one needs to factor in their past contributions to society both in the form of direct net payments to the government and in other forms, such as defending the country during World War II.

Generational accounts are designed neither to resolve nor to address the mega-equity questions of whether females are being treated unfairly or whether the current elderly have been given too much of a good deal in the past. Rather, as noted above, they start with the status quo, namely current public policy, and ask two fundamental questions: *First, if we follow current policy and do not extract more from those generations alive today, including those who have just been born, how will the treatment of future generations compare with that of current newborns? Second, if we do change policy, which of the different generations now alive and coming in the future will gain and which will lose (and by how much)?*

These two comparisons—comparing the accounts of future generations with those of newborns and comparing the policy-induced changes in the accounts of different generations—should be the focus of attention. Importantly, these two comparisons are *label-free;* regardless of which words the government uses to label what it takes in (taxes or borrowing) and pays out (transfers or repayments), these two comparisons always yield the same answer. However, while the use of generational accounts to make these two comparisons is label-free, the initial levels of the accounts displayed in Tables 5–1 and 5–2, with the exception of those of newborns, are not. They do depend on the way the government labels its receipts and payments.

To see why, consider again the negative $42,700 account of seventy-year-old males. Now think how much larger (less negative) that number would be had the government historically called Social Security contributions "loans" rather than "taxes" and Social Security benefits "repayment of principal plus interest on the loans" plus an "old-age tax," where the old-age tax adjusts for the fact that benefits may not equal principal plus interest on contributions. With this alternative language, today's seventy-year-old's generational account would be a lot larger (a lot less negative), because it would exclude the $61,900 in present value of Social Security (OASDI) benefits indicated in Table 5–1 and would include the present value of the "old-age tax."

Moreover, the accounts for newborns don't depend on the government's labels because the government has yet to take or give any money to any newborns. That is, there is no basis as yet on which an arbitrary labeling decision can be made. For a newborn, the present value of his or her future Social Security contributions less the present value of his or her future Social Security benefits has the same value regardless of how those future contributions and benefits are labeled, because both the contributions and the benefits are in the future. In contrast, for the seventy-year-old male, the contributions made in the past will not be included in his generational account as of age seventy; thus, his account is quite sensitive to what words are being used to describe his future benefits.

The same reasoning explains why changes in generational accounts arising from new policies are invariant to government labels. In the case of changes in policy, everyone looks like a newborn; whatever additional net payments the government may extract, these will occur in the future, and their net present value will be the same regardless of the words the government attaches to the dollar amounts. To see this, consider again our seventy-year-old. Suppose the government announces today that it is going to reduce the seventy-year-old's Social Security benefit by $100 a year. Under the conventional set of labels, the present value of transfers calculated in the process of determining his generational account would *fall* by the present value of $100 per year for the rest of his life. Under the "principal plus interest" plus an "old-age tax" labeling of benefits, the present value of the seventy-year-old's old-age tax payments would simply *rise* by this amount. In both cases the seventy-year-old's generational account increases by the same amount.

Focusing on the differences in the accounts either across current and future newborns or for the same generation but across policies is the "appropriate use" of generational accounts referred to in Chapter 1. In making too much of the initial levels of the accounts, rather than these differences, one can make the same mistake that arises in using the deficit, namely, confusing words with substance.

HOW ARE THE ACCOUNTS ASSEMBLED?

Before looking more closely at the two fundamental questions—the burden on future generations relative to that on today's newborns and how different policies would change the accounts of different age groups—it may be helpful to learn a little about the way the accounts are constructed.[6] It is a two-step process. The first step is simply to project each generation's average taxes less transfers in each future year during which at least some members of the generation will be alive. The second step converts those projected average net tax payments into a present value, using an assumed discount rate and taking into account the probability that the generations' members will be alive in each of the future years (actuarial discounting for both mortality and interest).

The initial step requires a bit of work. In a nutshell, the procedure involves first determining by age and sex this year's average taxes less transfers in a manner that is consistent with the government's total reported transfers and taxes, and second, projecting how these age- and sex-specific average net taxes evolve through time. This projection must take into account how specific taxes and transfers are slated to change, according to current policy, as well as the fact that many of the taxes and transfers will grow as a result of economic growth. One transfer program whose future growth is rather uncertain is Medicare. The tables in this chapter are based on the perhaps unrealistic assumption that Medicare expenditures will not continue to grow relative to the size of the economy. As Chapter 8 will explain, continued excessive Medicare growth will imply a very much greater shifting of fiscal burdens onto the current young and future generations than the burdens reported here.

Since the government already forecasts the totals of its

various taxes and transfers for many years ahead, the additional work involved in generational accounting is primarily in allocating these projected totals by age and sex. Thus, although there are a few additional elements, and the requisite projections extend farther into the future, generational accounting uses mostly the same numbers the government uses, only in a different manner. The second step is easy, given a computer. Computers being what they are—fast—the time required to do the calculations, showing how different generations are affected by alternative proposed policies, takes only seconds.

THE BURDEN ON FUTURE GENERATIONS

Let's now compare the generational accounts of future generations with those of newborns. As mentioned, for both males and females the growth-adjusted accounts for future generations are 21 percent higher than the corresponding accounts for male and female newborns. The equal male and female differentials are no accident; this equivalent percentage treatment of future males and females was assumed for purposes of clearly identifying the imbalance in generational policy. What exactly does it mean that future newborns will be handed bills that are larger, even after adjusting for growth, than the bills that will be handed to today's newborns? Simply put, it means that those of us alive today, including today's newborns, aren't slated to pay enough to keep the fiscal burden on future generations from rising.

Recall that the 21 percent figure was calculated by considering how much future generations need to pay to cover the government's present value net payments shortfall. This shortfall is the difference between what the government intends to spend and the amount of this spending that can be covered by its current net worth (total government assets minus debt outstanding) and the generational accounts of those alive today, multiplied by today's generation-specific population totals. (By the way, demographics enter into the calculations through these current population totals, through the survival probabilities, and through projections of the number of members of future generations who will co-share the fiscal burden not borne by those now alive.) If we spread the burden in a proportionate manner across everybody coming along in the future it means that, even after taking growth into account, future generations will all pay 21 percent more than current newborns in net tax payments over their lifetimes.

What does "adjusted for growth" mean? Well, suppose the economy's growth rate of output per worker is 1 percent per year. Then the payment scenario being discussed means that next year's newborn, call him baby Alex, will pay 1 percent more than this year's newborn because of growth and 21 percent more on top of this growth-adjusted amount because of the intergenerational imbalance of fiscal policy. The following year's newborn, call her baby Phoebe, will pay 2 percent more because of growth and 21 percent more on top of this growth-adjusted amount because of the imbalance of policy. And so on.

What if we don't hit up babies Alex, Phoebe, and their successors for more money—indeed, 21 percent more money than these growth-adjusted total amounts? What if we instead wait, say, ten years to start hitting up new babies? Then when we do generational accounting ten years from now, we'll learn that the 21 percent figure has grown to 35 percent. And if we wait twenty years to start extracting more from future generations, those born in 2010 and thereafter will face a 57 percent growth-adjusted larger hit than today's newborns. This is the zero-sum nature of our collective bills. If those of us alive aren't going to pay them, or more of them, and if we aren't going to make those coming along in the short term pay them, we're going to stick it in spades (pass the buck) to those coming along later.

THE ALTERNATIVE TO PASSING THE BUCK

What would it cost those of us alive to keep future generations from paying at least a 21 percent bigger share of their lifetime incomes to the government than the share current newborns are scheduled to pay? One way to answer this is to calculate the size of the immediate and permanent increase in income or other tax rates that would equalize the burden on current and future newborns. An immediate increase in, say, income tax rates or sales tax rates would obviously make almost everyone currently alive pay more over their remaining lives, not only those who have just been born.

If we chose to raise income taxes, the required increase in the average tax rate would be 5.5 percent (from a rate of 14.5 percent to one of 15.3 percent).[7] This assumes that state and local income taxes would be increased as well as federal income taxes. Simply raising federal income taxes to equalize generational burdens necessitates a 6.5 percent increase in the average federal income tax rate.[8]

If we chose to relieve the excess fiscal burden on future generations by raising all payroll taxes now, they'd have to rise by 7.8 percent, from a 12.8 percent average tax rate to 13.8 percent.[9] Alternatively, average sales and excise tax rates could be increased by 10.2 percent, from a rate of 13.2 percent to a rate of 14.5 percent.[10] Finally, if we choose to raise capital income taxes, the average capital income tax rate would climb by 14.3 percent, from a rate of 25.1 percent to a rate of 28.7 percent.[11]

Each of these different methods of achieving generational balance, and each combination thereof, produces different tax receipts and different deficits this year and over time. *This is just one more indication that generational balance and budget balance bear no intrinsic relation.* The largest increase in immediate annual revenue—$37 billion—would arise in the case of payroll taxation, the smallest increase—$33 billion—would occur if we used capital income taxation.[12]

Of course, permanently raising average tax rates now, regardless of which ones, means that future generations will pay these higher taxes as well. If income taxes are raised to equalize the generational accounts of current and future

128

newborns, the equalizing present value is $76,089. For pay-roll taxes it is $76,350; for sales and excise taxes it is $76,576; and for capital income taxes it is $75,641. But such seem-ingly large burdens must be put into perspective. Even the largest of the four figures is only 4 percent bigger than the $73,716 today's newborns will pay with no change in poli-cies; put another way, if we all pay a bit more now, we can eliminate the need for future generations to pay a lot more later.

Table 5–3 indicates how much more different generations will pay under the four different approaches to equalizing generational burdens.[13] The numbers are present values in thousands of dollars. The required payments aren't stagger-ingly large, but they aren't trivial. Take the case of an in-crease in the income tax. If you are a middle-aged female, your additional lifetime bill is equivalent to making a one-time payment to the government this year of $2,500. For middle-aged males the bill averages about $5,300. With the exception of the very old, who pay only a couple of hundred dollars more, raising the income tax would represent a good-sized hit on all those currently alive, with the biggest absolute burden falling on baby boomers. Measured against the costs to current generations, however, the gains to fu-ture generations are quite substantial. By paying for more of the government's spending, current generations would, in the case of an income tax increase, lower the burdens on fu-ture males (females) by a growth-adjusted $13,500 ($6,600).

Which tax is increased makes a big difference as regards which generation will be hit the hardest. For example, under the payroll tax increase males aged seventy pay only $300 more on average, while under the capital income tax in-crease, they pay $2,700 more. The choice of taxes also deter-mines how the burden is split between males and females. If the sales or excise tax is increased, the additional bills faced by current females of a particular age will be as large or al-most as large as those faced by current males of the same age.[14]

Table 5–3
Additional Present Value of Net Payments Needed to Equalize Generational Burdens
(thousands of dollars)

	Tax to Be Increased			
Age	Income Tax	Payroll Tax	Sales Excise Tax	Capital Income Tax
Males				
0	1.8	2.1	2.3	1.4
10	3.0	3.4	3.0	2.3
20	4.5	5.0	3.3	3.5
30	5.4	5.5	3.3	5.1
40	5.2	4.7	2.9	6.1
50	4.2	3.2	2.3	5.9
60	2.6	1.4	1.7	4.6
70	1.2	.3	1.1	2.7
80	.5	0	.6	1.4
Future generations	−13.5	−13.1	−12.9	−13.9
Females				
0	1.0	1.2	2.1	.5
10	1.6	2.0	2.7	.9
20	2.2	2.8	3.1	1.3
30	2.5	2.7	3.2	2.0
40	2.5	2.3	2.9	2.8
50	2.1	1.5	2.3	3.0
60	1.3	.6	1.6	2.5
70	.7	.2	1.1	1.1
80	.2	0	.6	.6
Future generations	−6.6	-6.3	−5.5	−7.0

PUTTING GENERATIONAL ACCOUNTING
THROUGH ITS PACES

Generational accounting is supposed to detect intergenerational redistribution no matter how well camouflaged. This section demonstrates that it does. The demonstration is based on four policies whose generational effects are displayed in the first four columns of Table 5–4. Like Table 5–3, this table records policy-induced changes in the generational accounts. The first of the four policies considered greatly alters the federal deficit; the other three do not. The four policies are hypothetical, but they might be chosen, especially in an election year.

A Deficit-financed Tax Cut

Imagine that the President sits at his mirror for his daily lip reading and his lips say "Do it! Do it again! Reagan got away with it, why not you? Cut taxes and hang the Democrats out to dry one more time." So the President revs up the supply-side groupies and pushes through a 20 percent reduction in federal income taxes for five years, after which time taxes are raised to pay off enough of the interest on the additional debt so that the additional debt is always an equal share of national income.[15] The supply-side groupies won't like the subsequent tax hike, but given the realities of the U.S. economy and tax structure, there is no such thing as a self-financing income tax cut.

Who ends up paying for this policy, which raises the federal debt by about $800 billion over the five-year period? The answer, in large part, is today's children. Today's kids are too young to benefit from the reduced tax rates over the next five years, but they'll face the full burden of the higher taxes when they start make a living.

Take Paul and Charlotte, who today are ten-year-old twins. They get saddled with about $2,000 each in additional lifetime net taxes ($2,600 for Paul and $1,400 for Charlotte). These are present value bills at age ten; if Paul and Charlotte

Table 5–4
Changes in Generational Accounts
Due to Four Hypothetical Election-Year Policies
(thousands of dollars)

Age	5-Year Tax Cut	20 Percent Social Security Benefit Increase	Shifting from Payroll to Sales and Excise Taxes	Eliminating Investment Incentives	1990 Budget Deal
Males					
0	1.6	2.7	.8	.9	.1
10	2.6	3.9	−1.7	1.5	.2
20	1.7	5.3	−6.6	2.3	.6
30	.3	4.8	−8.4	2.1	.9
40	−2.2	2.0	−6.8	.2	.9
50	−3.5	−3.1	−3.2	−2.5	1.0
60	−3.8	−10.4	1.1	−4.7	1.3
70	−2.0	−10.5	3.1	−5.0	1.1
80	−1.2	−6.0	2.3	−4.0	.7
Future generations	1.5	3.1	.5	.2	−6.4
Females					
0	.8	1.0	3.3	.4	.1
10	1.4	1.5	3.0	.6	.2
20	.4	1.8	1.3	.8	.4
30	.2	.7	1.8	1.2	.6
40	−.8	−1.2	2.3	.6	.7
50	−1.5	−4.7	3.0	−.5	.7
60	−1.6	−10.0	3.7	−1.8	.9
70	−1.1	−10.0	3.6	−2.4	.9
80	.7	−6.4	2.4	−2.4	.6
Future generations	.8	1.1	3.7	.1	−3.1

wait to pay them, which they surely will (right now they're more into Ninja turtles than writing checks to Uncle Sam), these bills will grow, because interest on the bills must be tacked on to ensure that the future payment of the bills has no smaller present value than would payment today. Say, Paul and Charlotte wait till age forty, at which time they completely pay off the bills. Well, by that time the bills will have grown to $14,933 for Paul and $8,041 for Charlotte.[16]

Now consider how the tax cut affects Paul's and Charlotte's parents, Neal and Michelle, both of whom are now forty. The tax cut policy is equivalent to the government's handing checks to each of them, specifically a $2,200 check to Neal and an $800 check to Michelle. Why are Neal and Michelle getting something on balance from this policy? Won't they have to pay the higher taxes starting six years from now? Yes, but in the short run—the next five years—Neal and Michelle will save a lot on their income taxes, and the present value of their near-term tax savings exceeds the present value of their additional future tax payments.

The tax cut policy is an even bigger freebie for Paul's and Charlotte's sixty-year-old grandparents, Christophe and Marie. These grandparents will be fully retired by the time taxes go back up. Yes, they will eventually have to pay higher income taxes on their asset income, but escaping taxes on their immediate remaining labor earnings as well as their immediate asset income means a lot more in present value. This explains why the policy amounts to Uncle Sam's giving checks to grandpa Christophe and grandma Marie today—a $3,800 check to grandpa and a $1,600 check to grandma, to be precise.

Paul's and Charlotte's eventual children will also pay for the giveaway to Neal, Michelle, Christophe, Marie, and everyone else who today is in their mid-thirties or older. Take Michael and Beverly, the two children Paul will father around the turn of the century. Adjusting for growth, they'll face, on their birth date, additional bills of $1,500 and $800, respectively. Of course, they won't be writing checks in the delivery room. If they wait until age forty to write the checks, their respective required payments will have grown to $15,428 and $8,228.

Here, then, is indeed a case in which the burden on future American generations goes up and, because of the official labels chosen for the government's receipts and payments, the official deficit rises as well. The next three policies produce as large or larger intergenerational redistribution, but, because of the labels chosen, leave the official deficit unchanged.

"Pay-As-You-Go-Finance"

The President, of course, cares about our progeny even if some of us want to take the money and run. So he'd ignore his hips—oops!—lips. But now imaging the voice of Wilbur Mills comes to him in the Oval Office and says, "You want to win really big? Raise Social Security benefits! The old vote in droves; they've got nothing better to do. Do it! What, you're worried about the deficit? Don't run a deficit. Pay as you go."

So the President out-democrats the Democrats and permanently raises Social Security benefits by 20 percent just before the election. What happens? The numbers in the second column in Table 5–4 is what happens. Our ten-year-olds, Paul and Charlotte, get nailed for $3,900 and $1,500. And Paul's kids, Mike and Bev, have to fork over $3,100 and $1,100. Grandpa Christophe and Grandma Marie sense this may not be so great for their grandkids, but since nobody's told them exactly how bad it will be, they don't get too worried. Furthermore, their great-grandchildren, Mike and Bev, aren't even a twinkle in little Paul's eye. Besides, they're delighted by the big checks the President, in effect, just handed them—$10,400 for Grandpa and $10,000 for Grandma. They, their fellow readers of *Modern Maturity*, and most of those in their middle ages smile all the way to the polls.

Changing the Tax Base

The Social Security scenario is a good political move, but it's been tried in the past. Besides, the Chairman of the Council of Economic Advisers has given the President his recent book on the troubling economic consequences of playing this game.[17] But the election is getting close. "What to do?" the President wonders. "The Democrats might actually win three states. Hey, there are all those baby boomers out there. Let's do something for them. Let's lower taxes on wages by 30 percent and raise sales and excise taxes on consumption to break even. Time to give the workers a break. Let's do it!"

So the President calls in Americans for Generational Equity (AGE), the boomers' counterpart to the American Association of Retired Persons (AARP), to remind the boomers where their bread is buttered. The result is a fifty-state landslide, not counting Kuwait, which just couldn't resist voting.

But female boomers and the elderly, if they were voting their pocket books, should have thought twice. As Column 3 in Table 5–4 shows, this policy is terrific for male boomers but takes female boomers as well as male and female elderly to the cleaners. Female boomers are worse off, because they were, to begin with, paying much less in payroll taxes than male boomers, but roughly the same amount in sales and excise taxes. Hence, cutting payroll taxes by a given percentage reduces the absolute net tax payments of male boomers more than it reduces the absolute tax payments of females. On the other hand, raising sales and excise taxes by a given percentage increases the absolute net tax payments of male and female boomers by roughly the same amount.

What does this all mean for Paul and Charlotte, Neal and Michelle, and Christophe and Marie? It means Paul is up $1,700, Charlotte is out $3,000, Neal is up $6,800, Michelle is out $2,300, Christophe is out $1,100, and Marie is out $3,700. And what about Mike and Bev, Paul's unborn children? The answer is that they're out an additional $500 and $3,700, respectively.

Redistribution Through Financial Markets

"Can't do it." Barbara says to George as she turns down the volume of "Proud to Be an American." "All our friends who

135

had the good sense to retire ten years ago are writing me that they didn't save all their lives to spend it on federal sales taxes."

"You're right," the Pres says. "The elderly are in bad shape already. Most of them can't even jog as far as the press. Plus we can't risk losing their vote. Let's see. What else would be popular, especially with the give-me generation? Umm, everyone wants to cut the deficit. Who can pay for this who doesn't vote? I've got it! Corporations! Most of them are owned by the Japanese anyway, right? Time to reform the corporate tax. Let's do it!"

So the President goes after all remaining corporate tax "loopholes," thereby eliminating remaining accelerated depreciation allowances and all other investment incentives. The result: Even Mike Dukakis campaigns for him, and residents of Massachusetts vote for him twice.

Is this neutral for the elderly and good for boomers and future generations? Absolutely not! Indeed, as column 4 in Table 5–4 indicates, the policy represents huge windfalls to those around fifty and older, and huge losses to those now under thirty. Why are the elderly and the near-elderly better off? Well, by and large, they own the corporations and other business that lose their investment incentives. But, don't forget, the incentives pertain to new investment, not to past investment (old capital). Since the past investment (the old capital) has to compete with the new investment, and the new investment just lost its government subsidy, the market value of past investment rises.

Thus, in sticking it to the corporations and other businesses, the President hands older Americans, including Paul's and Charlotte's parents and grandparents, a huge capital gain, which collectively totals $609 billion. But who pays for this windfall? The answer is primarily the current young and middle-aged, to whom the elderly eventually sell their titles to the country's past investment, but now at a higher price, thanks to the President. The moral: What's bad for new business can be very good for the owners of old business.

Generational accounting records this capital gain to the elderly by treating the elderly as if they had experienced no capital gain but, instead, had enjoyed a reduction in their *inframarginal* capital income taxes—the taxes on their old capital. And it treats young and future generations, who must pay a higher price for the elderly's old capital paid, as if they are able to purchase the elderly's old capital at the same price, but must pay higher *marginal* capital income taxes on this capital after it has been acquired. For the owners of old capital, getting a break on their inframarginal capital income taxes leaves them in the same boat as getting their capital gain, and for new purchasers of this old capital, buying the capital at its initial price but paying higher marginal taxes on its return is equivalent to buying the old capital at a higher price, but not paying higher marginal taxes on its return.

The fact that we can use different words here to describe the same economic reality (e.g. "reduced inframarginal taxes" instead of "capital gain") is the same point being argued throughout the book. A good analogy is the different words we use, depending on our native tongues, to name the same jar of spicy yellow sauce. Some of us call it mustard (English), some moutarde (French), some senf (German), some mostaza (Spanish), some cogumelos (Portuguese), and on and on it goes. But whatever words we use, the spicy yellow sauce tastes just the same.

The interesting economic question is not what we call what we get to eat, but how much we get to eat. In the case of this policy Paul and Charlotte have just been weaseled out of a chunk of their lifetime consumption. Little Paul has lost $1,500, and little Charlotte has lost $600. The loss to Paul's kids is pretty small, only $200 for Mike and $100 for Bev. The parents, Neal and Michelle, also lose a bit. Neal is out $200 and Michelle is out $600. The big winners in this family, though, are the grandparents. Christophe and Marie are up $4,700 and $1,800, respectively.

Unfortunately for the President, but fortunately for the country, this policy won't fly either. Rather than realize that the abolition of investment incentives will lead to huge capital gains for their bosses (the shareholders of their firms), the country's top CEOs will start writing op-ed pieces in *The Wall Street Journal* to the effect that business is being taxed to death. They'll fail to realize that taxing new investment is a good, not a bad, thing for old investment, and that what their bosses really care about is the value of what they already own, not the subsidy to something (new investment goods) that they and all manner of other competitors might buy. The President will get the message in the form of smaller than expected campaign contributions from corporate officers.

Comparing the Four Policies

Before learning how the President resolves his search for a campaign-winning economic reform, let's examine again the first four columns of Table 5–4 and observe the following four points:

First, the magnitude and pattern of intergenerational redistribution bears no necessary relation to the reported deficit. The tax cut policy of Column 1 generates more than three-quarters of a trillion dollars of official debt, but does substantially less damage to younger and future generations than the pay-as-you-go Social Security benefit increase in Column 2, which leads to zero increase in official IOUs.

Second, some generational policies that redistribute to current older generations do so primarily to the detriment of current young generations, rather than future generations. Column 4, involving the elimination of investment incentives, illustrates this point. This policy does most of its damage to generations who are now young. Of course, policies that just redistribute from the current young to the current old could end up hurting future generations as well if these policies are reactivated shortly after future generations arrive on the scene.

Third, by using generational policies that don't show up in the official deficit, one can easily offset the generational im-

138

pact of policies that do. For example, one could overcome the generational impacts of the tax cut of Column 1 by running the reverse of the policy in Column 4, that is, by increasing rather than decreasing investment incentives and thereby reversing the signs of all the numbers in Column 4.

Fourth, since changes in our consumption–spending decisions depend on changes in our total projected lifetime incomes, generational accounting like that in Table 5–4 indicates the true stimulus to national consumption of policy changes. In contrast, as the examples in Table 5–4 show, the deficit need bear no relationship to the underlying stimulus to consumption. Thus, generational accounting, rather than the deficit, provides the proper guide to stabilizing the economy.

DID THE 1990 BUDGET AGREEMENT ACHIEVE GENERATIONAL BALANCE?

Having spent too long considering and rejecting alternative new initiatives, the President has no time left before the election to reform yet again the fiscal system. So the President's advisers counsel that he simply resell the previous reform, the 1990 budget deal. "After all," they point out, "the 1990 budget deal was a very significant piece of legislation. It causes some pain, but has a lot to recommend it in terms of the stance of generational policy." The president agrees and wins in a landslide with his vigorous defense of the 1990 budget deal (including its major tax increases), his hit campaign song "The Democrats Made Me Do It," and his evocative campaign pledge "I Failed You Once, But Never Again: No More New Taxes!"

Should we applaud the budget deal, and should its chief sponsor be reelected on the basis? Well, let's take a look at what the new law will do. The new law raised income tax rates and Medicare tax collections, curtailed mortgage and other deductions, imposed a 10 percent excise tax on luxuries, increased the federal gasoline tax, stipulated cutbacks in Medicare benefits, and scheduled reductions in government consumption spending, particularly on defense. If everything that is supposed to happen actually does happen, the new law could make a good-sized dent in the burden facing future generations, albeit at the cost of bigger burdens on ourselves.

The new legislation hits a broad spectrum of age groups, although the degree of pain inflicted on contemporaneous age-sex cohorts is fairly moderate. The last column in Table 5–4 shows what sticking to the budget deal for the proposed five full years is likely to mean to members of different generations. Our by now familiar children, Paul and Charlotte, each have to pay a modest $200 more. Their parents, Neal and Michelle, aren't so well treated. They have to pay an additional $900 and $700, respectively. And the grandparents get hit even harder: $1,300 for Grandpa Christophe and $900 for Grandma Marie. All this, however, is to the considerable benefit of Paul's children, Mike and Bev, and other children coming along through time. Mike's growth-adjusted lifetime bill is reduced by $6,400, while Bev's is reduced by $3,100. This leaves only a 12 percent growth-adjusted difference in the generational accounts of future generations and current newborns. Thus the new federal law, if kept in place for five years, *could* do about one-third of what needs to be done to restore generational balance to U.S. economic policy.

The "if" and the "could" in the last sentence refer to two concerns. First, the government may cite the recession, national defense, or other excuses to avoid sticking to its fiscal game plan. Second, the new law permits Congress and the Administration to expand their transfer programs so long as the expansion is financed on a "pay-as-you-go" basis.[18] Thus the new law is perfectly consistent with the government's this year dramatically raising Social Security benefits and the taxes to pay for them. As Table 5–4's second column makes crystal clear, this would cause a massive intergeneration transfer to current elderly and away from all other incumbent and incipient generations.

The fact that the federal government in 1900 subjected the country to month after month of deficit hysterics and at the end held a budget "summit" at which it enshrined "pay-as-you-go" finance as fiscally prudent is testimony to the depth of our political leaders' misunderstanding of the process by which we transmit generational burdens. The next chapter will indicate that deficit-financed tax cuts and pay-as-you-go transfer policies are not actually different policies that have similar impacts, but are fundamentally the same policy being described with different words. It clarifies the point made in previous chapters that the deficit reflects the government's words and not necessarily its policies, and shows why this critique of the deficit is not dependent on special assumptions about the economy or government behavior.

6

DEFICIT DELUSION

——— ∎ ———

Government announcements of fiscal initiatives receive enormous media attention and public discussion, virtually all of which takes for granted the notion that the government's economic deeds are, in fact, those suggested by its words. But are they? How do we know, for example, that the Reagan tax cuts and associated deficits of the early 1980s did not merely represent a relabeling of existing policies under which we "lent" the government the same amount of money we would otherwise have given it in "taxes," and now and in future years are using the "interest and principal" earned on that money to pay the government higher "taxes" than we would otherwise have paid? Judging whether the combination of the Reagan tax cut and other policies of the 1980s really made different Americans better off, in other worlds, were more than simply a relabeling of previous policies, requires the forward-looking generational accounting and distribution analysis already discussed.[1]

The temptation to take seriously the government's descriptions of its policies—its words—is hard to resist. The message underlying the words is never questioned, with the result that the words themselves become the message. Imagine, if you will, a lonely tailor at the annual convention of the Emperor's tailors lobbying for a little underwear when ev-

143

eryone else is marveling over the latest "emerald train," and you'll see the point.

The goal of this chapter is to erase from your, the readers', minds the government's subliminal message that its budget deficit necessarily tells you something meaningful about the economy. The method is to show that with the proper choice of words the government's budget deficit can literally be anything and that this proposition holds in essentially all economic settings, including our own.

THE MARTIAN PERSPECTIVE

For a better appreciation of the arbitrariness of deficit accounting, consider the government's activities from the point of view of a Martian economist named Marty. Marty is on a field trip to earth to study our fiscal affairs. Like other Martians, Marty has special powers. He can hover in the air endlessly; he can make himself invisible; and he can see everything.

Right now Marty is hovering invisibly over the United States and watching the transactions between federal, state, and local government agencies and the public. Actually, he's been doing this for years—which, for Martians, is really no time at all. What has Marty been seeing? Well, he's been seeing the government and the public hand each other a lot of paper. He's also been seeing the public hand the government real goods and services. Over the years Marty has carefully recorded each of these transactions. He's written down the color and size of the paper as well as the words and numbers written on the paper. He's also recorded the type of goods being given to the government.

Marty's Case Study

Despite endless analysis of his data, Martian Marty is still not sure he understands what's going on. He sees the government getting the goods and services, and he knows that more consumption spending by the government means less of the

144

economy's output is left over for the private sector. But he's confused about which members of the public end up consuming less when the government consumes more. He's convinced it has to do with all the paper exchanges, but doesn't know exactly how. A lot of the paper exchanges don't seem to have any purpose. Many times the same people seem to be both giving paper to and getting paper from the government. And sometimes it's the same type of paper. All of this has given Marty a big antenna ache.

As a last-ditch effort before blackholing to a more sensible planet, Marty has decided to do a case study of one forty-year-old American earthling named Sam. Marty's plan is to consider every transaction between Sam and the U.S. government over Sam's remaining life and then to relate these transactions to Sam's lifetime consumption of goods and services. Marty is also resolved to keep careful track of how the government's transactions with Sam affect its books. Finally, Marty will use his special powers to rerun history as many times as he wants. Each run of history is a little different, and these differences are basically out of Marty's control. But by squeezing his little green hands together, Marty is able to keep his histories simple, without changing anything important. Simple here means that the interest rate is zero, there is no inflation, and the government transacts with Sam only twice in Sam's life, when he's age forty and then age fifty.

Marty's Observations

Case 1

In Marty's initial observation of the life of Sam, he sees Sam hand the government a check for $1,000 at age forty and receive back from the government a check for $1,000 at age fifty. Marty notes that the present value (as of the time Sam is age forty) of Sam's remaining lifetime net payments (Sam's own account) is zero; Sam pays $1,000 at age forty but get back $1,000 at age fifty, and, since the interest rate is zero, the present value of the $1,000 he gets back later equals the present value of the $1,000 he gives up now.

Marty next looks at the government's books and notices that the government recorded its $1,000 receipt from Sam as a "tax" receipt and its $1,000 payment to Sam as a "transfer." He also observes that in the two years, when Sam is age forty and age fifty, the government's budget, including the taxes from and transfers to Sam, is balanced. Marty records this and subsequent information about the labeling of Sam's net payments and the government's deficit in Table 6–1.

Case 2

Marty's second case study also involves Sam's handing the government, on net, $1,000 at age forty and getting back, on net, $1,000 at age fifty. And since Sam's present value treatment by the government is the same as in the first case, Sam's consumption in each of his remaining years of life is

Table 6–1
Martian Marty's Observations of the Government's
Transactions with Sam

Case	Labeling of Govt.'s $1000 Net Receipt from Sam	Labeling of Govt.'s $1000 Net Payment to Sam	Govt.'s Deficit When Sam Is Age	
			40	50
1	"taxes"	"transfers"	$0	$0
2	"borrowing"	"repayment"	$1000	−$1000
3	"borrowing" of $20,000 less "transfer" of $19,000	"repayment" of $20,000 less "taxes" of $19,000	$20,000	−20,000
4	"taxes" of $60,000 less "loan to Sam" of 59,000	"transfers" of $60,000 less "repayment by Sam" of $59,000	−$60,000	$60,000

the same as before. But in this case, Marty notices that the government's books are different. Rather than call the $1,000 Sam pays at age forty a "tax," the government calls it a "loan"; it says it's *borrowing* the $1,000 from Sam. And rather than call the $1,000 it gives Sam at age fifty a "transfer," it calls these funds a "repayment" of the money it borrowed from Sam. Although Sam's economic behavior and that of the government are completely unchanged, by using these different *words* the government now reports a $1,000 deficit when Sam is age forty and a $1,000 surplus when Sam is age fifty.

Case 3

Marty's antennae start to tingle as he contemplates the fact that cases 1 and 2 feature the same economic behavior, but different sequences of deficits. But his third rerun of history makes his antennae really buzz. In the third case Marty again sees a net amount of $1,000 first being passed from Sam to the government and then, ten years later, being passed from the government to Sam. But in this case the government and Sam go through some additional gyrations. In giving the net amount of $1,000 to the government, Sam first hands the government $20,000, and then the government hands back $19,000 to Sam. The government calls the $20,000 it receives from Sam borrowing, and it calls the $19,000 it hands back to Sam a transfer. This leads the government to report a deficit of $20,000 in the year that Sam is forty. How's that? Well, not counting the government's treatment of Sam, there was, in this year, a $1,000 deficit, and now there is an additional $19,000 of transfer payments. Thus, including its dealings with Sam, the government reports a $20,000 deficit when Sam is forty.

When Sam is fifty the government hands Sam $20,000, calling it repayment of its past borrowing, but then takes back $19,000 from Sam in what it calls taxes. As a consequence, the government reports a surplus of $20,000 in the year Sam is fifty, corresponding to the $1,000 excess of taxes over transfers it has in dealing with the rest of the public, plus the $19,000 in taxes it receives from Sam.

Case 4

Marty's antennae have now become fully erect, as he realizes something's not *usroepish* (kosher in Martian) about the government's bookkeeping. But before he can figure it out, yet another rerun of history unfolds before his eyes. Like the previous three cases, this one has the same economic outcomes, but instead of reporting a deficit of $0, $1,000, or $20,000 when Sam is forty, the government now reports a surplus of $60,000; and instead of a surplus of $0, $1,000, or $20,000 when Sam is fifty, it now reports a deficit of $60,000. The government's trick in this case is (1) to call its $1,000 net payment from Sam "taxes of $60,000 less a loan to Sam of $59,000" and (2) to call its $1,000 net payment to Sam" a transfer of $60,000 less a $59,000 repayment by Sam of the $60,000 loan he received."

Marty's Deductions

Marty has seen enough reruns to reach the following conclusions. First, from his vantage point, he sees that the economic situation in each rerun is the same; the words are different, and different types of paper change hands, but the net amounts Sam gives at age forty and gets at age fifty are the same, always $1,000. Second, Marty realizes that the government is free to call its receipts taxes or borrowing, and is free to call its payments transfers or loans, and thereby to report any size deficit or surplus it wants. Third, he sees that there is nothing special about the amounts Sam pays at age forty and gets at age fifty; any amount (including zero) given at age forty and any amount (including zero) received at age fifty can apparently be labeled in an infinite number of ways.[2]

Fourth, he realizes that this embarrassing riches of words

148

has nothing whatsoever to do with standard critiques of the deficit (such as the failure to correct for inflation and growth) about which Marty has painstakingly been reading. Nor, Marty surmises, can this free choice of vocabulary be circumvented by capital accounting (keeping track of the government's net worth—its assets less debts), since one set of words leads to positive reported net worth and another leads to negative reported net worth.

Marty also notes that Sam is only one of millions of living Americans whose receipts and payments could be relabeled so as to change the reported deficit. Finally, he understands that the labeling choices the government makes over time— e.g. how it labels its treatment of Samantha (Sam's daughter) and Sammy (Sam's grandson), and so forth—will make all the difference in the world for the level through time of government debt.

In the end, Marty decides that the deficit is beside the point; what really matters for Sam's remaining consumption is not the deficit, but the present value of Sam's remaining lifetime net tax payments, which is zero in each of the four cases. Marty concludes that the net present value of the numbers written on the pieces of paper marked taxes less those marked transfers is the government's way of telling particular individuals how much they'll have to pay for government spending over time. Having finally cracked the earthling's fiscal code, Marty rockets back to Mars, but not before zooming around remote places like West Texas to tease the natives.

OBJECTIONS TO THESE MARTIAN CHRONICLES

Did Marty leave too soon? Did he ignore some complexity of the real world that would make the deficit a meaningful measure of the government's treatment of Sam and other citizens? Let's consider the following questions, objections, or counterarguments one might raise to Marty's case study as well as the responses to them.

Would the Government Engage
in Such Verbal Shenanigans?

The use of words *per se* cannot be a shenanigan, because the government needs to describe its actions with some words. If the government is engaging in verbal shenanigans, it's in the *choice* of words. But which words represent the shenanigans? Is one set of words really more appropriate than another? Unfortunately, there is nothing in economic theory to guide us in choosing how to label government transactions, just as there is nothing in economic theory that tells us whether we should discuss economics in French or English. While cases 3 and 4 may seem more contrived than cases 1 and 2, because the government seems to be both taking money from and giving money to Sam within the same period of time, the same changes in reported deficits arise if the party being taxed and receiving the subsequent transfer differs from the party from whom the government borrows and to whom the government repays its borrowing. In any case, the back and forth exchange of money between the public and the government sector is ubiquitous. Students pay sales taxes and receive loans from the government. Middle-aged workers buy government bonds, and the corporations they partly own receive investment tax credits. Retirees receive Social Security checks and use the funds to purchase government bonds.

Thus, in case 3, we can let Sam lend the government $20,000 at age forty and receive the $20,000 repayment ten years later, and have the government (1) use its $20,000 loan from Sam to cover the $1,000 it needed, plus finance a $19,000 transfer to Sally (no relation to Sam) and (2) finance its subsequent $20,000 repayment to Sam with the $1,000 surplus it otherwise has, plus a $19,000 tax on Sally. Note that this version of case 3, like the previous version, involves no change in the present value of remaining lifetime net payments to the government by either Sam or Sally.

The government might try to clean up its act by restricting what words it uses—by, for example, forbidding any government official ever to use the words "borrowing" and "repayment of borrowing." But given the Bill of Rights, there is nothing to stop each of us from using different words in describing the government's actions and, as a consequence, entertaining different historic and current values of the deficit.

Argument: The Government Doesn't Change Its Labels over Time

According to this objection, whatever words (labeling convention) the government chooses, it sticks to them (it) over time, so the reported deficits, even if they are based on a special set of labels, are reliable measures of changes in government policy. The first response to this objection was given above, namely, that even if the government is somehow consistent in using the same labeling convention through time, there is no *a priori* reason to value the government's choice of words over anyone else's. Since different sets of words will lead to different deficits, both historically and in the present, we are still left with the conundrum of not knowing which set of words to use and, therefore, which sequence of deficits to consider.

The second response cuts deeper. If there is nothing economic to guide us in the choice of labels, how do we know the government isn't changing its labels through time? Asked differently, what does sticking to a labeling convention mean when there is no basis for establishing a convention in the first place?

The fact that the government may change its labels through time raises the possibility that a change in labels could be mistaken for a change in policy. Return to Marty's case study and suppose the government extracts the same zero present value of payments from Sam and his daughter, Samantha, but uses the labels in case 1 to describe its treatment of Sam and uses the labels of case 3 to describe its treatment of Samantha. Then, when Samantha reaches age forty, the government will suddenly switch from reporting a

151

balanced budget to reporting a $20,000 deficit. People who are transfixed with the deficit will believe the government has changed policy when, in fact, it has only changed words.

An unambiguous real-world example of a labeling game involves the government's current proposal to stimulate private sector saving through the adoption of Family Savings Accounts (FSAs).[3] Like Individual Retirement Accounts (IRAs), FSAs would allow individuals to save at tax-free interest rates. The FSAs exempt interest from taxation when funds are withdrawn, while the IRAs provide, in effect, an up-front deduction for payment of future taxes on accumulated interest. While those partaking in FSAs and IRAs would enjoy the same present value tax treatment, the IRAs generate larger short-run deficits and smaller long-run deficits than FSAs.

This, of course, is exactly what occurs in moving from case 2 to case 1. The switch from FSAs to IRAs leads the government to collect the same funds from the public in the short run, but to call more of them borrowed and to leave the public with the same funds in the long run by offsetting the additional long-run taxes with the return of principal plus interest on the short-run borrowing. Thus, while any economist worth the title will tell the government that the FSA and IRA plans are economically equivalent, no one in Congress or the Administration will dare advocate simply the expansion of IRAs because of their concern with saying the wrong words (increasing the current deficit). Therein lies the newfound *political* advantage of FSAs!

Argument: The Labels Matter Because Taxes Are Involuntary and Loans Are Voluntary

How, some might ask, can one switch words so easily when there is clearly a legal distinction between taxes and borrowing (transfers and loans). The payment of tax liabilities is compulsory, while the purchase of a bond is voluntary. Similarly, the receipt of transfers by the government typically does not have as strong a legal protection as does the return of principal plus interest on government bonds. The answer is that, despite its potential importance for lawyers, the voluntary/involuntary nature of economic transactions may be of no economic import.

To see why the same economic choices might be made in circumstances that do and do not involve legal coercion, put yourself in the following situation. Suppose you're walking across the street with $100 in your pocket. You expect to spend $20 today and the remaining $80 over the course of the week. A policeman comes up to you, demands you give him $10 on pain of a jaywalking ticket, but assures you he'll return it to you when he sees you tomorrow. This is not the first time the policeman has forced you to save him making a trip to his bank for cash, and even though you detest his crude behavior, you know he'll make good on his promise.

You may hate the policeman, you may feel used and abused, but the important question here is not your feelings, but rather your economic actions. The question is whether being forced to give the policeman the $10, which you know he'll repay, leads you to spend more or less than $20 today. Clearly, the fact that the transaction is involuntary rather than voluntary should not alter your decision regarding how much to spend today. Thus, notwithstanding the legal distinction, there is no economic distinction between your voluntarily lending the policeman $10 and being repaid tomorrow and your being involuntarily taxed $10 today and transferred $10 tomorrow.[4]

The same argument applies to the funds the government acquires from the private sector through involuntary taxes net of transfers. In the United States these funds total less than 20 percent of our national income and less than 5 percent of our national wealth.[5] Thus the U.S. public, as a whole, is not cash-constrained and is not forced to postpone consumption because the government, like the policeman, is forcibly changing the timing of the public's income stream. In terms of the above parable, the U.S. public, as a whole, is jaywalking with $100 in its pocket. It plans to spend $15 today (the ratio of annual U.S. private consumption to the sum of annual NNP and U.S. net wealth is about .15), and the policeman forces it to hand over $4 (the ratio of taxes less transfers to the sum of NNP plus U.S. net wealth is about .04).

Argument: Won't Labels Matter if Some People Are Cash-Constrained?

Of course, not everyone in the United States has the same income and owns the same amount of wealth. Certainly, a segment of society, including many welfare recipients, has access to neither formal nor informal (such as family) credit markets. This segment of society is cash-constrained, and its members would be forced to reduce their immediate consumption if the government forced them to pay it money now in exchange for an equivalent (in present value) amount of money coming in the future. However, in the United States at least, the cash-constrained members of society appear to account for only about 6 percent of total private consumption.[6] Additionally, many of these individuals are not affected or are affected only slightly by major fiscal policies, such as the big Reagan tax cut of 1981, that have been associated with large reported deficits. In the case of the Reagan tax cut, many of these individuals received little or no relief because they paid little or no income taxes. While Keynesian economists are fond of stressing the existence of cash-constrained individuals, the mere existence of such individuals does not immediately translate into the importance of these individuals for considering and measuring fiscal policy.

Many of you reading the previous paragraph may feel cash-constrained even though you don't spend all your income within a given year and have a positive level of net wealth. But the notion of cash-constrained being discussed here is not that you are budgeting tightly or that you wish you had more money. Rather, the question is whether paying perhaps $200 more to the government this year and getting it back in the future will materially alter your consumption this year of goods and services. The $200 figure is illustrative of the size of the cash-flow impact on average middle-agers of large federal fiscal policy changes.

How can the typical forty-year-old male, with an annual income of, say, $30,000, maintain his consumption purchases while paying the government an additional $200 this year? Well, he can reduce his annual deposits to his savings or money market accounts; he can purchase less stocks, bonds, and real estate; he can reduce his contributions to his employer's pension fund; he can hold off purchasing durable assets (which is primarily a form of saving); he can take out a personal loan from the bank; he can borrow from relatives or friends; he can use reserve credit on his checking account; he can pay off his bills more slowly; he can borrow on his credit card; he can withdraw funds from his saving and money market accounts; he can sell stocks and other assets; he can take out an equity line of credit; he can take out a bigger mortgage; he can finance the purchase of his car. In short, he can and will do a lot of things to maintain his current standard of living if he knows that the money he is now giving up will be coming back to him later with interest.

Financial institutions also can be counted on to increase their loans to the public if the government were effectively to change its fiscal labels by borrowing less now and, instead, taxing more now, but returning, in the form of "transfers," the amounts "taxed" plus interest.[7] To see how financial institutions would respond, let's start in case 2, where the government comes to Sam at age forty and borrows $1,000, then returns the funds with interest (which happens to be zero for purposes of simplification) to him at age fifty. Suppose rather than borrow money from Sam, the government decides to run case 1, which features initial "taxes," but with Frank, who is no relation to Sam. Also suppose that Frank, prior to being hit with the increased tax, is in fact cash-constrained, having borrowed as much as he could from the bank. Will Frank have to cut his current spending on goods and services to pay for what amounts to a forced loan from him to the government? Well, the funds that Sam would otherwise have lent to the government can now be lent to Frank through the private banking system. Of course in the real world any particular individual's money may end up being lent through the banking system to a huge range of different individuals, none of whom know each other. The way to think about this example is in terms of there being a large number of Sams and Franks whose payments to the government are altered by what amounts to simply a change in government labeling of its total receipts and payments.

Argument: The Labels Matter
When Fiscal Policy Is Uncertain

Another reason that might be advanced to rescue conventional fiscal accounting is that future taxes and transfers are uncertain, while the government's repayment of interest plus principal on its borrowing is not. According to this argument, the government's words mean something because they tell us about the likelihood that particular payments and receipts will occur.

But it's not obvious that real (inflation-adjusted) debt repayment is actually more certain than real future taxes and transfers. Yes, the U.S. government always repays nominal principal and interest on its borrowing. But those who lend money to the government aren't fundamentally concerned with the nominal amount of dollar bills they receive on their government IOUs. What they really care about is how much these nominal dollar bills will ultimately purchase in goods and services.

In truth, because of inflation, the real purchasing power of the monies one receives under the rubric "principal plus interest" is highly uncertain, as anyone holding U.S. government bonds in the 1970s paying low interest rates will tell you. As a consequence of that decade's relatively high rate of inflation, the federal government effectively defaulted on U.S. Treasury bills and bonds to the tune, in today's dollars, of more than $500 billion.[8] The fact that bondholders stuck with low-interest-yielding bonds were burnt so badly by inflation in the 1970s may explain why we've had such high nominal interest rates ever since.

But even if there was no inflation, so that the real return on government bonds was certain, the argument that the government's fiscal accounting is entirely arbitrary would be equally valid. To see why, let's go back to Martian Marty's case study of Sam and modify it slightly. Let's have Sam still pay the government $1,000 on net at age forty, but let's have him at age fifty receive from the government, on net, either $2,000 (outcome A) or zero (outcome B), with a fifty-fifty chance of each. (The argument goes through no matter what the likelihood is of the government's paying $2,000 rather than zero; nor is there anything special about the amounts $2,000 and zero.) Thus, we are dealing here with a case in which the government's present value treatment of Sam in uncertain. With equal probability, Sam's lifetime net present value payment (generational account) ends up equaling either plus or minus $1,000.

Now suppose the government calls the $1,000 Sam gives up at age forty taxes and the $2000 or $0 Sam gets back at age fifty a transfer payment. Then when Sam is forty, the deficit will (as in Case 1) still be zero; but when Sam is age fifty it will be either $1,000, if outcome A occurs and the transfer to Sam is $2,000, or −$1000, if outcome B occurs and the transfer to Sam is zero.

Next suppose the government says it's borrowing the $1,000 Sam hands over at age forty. Then, in the event it hands $2,000 to Sam at age fifty, the government can describe the $2,000 payment as a $1,000 return of principal (the interest rate is still assumed to be zero) on past borrowing from Sam plus a $1,000 transfer to Sam. Alternatively, in the event the government hands zero to Sam at age fifty, it can describe this amount as a $1,000 return of principal less a $1000 tax. With this second set of words, the government's reported deficit when Sam is age forty is $1,000; when Sam

157

is age fifty, it will be either zero under outcome A or −$2000 under outcome B. As in the comparison of cases 1 and 2 in Table 6–1, using the second set of words rather than the first leads to a $1,000 larger reported deficit when Sam is forty and a $1,000 smaller reported deficit (for both of the possible outcomes) when Sam is age fifty.

One can work through the uncertainty analogues to cases 3 and 4 in Table 6–1 as well as a zillion other examples and learn that, despite the uncertainty of economic policy, the government's choice of words can generate any sequence of deficits it wishes to report with no change in the underlying treatment of Sam. As with the illustrative second set of words, in using each of these zillion choices of words, the government can always honestly state that it is fully repaying its borrowing; that is, the words "borrowing" and "repayment of principal and interest" can always be attached to transactions that occur with certainty.

But if the words borrowing and repayment of borrowing are always associated with payments and receipts that occur with absolute certainty, why is it that in the above example and in other potential examples the government can announce any level of borrowing it desires? The answer is (1) that payments and receipts that occur with absolute certainty can also be called taxes and transfers, and (2) that any uncertain payment or receipt can equivalently be described as the combination of a payment (or receipt) that occurs with absolute certainty plus an additional payment (or receipt) that is uncertain.

In the case of Sam, the $2,000 or $0 he receives at age fifty can be described as an absolutely certain receipt of $1,000, plus either an uncertain transfer of $1,000 or an uncertain tax of $1,000. The conundrum for deficit accounting is that the certain $1,000 Sam gives up at forty and the certain $1,000 Sam receives at fifty can be labeled in all the different ways described in and suggested by Table 6–1. In sum, the fact that the economy and/or economic policy is uncertain in no way limits the government's ability to alter its reported deficit simply by altering its choice of words.

Argument: The Labels Matter Because Taxes and Transfers Alter Incentives

A final defense that might be offered on behalf of the government's fiscal taxonomy involves the incentives associated with particular government payments and receipts. Take the IRAs and FSAs mentioned above as examples. Here the government is attempting to induce individuals to save more. It does so by telling them that if they place money in these accounts and leave it there for a specified period of time, the government will make sure they end up with more lifetime income than had they saved an equivalent amount outside of those accounts. But as the comparison of the IRAs and FSAs indicated, the same saving incentives can be provided in a variety of ways with completely different implications for the reported time path of deficits.

In the case of IRAs the government gives, in effect, individuals money up front to induce them to save in these accounts. In the case of FSAs, the government gives, in effect, individuals money in their retirement years when they start withdrawing funds from their FSA accounts. The government could just as well provide the financial inducement at some intervening dates along the way.[9]

It may help to relate this example to the situation of Sam. So far we haven't discussed how Sam comes to pay the government $1,000 at age forty and receive $1,000 at age fifty. Let's suppose Sam pays the $1,000 at age forty in the form of income taxes and receives the $1,000 at age fifty in the form of a tax credit for his saving in a special saving account.[10] As before, Sam pays zero in net present value to the government. With respect to the deficit, this situation corresponds to case 1 in Table 6–1, since a tax credit is identical to a transfer payment.

Can we now, as in case 2, change the labels and describe the government as "borrowing" $1,000 from Sam at age forty and "repaying" the borrowing when Sam is fifty? And can we do this and still provide Sam with the same incentive to accumulate funds in the special saving account? The answer to both questions is yes. Here's one simple way: Rather than give Sam his tax credit at age fifty, we can give him the credit at age forty. This will make his total (taxes less tax credits) tax payments (payments entitled taxes) at age forty zero. Then the government can turn around and "borrow" the $1,000 from Sam at age forty and "repay" the $1,000 to Sam at age fifty. The impact of these circumlocutions is completely noneconomic—Sam has the exact same incentives as before and he saves the same amount in his account—but they move us from case 1 to case 2 in Table 6–1.

Let's consider one more move, this time from case 1 to case 4. Let Sam at age forty continue to pay the same $1,000 in income taxes as in case 1, but let's have the government assess a $59,000 tax on his contributions to his special saving account when he is age forty and provide a $60,000 tax credit for those contributions at age fifty. In this case Sam still has the same $1,000 ($60,000 minus $59,000) net lifetime incentive to contribute the exact same amount to the special saving account.[11] The government, in this scenario, uses the additional $59,000 it collects from Sam in taxes at age forty to finance a loan to Sam (or someone else, since this won't matter) and uses Sam's age-fifty $59,000 repayment of the loan, plus the $1,000 it otherwise had, to finance the $60,000 tax credit to Sam. Presto, we've got case 3, and Marty, on his return voyage, in a final look-back from deep space, notes that Sam and the government are still swapping $1,000, on net, when Sam is ages forty and fifty.

This last example may seem contrived. Would the government actually both tax and subsidize the same economic activity at different points in time? Yes, it would; in fact, the government does this all the time in its tax treatment of the investments we undertake, either through our own proprietorships and partnerships or through corporations that we, at least partially, own. In this case the subsidies typically come in advance of the taxes. Examples include investment tax credits and accelerated depreciation allowances. These provisions generally lead to net payments to the government on our investments that are smaller, if not negative, in the short run, and larger in the long run.[12]

Another example of the taxing and subsidizing at different points in time of an activity that occurs at a point in time involves Social Security's treatment of labor earnings. As mentioned in Chapter 4, the disincentive to working at any point in time arising from the 15 percent Social Security payroll tax is offset by the fact that, for most workers, every additional dollar earned increases their future Social Security benefits. So here we have a case in which today's labor supply is taxed today, but subsidized tomorrow.

The comparison of IRAs with FSAs, the Sam vignettes, the discussion of the tax treatment of investment, and Social Security's treatment of labor earnings all illustrate the same point, namely, that the time at which the government pays the public for taking particular actions can be quite different from the time at which the action is taken. But, as we've seen, the timing/labeling of these payments can make huge differences in the government's reported deficit.

THE NONRELATIONSHIP BETWEEN MARGINAL AND AVERAGE NET TAX PAYMENTS

A quite different reason why the government's structure of fiscal incentives bears no intrinsic relation to its reported taxes, transfers, or deficits is that these incentives are determined by *marginal* taxes and transfers, not by *total* taxes and transfers. It is total taxes and transfers, however, that are used in computing the government's deficit. To see the difference between marginal and total taxes and transfers, suppose the government announces that, to encourage work effort, it is going to pay $500 to all those who have already earned $5,000 or more this year. For those already in that boat, this policy constitutes a windfall. They receive $500 and have no incentive to earn more money this year. Indeed, because the $500 windfall has made them richer, they may actually choose to work less this year! The total subsidy to

161

each of those thus affected is $500, but the marginal subsidy is zero.

If, in contrast, the government told workers it would match, 10 cents on the dollar, their annual earnings beyond $5,000, this would give those who have already earned $5,000 a 10 percent subsidy on any additional earnings.[13] The total subsidy payments in this case would equal one-tenth of the total amount of earnings above $5,000. If the limit beyond which earnings were subsidized was increased to $6,000, virtually all U.S. workers (most of whom earn well beyond $6,000) would experience the same marginal subsidy, but total transfer payments for this subsidy would decline, for most workers, by $100. This again illustrates that total and marginal transfers are not fundamentally related.

Actually, marginal subsidies could be associated with increased total tax payments and marginal taxes could be associated with increased total transfer payments. In its quest to stimulate labor earnings the government could require (1) that all workers pay a $5,000 tax regardless of how much they earn and (2) that the government reduce this tax by ten cents for every dollar they earn. Since workers who earn less than $50,000 would end up paying money, on net, to the government, and since most workers earn less than $50,000, this policy, which subsidizes, at the margin, earnings at a 10 percent rate, would surely produce more total tax revenue. By running the reverse of this policy, the government could increase its transfer payments while taxing, at the margin, earnings at a 10 percent rate.

Taken together, the above examples lead to the following conclusion: *The government can effect any set of incentives it wants while simultaneously reporting whatever time path of deficits it wants.*

Argument: The Official Deficit May Have Flaws, but It's Tracked U.S. Generational Policy Fairly Well

This final argument for the deficit usually crops up in conversations with its defenders at the end of the foregoing list.

162

Suppose it were true that the official deficit, while it need bear no relationship to actual generational policy, was nonetheless very well correlated with actual changes in generational burdens. Then its continued use might be justified, not because it tells us what we need to know, but because it is somehow related to what we need to know. But it really can't be. The deficit is a single number and, as such, can't be telling us about the quite different treatment of multiple generations alive at a point in time. At best, the deficit could be correlated with the true measure of the treatment of current generations relative to future generations. But, at least for the postwar period in the United States, the official National Income and Product Accounts federal deficit has not been correlated with changes in the relative treatment of current and future generations!

The next chapter will discuss the major changes in generational policy in each of the decades since 1950. It shows that, as a share of the GNP, the federal deficit fell during periods when significant burdens were shifted from current to future generations and rose during periods when significant burdens were shifted from future onto current generations.

7

POSTWAR GENERATIONAL POLICY

——— ■ ———

Since the official U.S. federal deficit is simply a figment of vocabulary, there is no reason to expect its value through time to bear any relationship to the actual course of generational policies. In point of fact, there hasn't been a consistent relationship in the past, and there won't be one any time soon. Post–World War II declines in the federal deficit, as measured by the National Income and Product Accounts (NIPA), have not been coincident with an easing of fiscal burdens on younger and future generations. Nor have postwar increases in the deficit spelled an increased passing of the generational buck. The U.S. deficit has, generationally speaking, been off the mark not only in particular years, but in decade after decade. This chapter uses generational accounting to establish these facts.

In the 'fifties, 'sixties, and 'seventies the government, under cover of essentially balanced budgets, substantially redirected the bills it was handing to different generations. In the 'eighties the official federal deficit rose by amounts never imagined in peacetime. This fact notwithstanding, much of the cross-generation redistributive impact of fiscal policy in the 1980s resulted from policies that weren't even recorded in the federal deficit. As we move into the mid- and late 1990s, the deficit is likely to go into surplus because of the large number of baby boomers' making Social Security "tax" payments.[1] A huge Social Security surplus, for this reason, has been anticipated for years. Indeed, the Social Security Administration has been counting on these funds, at least since the late 1970s, to help pay for the boomers' retirement benefits. Its occurrence will not reflect any change in generational policy, although it is very likely to be misread as doing so.

STUDYING GENERATIONAL POLICY IN A COMPREHENSIVE MANNER

The examination here of postwar U.S. generational policy is based on the government's official statistics, which, of course, incorporate its historic labeling of its receipts and payments. Still, the focus will be on the receipts and payments arising from all policies, not just those recorded in the official deficit. By examining in a comprehensive manner all the government's actions, we can get a pretty good sense of how generational policy has changed through time. The main lesson of this chapter is that looking at the government's deficit is no substitute for considering the entire range of policies being pursued. This point ties in with the lessons of the previous chapter, namely, that with different words (1) those policies that didn't show up in the official deficit could have shown up and (2) those policies that did show up could easily not have shown up. No matter how the government defines its deficit, considering the deficit by itself will always miss major elements of the generational policy.

GENERATIONAL POLICY IN THE 1950s

If we were to let U.S. federal debt serve as our guide to generational policy in the 1950s, we'd quickly conclude that the Eisenhower Administration spent its time in office dramati-

cally reducing fiscal burdens on younger and future generations. Based on NIPA data, nominal federal debt remained
essentially unchanged over the decade, but in real (inflation-
adjusted) terms it declined by 18 percent.[2] Meanwhile, real
U.S. output increased by 41 percent.

Changes in federal debt are, however, only part of the
story. Generational accounting requires that one consider
changes in total (federal, state, and local) government net
wealth. Since state and local governments ran deficits in
nine of ten years in the 1950s, the reduction in total government debt relative to output in that decade was somewhat
smaller than that suggested by considering only federal
debt. Still, between 1950 and 1960 the ratio of total government debt to output fell by nearly half, from .617 to .367.

Whatever net tax burden was lifted from existing and future generations by the decade's real federal debt reduction
was more than made up by a dramatic increase in total (federal, state, and local) government spending on goods and
services.[3] This spending increase was "tax-financed," so it
didn't add to federal, state, or local deficits. Compared with
the late 1940s, government spending as a share of national
output rose by almost 50 percent, from under 17 percent to
around 23 percent of NNP.[4] In terms of the government's
peacetime direct consumption of the economy's production,
the Eisenhower Presidency, then, actually and truly her-
alded the age of big government.

Why did the roughly 6 percentage point rise between 1950
and 1959 in government spending relative to NNP increase
generational burdens more than the concomitant 25.0 (61.7
− 36.7) percentage point decline in total government debt
relative to NNP? The reason is that the spending increase
was permanent, i.e., spending was higher, and the burden of
paying for that spending was larger, not just in the 1950s,
but in each decade thereafter. Recall that what matters for
generational accounting is the present value of government
spending over time, not simply government spending in the
immediate future. *As of 1959 the present value increase in
projected future government spending due to Eisenhower-*

era policy was roughly five times larger than the decade's accumulated reduction in federal debt.

The fact that this rise in government spending raised, as shown below, the lifetime payment burdens of different generations does not, in itself, imply that the increased spending made these generations, on balance, worse off. For a generation to be worse off, it must value the increased spending less than the additional net present value payments it is forced to pay. Trying to assess the generation-specific benefits of government spending and to incorporate this information in generational accounting is not easy. Although the benefits of certain types of age-specific government spending, such as education expenditures, can readily, if roughly, be allocated to different generations, it is harder to allocate the benefits of spending on what economists call *pure public goods*, such as defense. Pure public goods are commodities or services that can be consumed by the entire populace without anyone's consumption reducing the amount available for consumption by others. Much of the increase in government spending during the Eisenhower years was, by the way, on defense.

The generational accounting in this chapter and, for that matter, in the rest of the book doesn't delve into the question of which generations have benefited and will benefit from past, present, and future government spending. Rather, the analysis is restricted to which generations have paid for and will pay for that spending. As described below, the postwar increase in government spending as a share of U.S. output primarily occurred in the 1950s. In the subsequent decades government policy involved, in the main, changing who would pay for a roughly constant rate of government spending.

Obviously, a full assessment of generational policy requires an understanding of which generations are the beneficiaries as well as which are the financiers of government spending. Research on the beneficiaries is under way. But whatever the outcome of that research is, it will be irrelevant for assessing much of what occurred in the 1950s and virtually everything that has occurred since the 1950s. In addition, it will be irrelevant for essentially all of the policy changes considered in Chapter 5 and those considered in the next chapter, Chapter 8, since these policy changes involve either no change or very minor changes in government spending.

Returning to the assessment of generational policy in the Eisenhower years, a second reason why the Eisenhower years were bad news (if one ignores the benefits of government spending) for younger and future generations is the change in the tax structure.[5] In 1950 taxes assessed on labor income (excluding payroll taxes) were about three-quarters the size of taxes assessed on capital income. By 1960 they were 23 percent larger. The relative decline in capital income tax revenues is reflected in the relative decline in corporate income tax receipts. Since the elderly pay a much higher share of capital income taxes than they do of labor income taxes, this shift in the tax structure was good for the elderly of that period, but bad for their progeny.

A more important aspect of the Eisenhower-era treatment of different generations was the expansion of pay-as-you-go Social Security. Between 1950 and 1960, Social Security benefit payments relative to Net National Product (NNP) rose by a factor of more than 5, from .005 to .026. To place these figures in perspective, the current ratio of Social Security benefits, including Medicare benefits, to NNP is .074, about three times greater than the 1960 level. The expansion of Social Security in the 1950s accounts, therefore, for more than one-third of the total postwar growth in this program. To get a sense of the generational impact of Social Security policy in the 1950s, refer to the second column in Table 5–4. If one expanded Social Security today to the same degree as it was expanded in the 1950s, the impact, roughly speaking, would be that given in the second column in the table multiplied by 1.4.[6] To illustrate, for sixty-year-old males the calculation suggests a windfall of $14.6 thousand; for twenty-year-old males it suggests a loss of $7.4 thousand.

Another piece of rather bad fiscal news for younger and

future folks during the Eisenhower years was the relative decline in welfare payments. In 1950 welfare benefits were 1.89 percent of NNP. In 1960 they were only .73 percent of NNP. Since the young—particularly younger females—are the chief recipients of welfare benefits, this decline hurt those who were young in the 1950s and those yet to be young. On the other hand, it benefited the older folks of the 1950s, who were excused from the burden of helping to maintain the level of real welfare benefits.

These adverse shifts in fiscal burdens for younger and future generations were offset somewhat by the introduction in 1954 of accelerated depreciation allowances. This increase in investment incentives is predicted to have reduced the market value of existing U.S. business capital by about 4.0 percent.[7] Measured as a percent of NNP, this capital loss was about 4.5 percent. Since most of this capital was owned by older generations, this government-induced capital loss hurt those who were elderly in the 1950s to the benefit of the purchasers of this capital—succeeding generations.

POLICY IN THE 1950s: THE BOTTOM LINE

A detailed generational accounting for years prior to 1989 remains to be done. One can, however, get a feeling for the net impact of the various policies conducted in the 1950s by asking how they would affect today's generational accounts were they all to be added to the policies already in place. How does one add the policies of the 1950s to those of today? Well, take as one example the rise in the 1950s in Social Security benefits relative to the economy. Adding a comparable benefit increase starting in 1989 is accomplished by raising post–1989 Social Security benefits (as well as payroll taxes) so that by 1999 the ratio of Social Security benefits to output is larger by 2.1 percentage points—the increase in the benefit-to-output ratio between 1950 and 1960.[8]

The first column of Table 7–1 shows the results of this hypothetical exercise.[9] It indicates for 1989 the absolute change in lifetime net payments of different generations re-

Table 7–1
Assessing Postwar Generational Policy
(thousands of dollars)

		Changes in 1989 Accounts from Adopting Policies of the			
Age	1950s	1950s, But No Change in Govt. Spending	1960s	1970s	1980s
Males					
0	15.8	4.1	7.8	7.9	5.3
10	23.4	5.5	12.2	12.2	7.4
20	32.6	6.8	15.8	14.3	7.3
30	35.8	3.5	16.1	12.5	4.4
40	32.0	−1.9	12.3	7.1	−.7
50	21.3	−8.7	3.9	−2.8	−7.5
60	6.6	−15.3	−6.0	−13.8	−12.0
70	2.5	−10.3	−4.8	−9.7	−9.0
80	2.8	−4.4	−1.3	−3.7	−5.5
Future generations	15.0	3.6	6.6	7.2	−1.2
Females					
0	12.1	4.0	.1	.0	4.4
10	17.8	5.7	1.0	.5	6.1
20	23.1	6.2	2.4	.0	6.1
30	21.2	1.6	2.9	−1.8	4.8
40	16.8	−3.6	1.2	−4.9	2.1
50	8.4	−10.2	−4.2	−11.7	−2.8
60	−1.7	−16.3	−10.9	−19.3	−7.0
70	−2.7	−12.3	−9.0	−15.5	−6.1
80	−.2	−5.4	−4.2	−7.9	−3.7
Future generations	12.5	4.3	−1.2	−1.2	1.5

sulting from the enactment of the combined set of 1950s policies. The second column shows the impact of the 1950s policies leaving out that decade's increase in government spending and the taxes used to finance that increase. A comparison of these two columns leads to two conclusions. First, the government's increase in spending in the 1950s greatly increased the sum total of lifetime payments required of existing and future generations. Second, while everyone's bill went up, the bills of middle-aged, younger, and future generations rose much more sharply than those of the contemporaneous elderly. Indeed, abstracting from spending policy in the 1950s (Column 2), redistribution in the 1950s toward the old and away from the young and unborn was more significant than that of the 1980s.[10]

In sum, in fiscal affairs Eisenhower was, perhaps unwittingly, anything but the conservative Republican we've been given to believe. Rather than leave America's youth and its posterity better off in terms of their fiscal obligations than they were before he took office, President Eisenhower presided over a very large redistribution from these generations to the elderly of his day as well as to the government, whose rate of spending increased so dramatically.

Imagine Richard Nixon showing up at the 1960 Presidential debates not to proclaim that he and his boss had lowered the federal debt-to-NNP ratio by more than one-quarter, but rather to explain why, during the Eisenhower Administration, government at all levels had increased the net lifetime payments of future generations by about 23 percent, of newborns by about 27 percent, of twenty-year-olds by about 23 percent, of forty-year-olds by about 20 percent, and of fifty-year-olds by about 19 percent.[11] Imagine him further being forced to admit that he and Ike had played a big part in letting government (1) expand its direct consumption of the economy's output by more than one-third and (2) hand huge windfalls, relatively speaking, to those generations fortunate enough to be old in the 1950s.

Clearly Nixon would have had a lot of explaining to do. He might have gotten away with the increase in federal govern-

172

ment spending by claiming, quite correctly, that a good part of it was on defense. But explaining the magnitude of the cross-generation shifting of fiscal burdens would have been far more difficult. Fortunately for Nixon, no one in the opposition was doing generational accounting at the time, so he was free to portray a profligate fiscal decade as a decade of extraordinary fiscal restraint.

GENERATIONAL POLICY IN THE 1960s

The 1960s was a hot time for tax legislation. Keynesian economists dominated the policy discussion with their recommendations to use tax policy to "fine-tune" the economy. In hindsight, the fine-tuning may simply have exacerbated economic fluctuations.[12] In any case, two early initiatives to spur the economy were the introduction of a tax credit for new investment (the investment tax credit) and the reduction of income tax rates. By 1965 both of these recommendations had been carried out. They had the effect of reducing federal tax revenues by about 10 percent.[13] Some of this reduction simply made up for the fact that real revenues had been growing, due to both economic growth and inflation, which was pushing taxpayers into higher tax brackets.[14]

By the late 1960s our legislators were ready to undo most of what they had done in the early 1960s. The claim then was that the economy was overheating and needed fiscal restraint. There was also the lingering question of paying for the Vietnam War. In 1968 the Congress enacted an income tax surcharge. It also passed the Tax Reform Act of 1969, which, among other things, repealed the investment tax credit and slowed the rate at which businesses could write off (depreciate), for tax purposes, their new investment.

In addition to reforming and re-reforming the tax code, our leaders in the 1960s were busy crafting the "Great Society." They did so by expanding existing welfare programs and introducing new ones, including Food Stamps and Medicaid. Large sums of money were spent on those programs. Indeed, welfare payments rose from .73 percent to 2.45 percent of output over the decade. Most of these added payments was targeted to younger Americans.

Notwithstanding all the exciting new fiscal initiatives, many of the variables involved in assessing generational policy changed, through the 1960s, in much the same manner as they changed in the 1950s. Real federal debt continued to fall as a share of output. In absolute terms real federal debt actually declined by 11.6 percent over the decade, whereas real output grew by 37.3 percent. By the decade's end total government debt was only 20.5 percent of output, down significantly from 36.7 percent in 1950.

As in the 1950s, the tax structure continued to shift away from taxes on capital income and toward taxes on labor income. The ratio of labor income taxes, excluding payroll taxes, to capital income taxes rose over the decade from 1.2 to 1.6. Again, the reduction in the share of corporate (income) tax revenue in total tax receipts was responsible for the relative decline in capital income taxes. In 1960 corporate tax receipts were 16 percent of total government revenue. In 1970 the figure was just 11 percent.

A third similarity between generational policy in the 1950s and 1960s is the expansion of Social Security. As a share of NNP, Social Security benefits increased by 1.8 more percentage points between 1960 and 1970. Almost half of this increase was due to the establishment, in the mid-1960s, of Medicare. Even though Medicare was in its infancy, its propensity to absorb ever increasing amounts of federal dollars was well developed by 1970. The average annual rate of increase in real Medicare expenditures between 1968 and 1972 was a whopping 9 percent![15]

A fourth fiscal policy common to both decades was the imposition on wealth holders of capital losses resulting from the enhancement of investment incentives. There were, however, some up and downs in the provision of these incentives. Owners of existing capital lost 3.9 percent of the value of their investments in 1962 as the result of the introduction that year of the investment tax credit and the decision, also in that year, to shorten the numbers of years over which one

174

could write off many investments for taxes purposes. They lost 1.6 percent more of their investments in 1964, when the investment tax credit was liberalized.[16] But in 1969, when the government repealed the investment tax credit outright and restricted depreciation allowances, the government orchestrated, in effect, a 2.9 percent capital gain to existing capital assets. Over the entire decade, the net decline in the price of existing capital, which one would predict would have resulted from the favored treatment of new investment, was 2.6 percent.[17]

A final similarity between the two decades is that government spending as a share of NNP rose in the 1960s. But compared with the 1950s, the increase was small; over the course of the 1960s, government consumption spending as a share of output was only 1.3 percentage points larger than it was in the 1950s.

POLICY IN THE 1960s: THE BOTTOM LINE

The third column of Table 7–1 does for the 1960s what the first column does for the 1950s, that is, it indicates how the combination of policies of the 1960s would play out on the generational accounts of today. As in the 1950s, fiscal policy in the 1960s involved a huge intergenerational redistribution toward earlier generations. Today's elderly would surely like to have the government add to existing policies those of the 1960s, primarily because of the Social Security benefit increases and the changes in the tax structure. For today's typical seventy-year-old male, enacting the policy of the 1960s would be like having Uncle Sam send him a check for $4,800. His seventy-year-old wife, were he to be married to the typical woman that age, would, in effect, be handed a check for $9,000.[18]

In contrast, see what happens to those generations under age fifty. Both sexes would see their remaining lifetime net payments rise, but the bills for males would be significantly higher than the bills for females. For example, thirty-year-old males would, in effect, be handed an extra bill by the government totaling $16,100, while today's fifty-year-old women would have to come up with "only" $2,900. Such large differences are due primarily to significant increases in welfare benefits in the 1960s, which, as previously noted, primarily benefit young and middle-aged females and their children.

According to the data, future males were hurt by policy in the 1960s, though not as badly as by policy in the 1950s. For future males, the lifetime bill rises by $6,600, from $89,500 to $96,100. For future females, there is actually a slight decline in their generational account, from $44,200 to $43,000. The average (males and females) bill to future generations rises, in part, because of increases in government spending, but mainly because of Social Security and welfare benefit increases, which, together with the change in the tax structure, reduced significantly the net lifetime payments of existing generations. *Somebody had to pay the tab for letting those around in the 1960s off the hook, and it was the generations which, in the 1960s, were not yet born—some of whom may now be reading this and shaking their heads!*

The magnitude of the numbers of the 1960s are even more impressive when one considers that this redistribution came on top of the redistribution of the 1950s. Together, the policies of the 1950s and 1960s appear capable of more than explaining today's imbalance in fiscal burdens between newborns and future generations; that is, in the absence of the policy of those two decades, future generations would probably have been treated more favorably than current newborns.

GENERATIONAL POLICY IN THE 1970s

Many of the components of generational policy of the 1950s and 1960s continued through the 1970s. Federal debt was a smaller fraction of output at the end of the decade than it was at the beginning, but the decline was much less than in the 1950s. While growth in federal debt (net deficits) was almost keeping pace with growth in output, total government debt as a share of output fell by 6.9 percentage points during the 1970s because of surpluses run at the state and local levels.

Total government spending was higher in the 1970s than in the 1960s, but not by much. This spending averaged 24.6 percent of output in the 1970s, as against 24.3 percent in the 1960s. The 1970s also witnessed a change in the structure of non–Social Security taxes. The share of capital income taxes in non–Social Security tax revenues remained constant at 24 percent, but labor income taxes rose relative to sales and excise taxes. The ratio of the former taxes to the latter in 1970 was .99; in 1980 it was 1.28. Since the elderly pay a larger share of sales and excise taxes than they do of labor income taxes, this structural shift entailed more redistribution toward the elderly and away from the middle-aged, youngsters, and the unborn.

Yet more redistribution in the same direction resulted in the 1970s from a further dramatic expansion of Social Security benefits. Over the decade, total real Social Security retirement, survivor, and disability benefits rose by 84 percent, and total real Medicare benefits rose by 132 percent. This striking growth in transfers, made primarily to the elderly, occurred during a period when the population aged sixty-five and older rose by less than 13 percent. All told, between 1970 and 1980 Social Security benefits increased from 4.4 percent of output to 6.8 percent of output.

The growth of welfare benefits accelerated through the 1970s. In 1970 these benefits were equal in size to 2.45 percent of output, but by 1980 they had grown to 3.54 percent of output. This growth did not reflect an increase in the fraction of the young population. The share of the population under age twenty-five was actually slightly smaller in the 1970s than in the 1960s.

Like the 'fifties and 'sixties, the 'seventies featured the enhancement of investment incentives. In 1971 the federal government reversed course once again and reestablished the investment tax credit. It also accelerated depreciation allowances on new investment. In 1974 the size of the invest-

177

ment tax credit was raised to 10 percent. And in 1975 there was a small change in the corporate tax rate. The net impact of these tax changes was to lower the value of existing business capital by an estimated 6.1 percent.

This capital loss, measured in today's dollars, was about $270 billion—not exactly small potatoes.[19] Essentially all of this loss was engineered by the administrations of Presidents Nixon and Ford.[20] For Democrats reading this book, the irony of Republican Presidents unwittingly afflicting their wealthy supporters with huge implicit wealth taxes must be rather delicious. Surely, neither Nixon nor Ford would have touched with a 10-foot pole the suggestion of explicitly taxing Americans' wealth.

POLICY IN THE 1970s: THE BOTTOM LINE

The fourth column of Table 7–1 spells out the implications of the generational policies of the 1970s, assuming, as before, that they are added to current policies. The changes in generational accounts are similar to those arising from implementing the policies of the 1960s. Once again there is a big redistribution to the elderly and away from future generations. Sixty-year-old males receive a $19,300 windfall. And young males in their twenties and thirties pay for a good portion of these windfalls with increased payments that range from $7,100 to $14,300. Young females in those age ranges benefit once again from the increase in welfare payments by experiencing a decline in their net payments ranging from zero to $4,900.

GENERATIONAL POLICY IN THE 1980s

Those of you Democrats who were pleasantly surprised to learn of the Nixon and Ford implicit wealth taxes of the 1970s may be even more pleased to discover that Ronald Reagan promulgated an even larger implicit wealth tax within his first few months of office.[21] In 1981 Congress passed and the President signed legislation providing the largest investment incentives in the nation's history. These investment incentives produced an estimated 6.5 percent capital loss to wealth holders, most of whom were elderly.

However, before any of you Democrats become too gleeful, you need to know that many of your leaders in Congress subsequently had a large hand in more than fully reversing the 1981 investment incentives. TEFRA, the Tax Equity and Fiscal Responsibility Act of 1982 (Don't you just love these titles?), scaled back the acceleration of depreciation allowances contained in the Economic Recovery Tax Act of 1981. And the Tax Reform Act of 1986, TRA, did more of the same. In addition, it canceled, yet again, the yo-yo investment tax credit and lowered tax rates on business profits, thus watering down the value of the remaining tax deductions available to businesses for engaging in new investment.

By helping pass these two pieces of legislation, Democrats unwittingly (no doubt) handed owners of U.S. capital a huge capital gain—$747 billion in today's dollars. The percentage size of this capital gain—13.1 percent—was larger than the combined percentage capital loss engendered by Nixon, Ford, and Reagan.[22] If we factor in all the policies of the 1980s, the predicted net impact of changes in the treatment of new investment versus old capital was a 6.6 percent capital gain to old capital, which went primarily to older people.

How do we we know that these predicted changes in the value of existing capital actually occurred? In particular, can we trace changes in the stock market—the market for the purchase and sale of much of existing U.S. business capital—to changes in investment incentives? Unfortunately, it's hard to ascribe capital gains and losses on the stock market in any particular day to changes in investment incentives, because changes in investment incentives don't occur overnight. The impact of new investment incentives on stock values occurs gradually as enactment of the new incentives becomes more likely. As this process goes on, there is an array of other factors impacting on values in the stock market.

Still, there may be some rough confirmation that invest-

ment incentives affect stock values in the fact that U.S. equity values were depressed in the early 1980s and were quite
high in the late 1980s—precisely as one would predict based
on the changes that took place in investment incentives. Certainly, it's safe to assume that the financial and business
community would not ignore the tax advantages from these
incentives, which, in the case of the 1986 Tax Reform Act,
were worth upwards of three-quarters of a trillion dollars.

In any case, the public's attention in the 1980s, when it
came to economic policy, was certainly not focused on investment incentives. Instead, it was on the decade's seem-
ingly colossal accumulation of federal debt. The 1980 to
1989 rate of increase in these liabilities was 303 percent in
nominal terms and 136 percent in real terms. By the end of
1989 federal debt was a 20-percentage-point larger fraction
of the nation's output than it was in 1980. For those who believe, even this far into this book, that the recent buildup of
federal IOUs will, in and of itself, lead to economic catastro-
phe, it many be comforting (or disheartening as the case may
be) to bear in mind that the past decade's increment to federal debt is small compared with the increase in federal debt
during World War II, between 1940 and 1945. During those
war years the rise in federal debt as a share of output was
more than five times the increase observed in the 1980s.
Having a federal debt in 1945 that was worth more than a
year's output did not prevent the U.S. economy from going
great guns for the next twenty-five years. Nor will today's
much smaller (.396) federal debt-to-output ratio, by itself,
prevent another sustained period of economic advance.

All the attention paid to federal debt has also missed the
point that state and local governments were running rather
hefty surpluses in the 1980s. According to the NIPA, through
the course of the decade federal debt rose by $1,455 billion,
whereas state and local debt fell by $480 billion. As a conse-
quence, the increase in the total government debt-to-output
ratio was much smaller than the federal debt-to-output ratio. The increase in the total government debt-to-output
ratio was from .136 in 1980 to .267 in 1989. It's worth bearing

in mind that the .267 debt-to-output ratio, while somewhat larger than the .205 figure in 1970, is notably smaller than the .367 figure in 1960 and quite a bit smaller than the .617 figure in 1950. That is, total government debt, as derived from the deficit series of the NIPA, is certainly not historically large compared to the size of the economy.

The distinction between federal debt based on the NIPA data and gross federal debt based on federal budget data needs to be drawn. Most of those claiming that the sky is falling because of the past decade's increase in federal debt are basing their claims on the increase in gross federal debt. This increase, which totaled $1.959 billion, is $504 billion (or 26 percent) larger than the increase in federal debt reported by NIPA. Much of the distinction between the two figures relates to the word "gross." Suppose the government borrows money from Mr. X and then lends it back to Mr. X. The transaction would raise the government's gross debt, although it would have zero economic significance. Such transactions are excluded from the NIPA measure of the size of the debt. Through the 1980s the federal government increased its borrowing from some segments of the public only to turn around and make loans to other segments of the public. The role the feds were playing here was simply that of a bank, which intermediates between those who want to borrow and those who want to earn a return on their savings. While your writer-at-large thinks all definitions of the debt are silly, he concurs with the national income accountants that the gross federal debt is sillier than most.[23] In any case, those still fixated on the federal debt may breathe easier knowing that its growth in the 1980s was 26 percent less than commonly believed.

Another reason the recent debt accumulation is less problematic than most believe is that, to some extent, this run-up in debt simply represented a labeling game. This is precisely the case for those Americans for whom the earlier Reagan tax cuts and the subsequent Bush, as well as state and local, tax hikes were, in present value, a wash. *In the 1980s the government (federal, state, and local) simply called more of the*

181

money it took from these Americans "borrowing" and called less of the money it took "taxes." In the 1990s these Americans are turning around and using the "return of principal plus interest" on this "borrowing" to pay their increased "taxes." While the words changed, the net amount of money actually flowing between the government and these Americans in the 1980s and the 1990s did not.

Of course, for others of us, the Reagan tax cuts, the Bush tax hikes, and the recent tax increases of states and localities were not merely a (present value) wash. Rather, they constituted a real change in our lifetime net payments to the government. But even those of us who did receive a big present value gift from the combined Reagan–Bush policy are now and will be in the future handing back at least a portion of what was handed to us in earlier years in the form of higher taxes. While the deficits of the 1980s captured every dollar of the Reagan tax cuts, they did not record a single dollar of the additional taxes we are now paying and will be paying in the next several decades. An analogy here is Uncle Sam's giving you something with his right hand (the 1981 tax cuts) and taking something from you with his left hand (the tax increases scheduled in the 1990 budget agreement, not to mention those being imposed by the states and localities). From an economic perspective you care about the net amount the government hands you, so focusing only on Sam's right hand (the tax cuts recorded by the deficit) can be terribly misleading.

Besides changes in investment incentives and the deficits, what other fiscal action was there in the 1980s? Well, total government spending relative to NNP was .4 percentage points larger in the 1980s than in the 1970s. But the most important policy beyond those mentioned was the 1983 enactment of amendments to Social Security. As previously discussed, this legislation substantially reduced the present value of baby boomers' benefits. Measured in today's dollars the present value loss to baby boomers is $1.228 trillion. *To put this figure in perspective, consider this: It is more than four-fifths of the face value of all the debt added to the federal government's books in all of the 1980s.*[24]

The 1983 legislation affected Social Security retirement, survivor, and disability benefits to be received after the turn of the century. This new law added to the significant 1977 Social Security legislation that had stabilized the growth of non-Medicare Social Security relative to the economy. Indeed, at the end of the 1980s the ratio of non-Medicare Social Security benefit payments to U.S. output was slightly smaller than it had been at the beginning of the 1980s, even though the fraction of elderly in the population was about 10 percent larger. In contrast, Medicare payments as a share of output grew by six-tenths of one percentage point.[25]

Labor income taxes (other than payroll taxes) also continued to rise as a share of total non-payroll taxes through the 1980s. The increase in this decade, though, was smaller. In 1980 the labor income tax share was 42.8 percent; by 1990 it was 44.0 percent. At the same time the share of sales and excise taxes rose by 1.2 percentage points, and the share of capital income taxes fell by 2.4 percentage points. On balance, this small structural tax change represented a plus for older generations in the 1980s, but a minus for all succeeding generations.

One trend that did come to an end during the Reagan years was the increase in welfare benefits relative to output. These payments declined from 3.54 percent of output in 1980 to 3.08 percent of output in 1989. This relative reduction in non–Social Security transfers can be added to the list of anti-youth and anti-future-generations policies of the Reagan years. The complete list includes the increase in federal debt, the expansion of Medicare, the shift in the tax structure, and the reduction, on balance, in investment incentives, as well as the decline in welfare payments. On the other side of the ledger is the reduction in official state and local liabilities and the major reduction in Social Security benefits, which will hurt middle-aged boomers to the benefit of today's and tomorrow's children.

183

POLICY IN THE 1980s: THE BOTTOM LINE

The fifth column of Table 7–1 indicates the net impact on our current generational accounts of adding the policies of the 1980s. *Contrary to common belief, fiscal policy in the past decade did not place a huge payment burden on future generations.* The hit on future generations in the 1980s is near zero if one averages the male and female numbers. The average (over males and females) damage done in the 1980s to future generations was only 0.5 percent of the damage done in the 1950s, only 2.7 percent of the damage done in the 1960s, and only 2.5 percent of the damage done in the 1970s.

The big winners from fiscal policy in the 1980s were Americans over forty at the time. Americans under forty were hurt by the policies. Young women were particularly hard hit by the decline in real welfare benefits and the rise in excise taxation.

MISSING THE FOREST AND MOST OF THE TREES?

It may be useful to summarize the historic inverse relationship between the growth in federal debt and extent of redistribution from later to earlier generations. In the 'fifties, 'sixties, and 'seventies the ratio of federal debt to output declined steadily, from .670 in 1950, to .377 in 1960, to .213 in 1970, to .196 in 1980. In the early 1980s this trend ended, and federal debt began to rise relative to output. By 1990 the federal debt-to-output ratio was .396. Based on these numbers conventional wisdom would say that the 1980s was the decade in which the welfare of later generations was sacrificed in spades to the benefit of earlier generations and that the 'fifties, 'sixties, and 'seventies were decades in which the opposite generational redistribution occurred.

But, as is apparent in Table 7–1, *generational policy in the last four decades was precisely the opposite of that suggested by conventional wisdom!* The 1950s, the decade featuring the largest decline in the ratio of federal debt to output, is the decade with the least youth- and future-oriented policy. The 1980s, in contrast, is the decade in which the smallest damage was done to future generations.

To see more clearly how much of the generational policy one can miss by focusing solely on changes in federal debt, consider Table 7-2. This table compares the decade-specific changes in generational accounts reported in Table 7-1 with those that arise solely from changes in the ratio of federal debt to output. In this and the previous table, increases (decreases) in the debt-to-output ratio over a given decade are treated as a ten-year-long tax cut (increase) leading to a permanent tax increase (cut) starting in the eleventh year sufficient to maintain constant through time the debt-to-output ratio. Because some generations suffer (benefit) more from the subsequent tax increases (cuts) than they do from the more immediate tax cuts (increases), the change in generational accounts for different generations can be opposite in sign. The second column in Table 7-2 illustrates this point. It shows that the decline in federal debt relative to output in the 1950s benefited young and future generations but hurt older generations, who paid higher taxes than would have been the case had the federal government kept its debt from falling as a share of the nation's output.

The numbers in the columns labeled "Federal Debt Policy Only" differ dramatically from the numbers in the adjacent columns labeled "All Policies." Take the 'fifties, 'sixties, and 'seventies. The burden on future generations of males was increased in these decades by $15,000, $6,600, and $7,200, respectively. But, if one considers only the generational account changes arising from changes in federal debt, the burden was *reduced* by $2,400, $1,500 and $100, respectively. In contrast to these decades, for the 1980s consideration of the federal deficit by itself suggests a $1,900 increase in the burden on future males, but when all the policies of the 1980s are considered the burden on future males actually declines by $1,500.

Table 7–2
Postwar Generational Policy: All Policies Versus Federal Debt Policy Alone
(thousands of dollars)

| | Changes in 1989 Accounts from Adopting Policies of the | | | |
| | 1950s | | 1960s | |
Age	All Policies	Federal Debt Policy Only	All Policies	Federal Debt Policy Only
Males				
0	15.8	−1.9	7.8	−1.2
10	23.4	−2.6	12.2	−1.6
20	32.6	−1.3	15.8	−.8
30	35.8	.8	16.1	.5
40	32.0	2.6	12.3	1.6
50	21.3	3.8	3.9	2.3
60	6.6	3.6	−6.0	2.2
70	2.5	2.3	−4.8	1.4
80	2.8	1.5	−1.3	.9
Future generations	15.0	−2.4	6.6	−1.5
Females				
0	12.1	−1.2	.1	−.7
10	17.8	−1.6	1.0	−1.0
20	23.1	−.5	2.4	−.3
30	21.2	.5	2.9	.3
40	16.8	1.3	1.2	.8
50	8.4	2.0	−4.2	1.2
60	−1.7	2.0	−10.9	1.2
70	−2.7	1.6	−9.0	1.0
80	−.2	1.1	−4.2	.7
Future generations	12.5	−1.5	−1.2	−.9

Table 7–2 (continued)

| | Changes in 1989 Accounts from Adopting Policies of the | | | |
| | 1970s | | 1980s | |
Age	All Policies	Federal Debt Policy Only	All Policies	Federal Debt Policy Only
Males				
0	7.9	−.1	5.3	1.5
10	12.2	−.1	7.4	2.1
20	14.3	−.1	7.3	1.0
30	12.5	.0	4.4	−.6
40	7.1	.1	−.7	−2.1
50	−2.8	.2	−7.5	−3.0
60	−13.8	.2	−12.0	−2.9
70	−9.7	.1	−9.0	−1.8
80	−3.7	.1	−5.5	−1.2
Future generations	7.2	−.1	−1.2	1.9
Females				
0	.0	−.1	4.4	1.0
10	.5	−.0	6.1	1.3
20	.0	.0	6.1	.4
30	−1.8	.1	4.8	-.4
40	−4.9	.1	2.1	−1.1
50	−11.7	.1	−2.8	−1.6
60	−19.3	.1	−7.0	−1.6
70	−15.5	.1	−6.1	−1.3
80	−7.9	.1	−3.7	-.9
Future generations	−1.2	−.1	1.5	1.2

187

HAVE OUR LEADERS UNDERSTOOD THEIR GENERATIONAL ACTIONS?

If the federal deficit has failed to track generational policy, have policy-makers misjudged their treatment of different generations? The answer is "yes and no." Take the massive buildup of pay-as-you-go Social Security in the 'fifties, 'sixties, and 'seventies. U.S. policy-makers certainly knew whom they were helping in raising real Social Security retirement and survivor benefits and in providing health insurance to the elderly through Medicare. The real question is not whether policy-makers knew whom they were helping, but rather whether they fully appreciated whom they were hurting. The answer is probably no. Indeed, prior to the seminal research of Harvard's Martin Feldstein in the mid-1970s, even most economists specializing in the field of public finance were unaware of the magnitude of Social Security's intergenerational redistribution.[26]

Surely the words the government used to describe (disguise) its generational policies were critical to Social Security's remarkable postwar growth. Had the politicians been forced to use different words and thereby to count Social Security's huge unfunded liabilities as official debt, Social Security, in all likelihood, would be a minor program today. Can anyone really imagine the U.S. government funding its Social Security benefit increases in the 'fifties, 'sixties, and 'seventies by accumulating trillions of dollars in official IOUs? By cloaking Social Security finance in the seemingly benign words "pay-as-you-go," politicians gave themselves and the public the impression that we were paying immediately for the benefits we received. The problem, of course, is that the "we" who received the benefits and the "we" who provided the tax finance were, and still are, quite different people.

If economists (the author included) specializing in matters of public finance were missing the economic equivalence of deficit and pay-as-you-go finance, one can certainly forgive the politicians for doing so. *The politicians have had a doubly hard time understanding this point because they've had Keynesians economists telling them that expropriating specific generations with one set of words was somehow different from expropriating them with another.*[27]

To many, pay-as-you-go finance seemed and still seems different from running deficits; it seems more like participating in a chain letter or a Ponzi scheme. Many people get snookered by chain letters, and this case is no exception. As with any chain letter, pay-as-you-go Social Security can appear, at first glance, like a great deal for all participants. Everybody who contributes thinks he'll get paid back. In the Social Security chain letter all contributors do get paid back, but in much smaller dollars, in present value, than the dollars contributed.[28] A mature pay-as-you-go Social Security scheme effectively pays a rate of return on contributions equal to the economy's rate of population plus productivity growth. In the United States this growth rate has been, and remains today, significantly lower than the real return available from investing one's Social Security contributions in productive capital.[29]

Although most politicians have yet to appreciate fully the adverse effects of the Social Security chain-letter game, they seem to understand intuitively that they're playing a chain-letter game when it comes to continuing to borrow from succeeding generations to pay interest on the government's debt. When the real return that must be paid on government borrowing exceeds, as it does, the economy's growth rate, such continued borrowing leads to an exponential growth in debt. In the case of Social Security, trying to give each new generation a market rate of return on its contributions leads to an exponential growth in benefits. Rather than let benefits grow relative to the economy, politicians in the late 1970s and early 1980s have, in the case of non-Medicare Social Security, broken the chain letter by choosing to pay its current and prospective contributors much less in benefits than is needed to provide a market return on contributions.

The continuing confusion concerning the generational implications of pay-as-you-go finance is, as mentioned, per-

189

fectly illustrated by the 1990 federal budget agreement, whose goal was to cut federal deficits by $500 billion over five years. While going to considerable lengths to ensure real deficit reduction of this magnitude, the new law permits unlimited increases in Social Security benefits provided they are funded on a pay-as-you-go basis. *If politicians, after years of vast intergenerational redistribution through Social Security, can today officially sanctify more of the same in a bill whose express purpose is to limit such redistribution, they are either very badly confused or engaged in a much more sophisticated duplicity than any of us have dared to imagine.*

Since the politicians are still missing the true dimension of their intergenerational redistribution through Social Security, it is unlikely that they understand the potentially equally large shifting of generational burdens arising from "revenue-neutral" changes in the age structure of taxes, from "revenue-neutral" changes in the age structure of transfers, from government-induced changes in asset values, and from announcements today of changes in future taxes and transfers.[30]

POSTWAR GENERATIONAL POLICY
AND POSTWAR U.S. SAVING

Generational policy is only one of a range of important determinants of national saving.[31] In addition to generational policy, national saving depends on the government's spending policy, distortionary policy, and distribution policy. It also depends on private preferences about saving and private labor supply decisions. National saving is also greatly influenced by such other factors as demographics, insurance arrangements, and credit institutions.

Given the number and complexity of saving determinants and the still rudimentary state of economic measurement, one cannot expect to connect changes in national saving on a year-to-year basis to changes in generational policy. Over a long period of time one would, however, expect to see the impact of generational policy showing up in national saving. The last forty years of U.S. generational policy has certainly been heavily biased against saving, and the trend in national saving has certainly been downward. While it is difficult to say empirically how much of the postwar decline in U.S. saving is due to generational policy, elaborate computer models of the economy suggest that generational policy could explain a good share of the decline in our nation's saving rate.[32]

We may never know precisely how much damage U.S. generational policy has been doing to our nation's rates of saving, investment, and growth, but both economic theory and common sense suggest the importance of putting a halt to the further burdening of those coming in the future to the benefit of those currently alive. Unfortunately, as described in the next chapter, a continuation in this decade of adverse generational policies is a very real possibility.

8

SOCIAL SECURITY
AND THE BABY
BOOMERS

———— ■ ————

If baby boomers aren't worried about financing their old age, they should be. There is a long list of reasons, many already mentioned, why the boomers' retirement years may be far less comfortable relative to their working years than was the case for their parents. Compared with their parents, boomers can expect to retire earlier, live longer, rely less on inheritances, receive less help from children, experience slower real wage growth, and replace a smaller fraction of their preretirement earnings with Social Security retirement benefits.

Boomers also face a type of competition different from that of smaller cohorts. The competition of boomers is with one another. It involves the boomers' purchase and sale of age-specific commodities. When one boomer is buying an age-specific commodity, such as a starter home, chances are other boomers are buying the same thing, leading to a rise in the commodity's price. The obverse holds true for commodities boomers are trying to sell. Since the number of boomers moving into certain age ranges occurs gradually, these increases in the prices boomers pay and declines in the prices boomers receive also occur gradually. This slow process of price change is hard to see in the data. Still, the basic laws of supply and demand operate here as elsewhere, and without a doubt boomers are substantially increasing the demands for what they are buying and supplies of what they are selling.

In recent years boomers have been buying homes. In so doing they have surely helped drive sky-high the price of houses in many regions.[1] They have also been selling, en masse, their labor services, thereby depressing their wages by an estimated 6 to 13 percent.[2] In forty or so years, boomers will all be renting out or selling off their accumulated capital—their equity and debt claims to plant and equipment, their land, and their housing. This collective behavior will depress the returns boomers receive on those assets as well as the sales prices of those assets.[3] For most boomers, their house will be the principal asset they will be trying to sell at the end of their lives. Could these price effects be large? Unfortunately for boomers, the answer appears to be yes. According to sophisticated computer models of the demographic transition, the decline in capital returns and asset prices received by boomers could be as large as 20 percent.[4]

GENERATIONAL POLICY AND THE BOOMERS

All this unpleasant news comes on top of the very substantial fiscal burdens that have been visited on the baby boom generation as the result of four decades of mostly under-the-cover intergenerational redistribution. As described in the preceding chapter, this redistribution was primarily away from the boomers and their progeny and toward their parents, grandparents, and great-grandparents. The fact that boomers have been heavily burdened is not to say that their parents, grandparents, and great-grandparents made out like bandits. After all, these are the generations that suffered through the Great Depression and fought World War II. In addition, the fact that the government helped, is helping, and will help these generations relieved the boomers of a good part of their filial obligation.

Still, boomers can legitimately object that had their older relatives known how much they were taking from their off-spring, they might well have limited their claims. Certainly there is little reason to believe that boomers as a group would voluntarily make transfers to their older relatives that are as generous as those now codified in law.[5]

One could spend a long time arguing whether the baby boom generation has been well treated or mistreated by past generational policy. But that argument would not change the fact that the redistribution that occurred in the past is not likely to be reversed by the political process. Indeed, much of what was given away in the past four decades could not be taken back even were there a consensus to do so. After all, many, if not most, of the beneficiaries of postwar generational policy are already dead.

Short of resurrection day, the deceased aren't coming back to repay past favors. This fact of death notwithstanding, some boomers have been smitten with the "I'm mad as hell, and I won't take it any more" syndrome. They espouse abolishing the institution that was associated with much of postwar intergenerational redistribution—namely, the Social Security system.[6] Even were elimination of Social Security feasible, such a move would be likely to do boomers a lot more harm than good. True, Social Security takes more from boomers in present value than it gives them back in present value. Yet the system provides several forms of insurance that boomers greatly need and might not otherwise get. The most important are inflation-protected annuity, disability, and life (survivor) insurance. Outside of employer-provided policies, private insurance markets for the first two of these three types of insurance are essentially nonexistent. And in the case of life insurance, there seems to be a great reluctance on the part of boomers and other Americans to confront the possibility of their ultimate demise and to purchase adequate amounts.[7]

The reason Social Security is not going to disappear can

be seen by referring back to Table 5–1, which shows the huge stake older Americans have in Social Security. Consider the typical seventy-year-old. His or her stake is about $90,000.[8] For many of the elderly Social Security represents their chief, if not sole, source of income. Baby boomers, as a group, would certainly oppose pulling the rug out from under today's elderly, who are in no position to recoup their losses by reentering the labor market.

HOLDING ONE'S OWN

If boomers must admit, however reluctantly, that bygones are bygones, they still need to keep a very careful eye out to prevent further erosion in their position (their generational accounts). In 1983 boomers saw about one-fifth of their Social Security retirement benefits wiped out at the stroke of a pen. The remainder of their retirement benefits could also be in jeopardy in this decade, *based* on the government's reaction to Social Security surpluses, and in the next decade, *depending* on the government's handling of Medicare's projected deficits.[9]

Other generations also need to watch out. Since the baby boom is such a large voting bloc, policies such as the Moynihan proposal (described below) that favor them to the detriment of other generations are likely to continue to be proposed. Fending off the baby boom generation is, of course, impossible for future generations, who are not around to defend themselves in the political debate. The best one can do for future generations is to ensure that those currently alive are fully aware of the burdens they may be shifting upstream. Some boomers, even in the broad light of day, will want to use fiscal policy to take money from their children and grandchildren. But most are likely to oppose such policies provided they see clearly that this is indeed what is taking place. Identifying the losers as well as the winners is precisely what generational accounting brings to the policy debate.

The goal of the remainder of this chapter is to give boomers and others a sense of their stake in Social Security policy over the next several decades. Toward that end the chapter evaluates four Social Security policies. One is Senator Moynihan's proposed short- and medium-run cut and long-run increase in Social Security payroll taxes. Each of the policies represents an alternative response to Social Security's short- and medium-term surpluses. Compared with the status quo, each has the potential of greatly affecting the welfare of the boomers as well as other generations.

The discussion of these four policies is followed by an analysis of Medicare's provision of health insurance to the elderly, particularly the unpleasant implications for boomers of the government's failure to gain immediate control of spiraling Medicare costs. Given the current growth rate in health care costs, the Medicare system will run short of funds around the turn of the century. If the politicians wait until then to address this problem, as is likely if history is any guide, they will effect a big transfer to those who will be over sixty-five in the 1990s. The bill for that transfer could well end up in the laps of the boomers. Hence, *the fact that Medicare payroll taxes will keep pace with rising Medicare health care costs for the next ten years should be a cause for alarm, not solace, to baby boomers for it is* their *dollars, in large part, that will be used to cover somebody else's larger health care benefits.* And it is *their* Medicare (HI) taxes that are most likely to be increased once Medicare runs short of cash. Were the government to curtail this ongoing pay-as-you-go expansion of Medicare, the resulting surplus of Medicare taxes over benefit payments could be set aside in the Medicare trust fund to help pay for the boomers' own old-age health care.

FOUR SOCIAL SECURITY POLICIES

The first of the four policies to be considered is Senator Moynihan's proposal to cut the Social Security payroll tax rate over the next three decades and to increase the tax rate thereafter. The second policy also involves the reduction in payroll taxes through the year 2020 as recommended by Senator Moynihan. But instead of raising tax rates after 2020, this policy reduces the Social Security benefits of the baby boomers by the same amount that payroll taxes would otherwise have increased. The third policy entails the indirect dissipation of the Social Security trust fund though an increase in government spending over the next three decades equal, on an annual basis, to the Social Security surplus. Over these decades funds to pay for the increased government spending are "borrowed" so that in 2020 the additional accumulated federal debt is equal in magnitude to the Social Security trust fund. The fourth policy is an immediate and permanent switch from payroll tax financing to income tax financing of Social Security.

The first two of these policies are quite beneficial to baby boomers; the third is highly detrimental; and the fourth policy is a mixed bag, helping some boomers and hurting others, in many cases by substantial amounts. Of course, whenever boomers as a group are helped, other generations are necessarily hurt. Of the four policies, the Moynihan proposal is the most detrimental to those yet to be born.

THE MOYNIHAN PROPOSAL

Let's listen in on a few statements by Senator Moynihan in his January 14, 1991, address to the U.S. Senate in which he introduced the latest version of his plan:

> Mr. President [of the Senate], I rise to introduce as S. 11 the Social Security Tax Cut Act of 1991, a bill to reduce Social Security contribution rates and return the program to traditional pay-as-you-go financing.
>
> It is the dirty little secret of last year's budget summit agreement that we will spend $500 billion of Social Security tax revenue on general government expenses over the next 5

years. This practice violates the integrity of the Social Security Trust Funds and makes government finance more regressive.

Mr. President, we must cut Social Security taxes. We don't need the money for Social Security, so let's give it back to the workers who earned it and need it.

We would schedule a series of rate increases for the next century as costs rise, consistent with pay-as-you-go financing.

We would then, in a sense, just smooth out, or fine tune the current arrangements.

A return to pay-as-you-go financing will strengthen the financing of Social Security, restore honesty and integrity to federal finances, stimulate the economy, and provide a fair tax cut to 132 million Social Security taxpayers.

The Charitable Interpretation

There are charitable and uncharitable interpretations of the Senator's scheme. Here's the charitable interpretation: The Senator is concerned that over the next three decades the Social Security surpluses will induce the government to spend more than would otherwise be the case. That is the "dirty little secret" to which the Senator refers.

"Wait a second," you might say, "the official deficit, or at least the latest version of the official deficit—let's call it the official official deficit—is supposed to exclude Social Security." Moynihan's response would surely be, "Yes, that's true, but Congress has set very high targets for the next five years for the official official deficit, which excludes Social Security surpluses, implicitly taking into account the size of the current and impending surpluses. In so doing, Congress is permitting spending to be larger than would occur with no Social Security surpluses. Redefining the deficit doesn't work. The only way to keep the government from looking at the surpluses and, as a consequence, increasing its spending is to actually eliminate the Social Security surpluses by cutting the payroll tax."

The Uncharitable Interpretation

The uncharitable interpretation begins with the assumption that the government's spending as well as other non–Social Security policies will be the same regardless of whether or not there are Social Security surpluses. Hence, in arranging to "just smooth out, or fine tune the current arrangements," what the Senator is really advocating is not holding down government spending, but simply giving baby boomers a tax break. But in giving boomers a tax break, the Senator is sticking it to their kids, grandkids, and so on with a whopping tax increase. *According to this interpretation, the dirty little secret of the Moynihan proposal is that "strengthening the financing of Social Security" will be done on the backs of the next generation.*

Which Interpretation Is Correct?

Both interpretations may be correct. In the 1990 budget agreement Congress and the Administration probably did plan a higher course of spending for the subsequent five years taking into account the Social Security surpluses. But since they have already chosen that spending plan, adopting, at the margin, the Moynihan proposal is not likely to change the course of federal spending, at least through 1995. Furthermore, those in Congress and the Administration who want to maintain spending levels can, if the Moynihan proposal is adopted, point to the official official deficit and argue that since cutting payroll taxes has not increased this deficit (recall that it excludes Social Security), there is no reason, certainly no political reason, to cut spending below what was planned.

For the time being, the Senate has rejected the Senator's proposal, which suggests, perhaps, that the majority of its members adopted the uncharitable view. Alternatively, many of the Senators may have considered the immediate adoption of the Moynihan proposal premature, since the Social Security Trust Fund, at the time of the vote on the proposal, was insufficient to cover even a year's benefit payments. Those Senators may in time change their votes on this proposal as the Security Security Trust Funds swell to up to more than five years of benefits.[10] A third possibility is that many Senators may have been concerned that in voting for the Moynihan proposal, they would be accused of jeopardizing the Social Security benefits of the current elderly. Of course, there is nothing in the Senator's proposal that would have altered the benefits paid to current recipients. Unfortunately, simply uttering the words "Social Security reform" sends shudders down the spines of many retirees. The concern that modifying Social Security's treatment of some generations will involve a change in the treatment of all generations is what one might expect in a society in which generation-specific policy is rarely discussed and, indeed, seems to be somewhat taboo.

The Uncharitable Interpretation: Who Pays?

The first column of Table 8–1 indicates what the Moynihan proposal would mean to different generations if it were adopted and if the course of government spending were not altered as a consequence. As a result of its short- and medium-term payroll tax cuts, the policy provides windfalls to Americans currently alive, with the exception of the very old and the very young. The baby boomers receive the largest windfalls, roughly $3,000 for males and $1,500 for females. These gains come at the expense of American children currently under ten as well as future Americans. If all future Americans are treated uniformly, up to the growth adjustment, their lifetime net payments would rise by $6,100, in the case of males, and $3,000 in the case of females. These are large numbers; *adopting the Senator's plan means an almost 7 percent increase in the present value net lifetime payments of future Americans.*

While boomers may favor the Moynihan proposal on purely selfish grounds, their enthusiasm should be tempered by the possibility that rather than raise payroll taxes

Table 8–1
Changes in Generational Accounts from Four Social Security Policies
(thousands of dollars)

Age	Senator Moynihan	Immediate Payroll Tax Cuts Financed by Future Benefit Reductions	Dissipating the Social Security Trust Fund	Switching from Payroll to Income Tax Finance
Males				
0	1.3	.3	4.1	−2.4
10	−.2	−.6	4.0	−3.6
20	−2.3	−1.8	2.9	−4.4
30	−3.4	−2.2	1.5	−1.0
40	−3.2	−2.5	.6	4.4
50	−2.0	−1.8	.2	8.4
60	−.7	−.7	0	9.6
70	−.1	−.1	0	7.7
80	0	0	0	4.5
Future generations	6.1	3.8	5.2	−2.5
Females				
0	.6	.4	1.9	−2.0
10	−.3	−.1	1.9	−3.1
20	−1.4	−.6	1.5	−4.2
30	−1.7	−.5	.9	−2.0
40	−1.5	−.6	.4	1.3
50	−1.0	−.5	.1	4.2
60	−.4	−.4	0	5.6
70	0	0	0	4.8
80	0	0	0	2.2
Future generations	3.0	2.2	2.4	−2.2

after 2020, the government might simply decide to cut the boomers' Social Security benefits by the amount that would otherwise have been collected in additional taxes. Such a policy delivers the generational account changes reported in the second column in Table 8–1. The gain to boomers, in this case, is reduced by about one-third for males and by about two-thirds for females. Female boomers lose relatively more because their share of Social Security benefits is larger than is their share of payroll tax payments. This reflects Social Security's dependent and survivor benefits, which are paid primarily to married and widowed women, based not on their own past Social Security tax payments, but rather on the extent of their husbands' past earnings that were subject to payroll taxation.

The Charitable Interpretation: Who Pays?

The third column in Table 8–1 shows what happens if Senator Moynihan's proposal is never enacted, and, as he predicts, the federal government indirectly dissipates the Social Security surplus by raising its spending beyond the amount projected in the baseline generational accounts. In the Senator's nightmare the government continues to accumulate its Social Security Trust Fund, but it also borrows to pay for additional spending with the annual amount of the borrowing equal to the annual Social Security surplus. Let's assume this process of deficit-financed increased spending continues through 2020. Let's also assume that after 2020 the government raises income taxes to pay interest (less an adjustment for growth) on the additional accumulated debt.[11]

This scenario is bad news for boomers. Those born around the peak of the baby boom lose about $1,500 in present value. It is also bad news for those coming down the pike. Future males lose $5,200, and future females lose $2,400. Note that these costs to future Americans are almost as large as those arising from the adoption of the Moynihan proposal.

If Senator Moynihan is right that, under the cover of Social Security's surpluses, the government has begun to loosen up on its spending, we can look forward to more of the same for years to come. Social Security's surpluses will continue for the next forty years.[12] Within a decade we will be running annual surpluses in the range of $200 billion to $300 billion. With such large surpluses Keynesians will be clamoring not only for more spending, but also for bigger transfers and lower taxes to reduce "fiscal drag." Extreme supply-siders will no doubt chime in that lower taxes are more important than ever to enhance work and saving incentives.

Actually, the pressure to loosen fiscal policy has already begun. The *New York Times* began in 1988 to advocate loosening fiscal policy in the 1990s with their editorial entitled "Trillions, Trillions All Around."[13] According to the *Times*, "Washington will have to take measures to offset the depressing effect of the big [Social Security] surplus on jobs and economic growth. . . . Fiscal drag is fiscal drag—less purchasing power and fewer jobs—no matter how the Government disguises the figures."

Even moderate economists may start to worry about allowing the Social Security Trust Fund to grow. By 2010 the Social Security Trust Fund is likely to be about half the value of national output.[14] This proportion should be compared with today's ratio of federal debt to output, which is just under two-fifths. It appears that the Trust Fund could end up holding so much of available Federal Treasury bills and bonds that it will have to invest some of its assets in nongovernment securities. This raises the specter of the U.S. government investing in the stock market and owning and even controlling U.S. companies. To be honest, the concern that building up the Social Security Trust Fund will lead to the effective nationalization of a good deal of U.S. commerce seems quite overblown. There is no reason that the Trust Fund will be forced to purchase U.S. stocks. It can hold its assets in state and local bonds as well as the bonds of well-managed foreign economies, such as those of Japan and Germany. It can also hold the bonds of major U.S. corporations, like General Motors, IBM, and AT&T.

Damned if You Do and Damned if You Don't

The above discussion has exposed the following dilemma: Adopting Senator Moynihan's proposal redistributes toward the boomers but makes the deficit (including Social Security) look large, which inhibits spending. Not adopting the plan makes the deficit look small and encourages spending. This is a no-win situation in which the country gets either column 1 or column 2 of Table 8–1 if it adopts the Moynihan proposal, or column 3 if it doesn't.

Are we really forced to choose between bad alternatives as a consequence of using an outdated and misleading fiscal indicator? Not necessarily. If we abandon the deficit and switch to generational accounting, the downsides of both the Moynihan proposal and the implicit dissipation of the Social Security Trust Fund will be crystal clear. Reliance on generational accounting will permit boomers to preserve what they have left in Social Security benefits, and to do so without further encumbering their children.

MAKING THE REVENUE BASE MORE PROGRESSIVE

A key element in Senator Moynihan's argument is that the tax system has become less progressive as payroll taxes have risen in importance relative to income taxes. His argument ignores the previously mentioned fact that the Social Security benefits one receives in exchange for one's payroll tax contributions are provided on a highly progressive basis. Consideration of only the tax side of Social Security is therefore very misleading. A true understanding of fiscal progressivity also requires the analysis of *all* fiscal programs, not simply Social Security and income taxes, and it requires comparing the treatment of individuals over their lifetimes, not simply over a single year. The critical, but as yet unresearched, question is whether, on a generation-by-generation basis, total net lifetime payment burdens have, over time, become more or less progressive. Because that research remains to be conducted, there is at the moment no solid basis for arguing that the U.S. fiscal structure has become less progressive over time.

This point notwithstanding, if the senior Senator from New York had complete latitude, he would probably eliminate the Social Security payroll tax altogether and finance Social Security benefits with income taxes. Whatever the increase in progressivity from a switch from payroll to income taxes, such a switch would be a bonanza for some generations but a disaster for others. Those under forty would win, and those over forty would lose. Why? Because, in contrast to payroll taxes, income taxes are levied on income from assets (including capital gains) as well as income from labor, and older individuals receive a much bigger share of asset income than they do of labor income.

The generational implications of using general revenue finance to pay for Social Security are indicated in the last column of Table 8–1. Consider, for example, sixty-year-old males and females. On average, they would be forced to pay $9,600 and $5,600 more in present value, respectively. Forty-year-old males and females would suffer present value losses of $4,400 and $1,300, respectively. In contrast, males and females who are now age ten would benefit by more than $3,000 each. The policy would also represent a more than $2,000 present value net payment break to future generations.

MEDICARE POLICY

The Explosion in Medicare Costs

Health care spending in the United States is, quite simply, out of control, as Figure 8–1 demonstrates. On a per person basis, our spending is almost twice that of France and Germany, more than twice that of Japan, and nearly three times

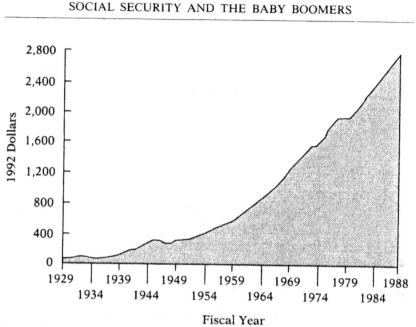

Figure 8–1 *Real per Capita National Health Expenditures (in 1992 dollars)*

Source: Health Care Financing Administration, Office of the Actuary.

that of Great Britain. After the United States, Canada is the country with the highest per capita health care spending, but the Canadians spend almost 30 percent less per person.[15] As mentioned, health care costs now absorb 12 cents of every dollar of U.S. output. By the turn of the century the figure is projected to be 17 cents. And if the growth of health care is unabated, the figure will reach 37 cents by the year 2030![16]

What explains the rapid growth in real per capita U.S. health expenditures? Since 1960 slightly over half of the growth simply reflects expanded use of health care services and facilities. Another third of the growth is due to a rise in the price of medical care relative to the prices of other goods and services. And the remaining 11 percent or so of health expenditure growth reflects the aging of the population.[17] This aging of America will, of course, intensify in the years ahead.

The growth of health care expenditures has potentially enormous implications for government outlays and the well-being of different generations. Consider the federal government expenditures on Medicare alone. These payments currently constitute 7 percent of total federal outlays. According to Office of Management and Budget (OMB) Director Richard Darman:

> Medicare is projected to exceed 30 percent of the federal budget by 2025. This means that to support current Medicare projections alone, either the federal budget would have to grow far beyond 20 percent of GNP or the rest of the budget would have to decline by more than 20 percent in real terms—in order to make room for Medicare.[18]

How will the projected growth in Medicare be financed? The most plausible scenario entails sticking future generations with all or most of the bill. As mentioned, given its labeling of receipts and payments, Medicare will be reporting cash-flow surpluses over most of this decade as the boomers' HI (health insurance) tax payments swell the Medicare Trust Fund coffers. But by the end of the decade the higher payroll tax receipts will be falling short of the increased Medicare spending, leading, in short order, to the exhaustion of the Medicare Trust Fund. At that point the government may raise payroll taxes, but the more likely scenario is that it will simply "borrow" from the Old Age and Survivor Insurance (OASI) Trust Fund, which pays Social Security retirement and survivor benefits, as well as the Disability Insurance (DI) Trust Fund, which pays Social Security disability benefits. The combination of the OASI and DI trust funds is referred to below simply as the Social Security Trust Fund.

Whatever one thinks of the likelihood of indirect dissipation of the Social Security Trust Fund, the potential for direct dissipation of the Trust Fund through this channel seems very great indeed. Interfund Social Security borrowing has occurred in the past, and the temptation to use the surplus OASDI monies to meet Medicare's bills will be overwhelming. "After all," the politicians will argue, "it's all one Social Security system, so why raise taxes to meet Medicare's bills, when we already have more taxes coming in than we need to meet current outlays?" The use of interfund borrowing may delay the eventual raising of payroll taxes for thirty to forty years. Assuming payroll taxes are finally increased in 2035 or so, the burden of these higher taxes will fall primarily on generations not yet born. By how much will taxes have to rise? Well, according to Medicare actuaries, the HI payroll tax may have to rise by anywhere from 6 to 16 percentage points.[19] *Since the combined employer–employee Social Security payroll tax is currently just over 15 percent, the uninhibited growth of Medicare expenditures could eventually require a doubling of Social Security taxes!*

While this scenario entails Medicare's raiding the Social Security Trust Fund, the important thing to keep in mind is not this change in bookkeeping, but rather the fact that the scenario has current and near-term elderly receiving larger health benefits over the next decade than would otherwise be the case and subsequent generations paying higher taxes over their remaining lifetimes to pay for those larger benefits. In other words, the scenario involves real changes in generational accounts, not simply changes in the bookkeeping entries of government trust funds.

Assessing Medicare Growth with Generational Accounts

The generational accounts considered thus far were based on the optimistic (perhaps naïve) assumption that the government will get health expenditures under control immediately and that these expenditures will grow no faster than the rest of the economy. In light of the past exponential growth of Medicare, less optimistic scenarios clearly need to be examined. Table 8–2 considers two alternative growth rates for Medicare expenditures over the 1990s. In the table Medicare outlays in the 1990s are assumed to grow at either

Table 8-2
Changes in Generational Accounts from Medicare Policies
(thousands of dollars)

Age	2 Percent Growth Rate			4 Percent Growth Rate		
	Future Generations Pay	Eventual Medicare Benefit Cut	Pay-as-You-Go Finance	Future Generations Pay	Eventual Medicare Benefit Cut	Pay-as-You-Go Finance
Males						
0	-.2	.4	1.6	-.5	.8	3.4
10	-.4	.6	2.1	-.9	1.2	4.6
20	-.6	.8	2.3	-1.4	1.7	4.9
30	-1.0	1.1	1.6	-2.2	2.3	3.6
40	-1.6	-.3	.4	-3.5	-.6	.7
50	-2.7	-2.2	-1.6	-5.9	-4.8	-3.5
60	-4.2	-4.2	-3.9	-9.2	-9.2	-8.5
70	-3.6	-3.6	-3.5	-7.7	-7.7	-7.5
80	-2.0	-2.0	-2.0	-4.3	-4.3	-4.3
Future generations	8.9	3.6	2.0	19.4	8.0	4.3

Females

0	−.3	.3	.7	−.7	.7	1.5
10	−.5	.4	.9	−1.2	.9	1.9
20	−.8	.5	.7	−1.8	1.0	1.5
30	−1.3	.6	.0	−2.9	1.2	.0
40	−2.1	−.7	−1.2	−4.7	−1.5	−2.6
50	−3.5	−2.7	−3.0	−7.8	−6.0	−6.6
60	−5.5	−5.5	−5.3	−11.9	−11.9	−11.6
70	−4.9	−4.9	−4.9	−10.7	−10.7	−10.6
80	−2.9	−2.9	−2.9	−6.2	−6.2	−6.2
Future generations	4.2	2.0	.8	9.0	4.4	1.9

a 2 or 4 percent higher rate than the rest of the economy. After the turn of the century the Medicare growth rate is assumed to equal the economywide growth rate. The 2 and 4 percent growth rates bracket the 2.77 rate of growth of health spending in excess of GNP observed between 1960 and 1989.[20] The 4 percent growth rate is consistent with projections of an increase, over the decade, from 12 to 17 percent in the share of U.S. health care spending relative to GNP.

For each growth rate there are three alternative financing scenarios. The first is that future generations will pick up the entire bill for this decade's projected higher Medicare growth. The second is that the growth in Medicare over the next decade is ultimately paid for by a reduction in Medicare benefits starting in the year 2020.[21] The third is that this decade's growth in Medicare is matched, on an annual basis, with increases in HI payroll taxes.

The Impact of Medicare Growth on Baby Boomers and Other Generations

The three scenarios have markedly different implications for baby boomers. Under the first scenario, baby boomers bear none of the burden of the higher health expenditures, but benefit from the eventual receipt of higher health care payments. In the second scenario, most boomers are worse off because of the net cuts in Medicare benefits at the time of their retirement. The third scenario is also problematic for boomers. They are forced to pay immediately, through higher HI taxes, for the increased Medicare benefits provided to those currently over sixty-five (the age of Medicare eligibility) as well as those soon to reach sixty-five. Boomers, in this scenario, do receive higher Medicare benefits when they reach sixty-five, but the present value of their additional tax payments far exceeds the present value of these additional benefits.

Many of the changes in generational accounts reported in Table 8–2 are fairly large. Why is that? After all, the policies under consideration simply involve higher Medicare growth for ten years. The reason is that even after Medicare growth is stabilized, the level of Medicare spending relative to the scale of the economy will be permanently higher. In forming present values, generational accounting takes full consideration of the permanently higher Medicare outlays resulting from temporarily higher growth.

Take a close look at Table 8–2, starting with columns 1 and 4, which presents the results of passing the entire bill for Medicare growth to future generations. Depending on the growth rate assumed, future generations end up paying from 10 to 23 percent more than in the base case reported in Table 5–1. If Medicare growth is 4 percent, the absolute increase in the present value bill handed to our male descendants is $19,400; it is $9,000 for our female descendants. These additional burdens raise substantially the ratio of total net payments of the unborn to those of newborns. *Rather than paying 21 percent more than newborns, future generations in the 4 percent Medicare growth scenario end up paying almost 50 percent more than newborns!*

The big winners in columns 1 and 4 are the current elderly and baby boomers. Sixty-year-old females, for example, gain $5,500 in present value if excess Medicare growth is 2 percent and $11,900 if excess Medicare growth is 4 percent. The corresponding windfalls for forty-year-old females are $1,300 and $2,900.

Before you boomers, particularly younger boomers, become too complacent about near-term excess Medicare growth on the basis of columns 1 and 4, take a look at columns 2 and 5. These columns indicate what happens if, instead of borrowing from the Social Security Trust Fund, Medicare pays for its prospective near-term generosity with longer-term (after 2020) benefit cuts. Young boomers, those around age thirty, stand to lose between $1,000 and $2,500 in present value. In contrast, older boomers, those around age forty, stand to gain modestly—a few hundred dollars. The losses suffered by younger boomers as well as those suffered by today's children reduce by more than half the financial harm done to future generations. Note also that today's older Americans experience the same large gains from Medicare growth as in the previous financing scenario for the simple reason that the projected Medicare benefit cuts don't begin for thirty years.

The third financing mechanism, which involves annual increases in HI payroll taxes, starting immediately, to pay for the excess Medicare growth, is explored in columns 3 and 6. This financing scheme is even worse for young boomers than the previous scheme. For example, the loss to thirty-year-old males ranges from $1,600 to $3,600. Older boomers also lose in this case, but their loss is less than $1,000. As in the previous cases, older generations enjoy roughly the same gain from the near-term growth in Medicare.

Social Security and the Boomers: Some Parting Lessons

Boomers should take several lessons away from this comparison of Social Security and Medicare policies. First, boomers face significant gains or losses from these policies. Second, they need to pay attention *now*, not thirty years from now, to issues like Medicare growth, because every additional dollar of current Medicare spending could well be coming out of their own pockets. Third, boomers ought to worry not only about themselves, but also about their children, grandchildren, and so on, if for no other reason than the possible limit to the size of the fiscal burden they can pass to their progeny.

Fourth, and most important, boomers should understand the real financial perils they face from the old-time politics of cash-flow budget balance. In other words, they need to heed Senator Moynihan's warning, if not necessarily support his plan. For if politicians don't indirectly dissipate the boomers' Social Security Trust Fund through increases in government spending, they are likely to dissipate the Trust Fund directly by using its reserves to bail out Medicare. Either way, boomers stand, in the future, to lose yet more of their hard-earned Social Security as well as non–Social Security income. As the last decade's Gramm–Rudman shenanigans made perfectly clear, politicians will go a long way to put off the hard decisions, and this decade's Social Security and Medicare surpluses provide them excellent cover to do just that. It's time for boomers and everyone else to look through the cover and let the politicians know that any further changes in fiscal policy must be considered in the context of a proper generational accounting.

TOWARD THE ADOPTION OF GENERATION-SPECIFIC POLICY

Once we, as a nation, move away from expropriating successive young generations, we can turn our attention to a number of generation-specific policies that truly could improve some generations' welfare without reducing that of others. Such policies would be designed for particular generations who would fully pay for any benefits received. What are examples of such self-financed policies? One is the restructuring of Social Security for baby boomers and subsequent generations to make it more equitable, efficient, and secure.[22] Another is a generation-specific catastrophic health insurance fund to which cohort members would contribute in their working years and be able to draw on in old age for nursing home and other large health expenses. A third example is taxing boomers with children to finance more spending on education. A fourth example is taxes on those aged 55–65 to pay for government-provided home health care later in life. A final example is a policy under which the federal government gives an equal tuition grant to all college entrants of a given cohort and pays for the grants by taxing the same cohort-members in future years at progressive rates.

These and other generation-specific initiatives would presumably be hotly debated by the members of the generations affected. But by using generational accounting to show that their initiatives are indeed self-financing, each generation can avoid having its proposals blocked by other generations who might otherwise worry that they would be stuck with the bill.

215

9

WHITHER GENERATIONAL ACCOUNTING?

———— ∎ ————

This book's has a single, basic message. It is the urgent need to switch from an outdated, misleading, and fundamentally noneconomic measure of fiscal policy, namely the budget deficit, to generational accounting—the direct description of the government's treatment of current and prospective generations over their lifetimes. Replacing deficit accounting with generational accounting means extra work for government accountants. So be it. For there is no real alternative. On a conceptual level, the budget deficit is intellectually bankrupt. On a practical level, there are so many official, let alone unofficial, deficits that "budget balance" has lost any true meaning and budgetary restraint has become a charade in which the changing of words substitutes for the changing of policies.

U.S. postwar fiscal finance is testimony to the perils of deficit delusion. For three decades, from 1950 through 1979, the U.S. government used the cover of a balanced budget to engage in massive intergenerational redistribution. In the 1980s this redistribution continued apace, but only a fraction of the decade's intergenerational transfers were picked up by the sensational rise in federal debt. In this decade Social Security and Medicare surpluses are providing the budgetary guise for even more expropriation of young and future Americans.

The legacy of four decades of mortgaging the future for the sake of the present is a nation financially strapped, saving at the rate of an LDC, relying on foreigners for much of its investment, and left with little capacity to address its real needs. The low rate of U.S. investment is, in part, responsible for our stagnating real wages and derisory productivity growth.

In the wake of postwar "pay-as-you-go finance" and "revenue-neutral tax reform," the baby boom generation has inherited tremendous fiscal liabilities. Yet the fiscal obligations confronting the boomers' children and grandchildren are even larger. Unless generational policy is adjusted and adjusted soon, future Americans will pay at least 21 percent more, even after adjusting for real income growth, than those who have just been born. This 21 percent figure is based on an optimistic scenario concerning prospective government health care expenditures. Ten more years of excessive growth in health care spending could, by itself, more than double the extra payments required of future Americans.

THE GOAL OF GENERATIONAL BALANCE

Do we really wish to make successive generations of Americans pay ever increasing shares of their lifetime incomes to the government? Such a policy, even were it morally defensible, is economically infeasible. At some point those born in the future would be forced to hand over their entire lifetime incomes to the government. The question then of stabilizing the share of lifetime income paid by successive generations—of reaching generational balance—is a question not of if, but of when.

Will we wait four more decades to stabilize the fiscal burden on future Americans, or will we choose policies now that put an end to the further immiserization of our descendants? Whatever choices we make in this regard, they should be made in the open, not concealed by smoke and mirror games and benign-sounding phrases like "pay-as-you-go finance." If we choose, as a nation, to impose on our children a larger proportional burden than we place on ourselves, let's at least have the decency to admit it publicly through a full generational accounting of our fiscal actions.

Such accounting cannot, however, be relegated to the private sector. Public officials can easily dismiss the calculations of private individuals. Not so the calculations of independent and highly respected government agencies, such as the Congressional Budget Office and the General Accounting Office. Will such agencies adopt generational accounting and use it routinely on their analysis of budget proposals? The answer depends on our elected officials, who are the ultimate clientele of those agencies. If a sufficient number of Representatives, Senators, and Administration officials request this accounting, it will be done and become a routine part of official economic analysis.

Are those in government likely to advocate generational accounting? Some already have, and others surely will.[1] But the pressure for generational accounting may ultimately have to come from us as taxpayers. Self-interest, if nothing else, should motivate our interest in generational accounting. Each of us, in our role as members of particular generations, can lose, and lose big, from policies that adversely impact our age-cohorts.

THE BENEFITS OF GENERATIONAL ACCOUNTING: A RECAP

The adoption of generational accounting offers advantages beyond simply indicating which generations pay for what the government spends. First, it will guide us to policies that are generationally balanced, that is, fair to each generation. Second, it will shift the policy focus from the short term to the long term. Third, it will distinguish those policies which truly stimulate private spending by reducing lifetime, rather than simply immediate, net tax payments. Fourth, in its treatment of government assets, it will eliminate the current bias against government spending on infrastructure.[2] Fifth, it will draw attention not only to those generations paying for, but also those generations benefiting from, government spending. Sixth, its lifetime perspective will influence how we think about and measure the government's impact on economic inequality and economic incentives. Seventh, it will pave the way for the enactment of generation-specific policies that do not involve redistribution across generations. Finally, and perhaps most important, generational accounting will provide individual Americans a much clearer sense of their own future treatment at the hands of the government.

WHITHER GENERATIONAL ACCOUNTING?

While there is reason to be optimistic that official generational accounting will ultimately replace official deficit accounting as the standard way to measure fiscal policy, the process will surely take time.[3] Old notions make comfortable bedfellows, and too many people have already declared the beauty of this particular emperor's clothes. In this vein, it may be best to close with the sobering last paragraph of "The Emperor's New Clothes":

> "Why, he hasn't got anything on!" the whole crowd was shouting at last; and the Emperor's flesh crept, for it seemed to him they were right. "But, all the same," he thought to himself. "I must go on with the procession." So he held himself more proudly than before, and the lords in waiting walked on bearing the train—the train that wasn't there at all.

AFTERWORD

———— ■ ————

T his paperback edition of *Generational Accounting* appears about two years after the hardcover's release. I am delighted to report that the book was reviewed widely and favorably, with roughly two dozen newspapers and magazines carrying stories about the book and its ominous message. I discussed generational accounting on various local and national television and radio shows, and I was asked to testify to three committees of the U.S. Congress on the subject.

More important has been the reaction to the book by the Office of Management and Budget (OMB) of the U.S. Government. In the summer of 1992, OMB's Assistant Director of the Budget, Barry Anderson, asked me and my colleagues, University of Pennsylvania economist Professor Alan J. Auerbach, and Cleveland Federal Reserve Bank Senior Economist Dr. Jagadeesh Gokhale, to coauthor, with Robert Kilpatrick, Robert Anderson, and other staff at the OMB, a chapter on generational accounting to appear in President Bush's Fiscal Year 1993 Budget.

The collaboration with OMB proved highly successful and led to our writing a second generational accounting chapter for President Bush's FY 1994 Budget presentation.

Indeed, the FY94 Budget Chapter was written up in a lengthy article on the second page of the *Wall Street Journal* and in an editorial in the Business section of the *New York Times.*

The appearance of generational accounts in the 1993 and 1994 Bush Budgets (and hopefully in future Clinton Budgets) means that the U.S. government is taking generational accounting seriously. This has prompted governments of other countries to do the same. To date, the Bank of Italy, the Norwegian Ministry of Finance, the Finnish Ministry of Social and Health Affairs, and the Bank of Japan have all initiated generational accounting projects for their own countries. Unofficial efforts by German and Canadian economists are also underway to compile generational accounts for their countries. I expect and hope that many other countries will soon join the bandwagon.

So much for the good news. The collaboration with OMB has had the additional result of providing me and my colleagues with OMB's latest long-term forecasts of taxes and spending as well as those of the Social Security Administration and the Health Care Financing Administration. These forecasts are *considerably* more pessimistic than the ones used in Chapter 5 of this book. Indeed, they are considerably even more pessimistic than the worse case scenarios described in Chapter 8. They show that unless radical changes are made in generational policy, and made soon, America's current and future children could well end up paying between *60 and 70 percent* of their lifetime incomes to the government in net taxes!

These extraordinarily high tax rates can be compared with the 20 percent net tax rate faced by generations born at the turn of this century, the 28 percent rate faced (so far) by generations born in the 1930s, and the 31 percent rate faced (so far) by generations born in the 1950s. Such extraordinarily high lifetime tax rates will leave our children and children's children with even less wherewithal from which to save than we have had. Consequently, our nation's already pitifully low rate of national saving could end up falling to zero.

While some parts of the U.S. government, some members of the media, and some segments of the public have understood the importance of switching to generational accounting as the means for guiding fiscal policy, most have not. Discourse about U.S. fiscal policy continues to be carried out in terms of the Federal deficit. As I write, the U.S. Congress is debating a $500 billion deficit reduction fiscal package. While the package represents progress in the right direction from my perspective, it is a very long way from eliminating the fiscal Sword of Damocles hanging over the heads of unborn Americans.

As in previous budget debates, none of the high officials advocating the proposed legislation have clarified why the particular amount of deficit reduction called for in the legislation is appropriate. In the present case, none of our leaders have told us why $500 billion is the right number to shoot for as opposed to, say, $800 billion or $3 trillion. Even worse, at the same time that our leaders are making pious efforts to stem the growth of official government debt, they are letting unofficial government debt continue to grow by leaps and bounds. I refer here primarily to the government's unfunded liabilities to pay Medicare and Medicaid health care benefits to current and near-term retirees. With exploding costs, a rapidly aging population, and fewer workers paying in, these benefit funds are set for disaster. In other words, generational accounting appears to be sinking in too slowly to save us from a rendezvous with fiscal disaster.

Washington desperately needs to change its ways. But to get Washington to change, we, the public, need to start asking our elected officials, from the President on down, a very simple question: How much are you planning to tax our kids? If enough people start asking this question, over and over and over again, the politicians will be forced to learn the answer. When they do, they'll find it terrifying. And maybe then they'll finally begin to design fiscal policy that meets a reasonable standard of generational morality.

NOTES

———— ■ ————

1. Smoke and Mirrors

1. Andrew Dean, Martine Durand, John Fallon, and Peter Hoeller, "Saving Trends and Behavior in OECD Countries," OECD Department of Economics and Statistics Working Papers, no. 67, June 1989. This article indicates that of twenty-one OECD countries the United States ranks second to last in the size of its saving rate. One needs to view these numbers with some caution; measurement differences across countries make precise international saving comparisons difficult. Fumio Hayashi carefully compared U.S. and Japanese saving and found that measurement problems may account for some of the differences in saving rates between the United States and Japan. Fumio Hayashi, "Why Is Japan's Saving Rate So Apparently High?" in Stanley Fischer, ed., *NBER Macroeconomics Annual 1986* (Cambridge, Mass.: MIT Press 1986), pp. 145–210.

2. For an analysis of the predicted effects of demographics on U.S. saving see Alan J. Auerbach, Jinyong Cai, and Laurence J. Kotlikoff, "U.S. Demographics and Saving: Predictions of Three Saving Models," *Carnegie-Rochester Conference Series on Public Policy*, 1991.

3. As described below, these benefit cuts take the form of gradual increases in Social Security's normal retirement age as well as projected increases in the federal income taxation of Social Security benefits.

4. Social Security's Office of the Actuary reports a $929.9 billion

225

reduction in OASDI closed group liabilities between 1983 and 1984. Memo, Office of the Actuary, September 4, 1990.

5. The 5 percent figure represents the average annual ratio of net investment to net national product observed for the years 1980–90. Data come from *The Economic Report of the President 1991*, pp. 304, 310.

6. Another part of the explanation is the increase over the last two decades in the rate of female labor force participation. Like the slowdown in investment, the larger female supply of labor has made labor more abundant in relation to capital and has put downward pressure on real wage increases.

7. *Boston Globe*, August 27, 1991, p. 3.

8. According to the U.S. Bureau of Engraving and Printing, a dollar bill is .0043 inches thick and 6.14 inches long.

9. Alan Greenspan, "Statement to the Deficit Commission," *The Federal Reserve Bulletin*, January 1989.

10. Statement made by Ted Koppel on *Nightline*, 1987.

11. Lawrence Malkin, *The National Debt* (New York: Henry Holt, 1987).

12. Leon E. Panetta, "Fiscal Year 1991 Budget Agreement, Summary Materials," House Budget Committee, October 27, 1990, p. 52.

13. In the 1990 five-year budget agreement, the administration and Congress tried to take some of the emphasis off of deficits by focusing instead on a set of floating "caps" and complex rules governing increases in outlays. But all of this apparatus was predicated on the notion that a positive deficit is bad and that a big positive deficit is really bad.

14. John Maynard Keynes, *The General Theory of Employment, Interest, and Money* (New York: Harcourt-Brace & World, 1936).

15. Keynes's economics was much more conservative prior to his writing *The General Theory*, and he seems to have reverted to this conservative stance in the post-Depression 1940s. David Colander's 1984 article "Was Keynes a Keynesian or a Lernerian?" *Journal of Economic Literature*, XXII, no. 4 (December 1984): 1572–75, suggests that Keynes reached his policy conclusions first and then made up verbal economic arguments (he called them theories) to promote them. Colander (p. 1574) quotes Keynes as saying, "It's the art of statesmanship to tell lies, but they must be plausible lies."

16. John Hicks, "Mr. Keynes and the Classics," *Econometrica*, 1937. It's worth noting that before he died Keynes allegedly stated, "I am not a Keynesian," thereby accusing his disciples of betrayal.

17. What Feldstein failed to stress was the wide range of other implicit government liabilities, such as the commitment to provide, in future years, welfare benefits to the needy or to maintain the Lincoln Memorial. He also failed to stress the wide range of implicit government assets, such as the government's projected stream of future income tax receipts, that could be used to help finance those liabilities.

18. Actually, given the Social Security legislation in place, one's right to collect Social Security benefits based on past contributions is a legal claim. Those currently eligible to collect benefits have a legal standing to claim those benefits. And those who will be eligible to collect benefits in the future can receive a determination of the amount of such future benefits that have been accrued based on past contributions by writing to the Social Security Administration.

19. Social Security's unfunded liability refers to the sum for all currently living adult Americans of the present value difference between future Social Security benefits and future Social Security taxes. According to the Social Security System's Office of the Actuary, the unfunded liability of the OASDI system owed to adult Americans (called the closed-group liability) was $7.119 trillion. Memo, Office of the Actuary, September 4, 1990. This figure does not include Medicare, the health insurance component of Social Security. Inclusion of Medicare's closed group liability, which is not officially calculated, would substantially raise the $7.119 trillion figure.

20. According to the most recent report of the U.S. Office of Personnel Management, entitled "Civil Service Retirement and Disability Fund" and prepared by Retirement and Insurance Group, September 30, 1988, the value of accrued vested liabilities of the Civil Service Retirement and Disability Fund was $578.6 billion and the fund's assets totaled $197.1 billion, leaving an 1988 unfunded vested liability of $381.5 billion. Measured in current dollars, that exceeds $450 billion. The Office of the Actuary of the U.S. Department of Defense reported in 1989 an unfunded accrued liability for the Military Retirement System of $512 billion (see "Valuation of the Military Retirement System," Office of the Actuary, U.S. Department of Defense, September 30, 1989). In today's dollars that liability exceeds $550 billion.

21. Board of Governors of the Federal Reserve System, *Balance Sheets for the U.S. Economy 1945-89*, Balance Sheets Flow of Funds, October 1989. The 1989 national net wealth figure is the latest available value. This value is adjusted to 1991 dollars.

22. Even with its astronomical property values, Japan's net wealth does not appear to be as large as that of the United States.
23. See Robert Eisner, *How Real Is the Federal Deficit?* (New York: Free Press, 1986), p. 29; and *The Economic Report of the President 1990*, p. 376.
24. According to the *Economic Report of the President 1991*, the inflation rate (measured by the CPI) was 5.40 percent between 1989 and 1990. The growth rate of real GNP between these two years was .92 percent. The adjustments to the deficit reflect the multiplication of .0632 (.0054 + .0092) times $2971.9 billion, which is 1990 gross federal debt less federal debt held by the Federal Reserve.
25. Robert D. Reischauer, "Taxes and Spending Under Gramm–Rudman–Hollings," *National Tax Journal*, November 1990, pp. 223–32.
26. Many of the Capitol Hill economists, who have opposed deceptive federal budgeting, work for the Congressional Budget Office, the Congressional Research Service, the Joint Committee on Taxation, the Senate and House Budget Committees, the Senate Finance Committee, and the House Ways and Means Committee. Others are in the administration working for the Council of Economic Advisers, the Treasury, and the Office of Management and Budget. Finally, Comptroller General Charles Bowsher of the General Accounting Office (GAO) has put GAO economists to work thinking through new budgeting procedures that would preclude many of the Smoke and Mirrors games.
27. Part of the problem was that the regulators failed to scrutinize individual loans with sufficient care. Another part was that the S&Ls were not forced to diversify their investments geographically. Indeed, certain government regulations restricted the ability of S&Ls to diversify geographically.
28. For an excellent analysis of the S&L debacle see G. Thomas Woodward, "Origins and Development of the Savings and Loan Situation," *Congressional Research Service Report for Congress*, November 5, 1990. The following passage was culled, in part and with permission, from a senior government economist's (deep econ's) written account of the S&L debacle.
29. *Time*, September 24, 1990, p. 50.
30. The arbitrary nature of the deficit is demonstrated in Laurence J. Kotlikoff, "Taxation and Savings: A Neoclassical Perspective," *Journal of Economic Literature*, December 1984; Laurence J. Kotlikoff, "Deficit Delusion," *The Public Interest*, Summer 1986; Alan J. Auerbach and Laurence J. Kotlikoff, *Dy-*

namic Fiscal Policy (New York: Cambridge University Press, 1987); Laurence J. Kotlikoff, *What Determines Savings?* (Cambridge, Mass: MIT Press, 1987); Laurence J. Kotlikoff, "The Deficit Is Not a Meaningful Measure of Fiscal Policy," *Science*, September 1988; and Laurence J. Kotlikoff, "From Deficit Delusion to the Fiscal Balance Rule: Looking for a Sensible Way to Measure Fiscal Policy," National Bureau of Economic Research working paper, March 1989.

31. What is uniquely defined in neoclassical models is the government's impact on the lifetime budget constraints of the models' agents. Hence, a unique description of fiscal policy requires describing fiscal policy in terms of its impact on the lifetime budget constraints of the economy's households.

32. This example assumes that the change in words does not alter the likelihood of either having to make contributions to Social Security or receiving benefits from Social Security.

33. One can take generational accounting a step further and ask how any single generation's burden is divided among its different members. This is the issue of intragenerational distribution policy, discussed later in the book.

34. According to the Social Security Office of the Actuary, for new retirees retiring at age sixty-five, the replacement of average past wages by Social Security benefits rose from 34.3 percent in 1970 to 54.4 percent in 1981 and then declined to 40.9 percent in 1985. I am grateful to Orlo R. Nichols of the Social Security Administration for providing this information.

35. These figures do not take account of in-kind services provided by the government. The imputation of such services to particular generations will be the focus of future research, as will generation-specific adjustments for government-mandated actions imposed on the private sector.

36. This ignores the uncertainty surrounding the government's future taxes and transfers.

37. In recent years a group of so-called New Keynesian economists have attempted, in many cases quite successfully, to use microeconomics to explore many of the issues raised by Sir John Maynard Keynes. Given their micro foundations, these contributions typically raise the same concerns about the use of the deficit as neoclassical micro models.

38. I had the added advantage of coming to these questions as a public finance economist rather than as a macroeconomist. The subfield in economics known as public finance considers the effects of government actions on the economy. It pays careful attention to the microeconomic distinctions between fiscal policies, something that often gets glossed over in macroeconomics.

39. Lucas and Sargent did object to the general method of Keynesian policy evaluation in which households were assumed not to anticipate the likelihood of the government's changing its policy.
40. See, for example, Fumio Hayashi, "Tests for Liquidity Constraints: A Critical Survey," in Truman Bewley, ed., *Advances in Econometrics, Fifth World Congress* (New York: Cambridge University Press, 1987), and Steven P. Zeldes, "Consumption and Liquidity Constraints: An Empirical Investigation," mimeo, Rodney L. White Center for Financial Research, Wharton School, University of Pennsylvania, 1985.

2. U.S. Economic Malaise

1. White-collar employment has grown much more rapidly in recent years than has blue-collar employment. Hence, the fraction of white-collar workers among the unemployed in the recession that began in 1990 is larger than was the case in previous recessions. In this sense the recession that began in 1990 might be viewed as somewhat more of a white-collar recession, even though the unemployment rates of white-collar workers did not rise at faster rates than did those of blue-collar workers. See Randall W. Eberts, and Erica Groshen, "Is This Really a 'White Collar' Recession?" *Economic Commentary*, Federal Reserve Bank of Clevand, March 15, 1991.
2. *The New Republic*, 1989.
3. Robert J. Samuelson, "Debt," *Newsweek*, December 31, 1990, pp. 22–23.
4. Peter Peterson, "The Morning After," *The Atlantic Monthly*, October 1987, p. 46.
5. Alan S. Blinder, *Hard Heads and Soft Hearts* (Reading, Mass.: Addison-Wesley, 1987), p. 5.
6. See, for example, John Kenneth Galbraith, "The 1929 Parallel," *The Atlantic Monthly*, January 1987, pp. 62–66.
7. *Economic Report of the President*, 1990, Table C-32, p. 330.
8. Bureau of the Census, U.S. Department of Commerce, *Historical Statistics for the United States from Colonial Times to 1970* (Washington, D.C.: U.S. Government Printing Office, 1975), and Bureau of the Census, U.S. Department of Commerce, *Statistical Abstract of the United States 1989* (Washington, D.C.: U.S. Government Printing Office, 1990).
9. *Economic Report of the President, 1991*, p. 335.
10. American civilians were not the only ones to react as if they were near the front. The Belgians reportedly began hoarding

foodstuffs at the beginning of the war, and the French began purchasing small arms in record numbers.

11. *Economic Report of the President 1990,* Table C-71, p. 376.
12. *Ibid.,* Table C-69, p. 374.
13. *Boston Globe,* January 22, 1991, page 1.
14. *Ibid.*
15. *U.S. Statistical Abstract,* 1990, p. 841.
16. Carlos F. Diaz Alejandro, *Essays on the Economic History of the Argentine Republic* (New Haven: Yale University Press, 1970), note 1, p. 1.
17. *U.S. Statistical Abstract 1990,* p. 840.
18. Paul Krugman, *The Age of Diminished Expectations* (Cambridge, Mass.: MIT Press, 1990).
19. Benjamin M. Friedman, *Day of Reckoning* (New York: Vintage Press, 1989).
20. Lester C. Thurow, *The Zero Sum Society* (New York: Penquin Books, 1981).
21. Peter G. Peterson, "The Morning After," *The Atlantic Monthly,* October 1987, pp. 43–69.
22. The countries considered here are the member of the OECD. The OECD includes the United States, Japan, and the economies of Western Europe and several other major industrialized countries.
23. This is the net national saving rate defined as net national product less private plus government consumption divided by net national product. Net output, NNP, rather than gross (before depreciation) output, GNP, is used throughout the book as the measure of the nation's income, since it is really the country's income after depreciation that it has available either to consume or to save.
24. By "trade deficit" I refer here to what is technically called the "current account deficit," which equals the difference between imports and exports (technically called the trade account) plus income earned by foreigners on their investments in the United States, less income earned by Americans on their investments abroad (technically called the capital account).
25. Technically speaking, net foreign investment is referred to as the current account deficit. The term "trade deficit" is used in popular discourse. It should not be confused with the balance of trade on goods and services, which together with net investment income and net unilateral transfers constitutes the current account.
26. *Economic Report of the President 1991.* The trade deficit here is measured as net national saving less net domestic investment. Net national saving is NNP less personal consumption

expenditures and government purchases of goods and services.

27. See Kevin Phillips, *The Rich and the Poor* (New York: Random House, 1990), for a detailed discussion of the sale of particular American firms to foreigners.

28. The data in this chart are from the U.S. Bureau of Labor Statistics. The productivity growth series is derived as the annual percentage change in the BLS's series on output per hour in the nonfarm business sector. The growth in capital per worker is derived as the annual percentage change in the BLS's series on capital services per hour in the nonfarm business sector. The rate of technological change is measured as the annual percentage change in the BLS index of multifactor productivity in the nonfarm business sector.

29. In his Table 5, Norman S. Fieleke, "The United States in Debt," *New England Economic Review*, Federal Reserve Bank of Boston, September–October 1990, pp. 34–53, compares output per labor hour in manufacturing in selected industrialized countries.

30. U.S. Bureau of Labor Statistics, *Monthly Labor Review*, vol. 13 (April 1990), p. 98.

31. U.S. Bureau of Labor Statistics, private nonfarm business sector index of capital per hour of all persons, 1948–1989.

32. U.S. Bureau of Labor Statistics, multifactor productivity series for nonfarm business sector, 1949–1989.

33. *Ibid.* The rate of technological change averaged 2.01 percent per year from 1950 through 1969 and 2.24 percent per year from 1970 through 1989.

34. Lawrence Malkin, *The National Debt* (New York: Henry Holt, 1987).

35. Robert B. Reich, "Succession of the Successful," *The New York Times Magazine*, January 20, 1991.

36. *Economic Report of the President 1991*, p. 336.

37. *Ibid.*, pp. 314, 324, 351. The employment numbers used to form total compensation per employee exclude members of the military.

38. *Ibid.*, pp. 288, 321.

39. The calculation underlying this figure assumes that labor's share of proprietorship and partnership income as well as labor's share of indirect business taxes equals labor's share of aggregate net national product.

40. *Economic Report of the President 1991*, pp. 321, 322. There is an 18 percent difference between the 1975 employment-to-population ratio and the 1990 employment-to-population ratio. This, together with the 3 percent increase in real total

compensation per worker and the fact that labor's share of national income has remained fixed, explains why per capita income rose by 18 percent + 3 percent = 21 percent.

41. *U.S. Statistical Abstract 1989*, p. 385.
42. F. Lawrence Katz and Ana L. Revenga, "Changes in the Structure of Wages: The United States vs. Japan," *Journal of the Japanese and International Economies*, vol. 3, no. 4, pp. 522–53, and see Table 1. Also see McKinley L. Blackburn, David E. Bloom, and Richard B. Freeman, "The Declining Economic Position of Less-Skilled American Males," NBER working paper no. 3186, November 1989.
43. *U.S. Statistical Abstract 1990*, p. 451.
44. As part of its calculation of personal income, the government subtracts from net national product (a well-defined concept) indirect business taxes and FICA taxes, and adds back transfer payments. Since these taxes and transfers represent payments and receipts that could be labeled differently, the definition of personal income suffers from precisely the same arbitrariness as the definition of the deficit.
45. Daniel T. Slesnick, "Gaining Ground: Poverty in the Post-War United States," mimeo, Kennedy School of Government, Harvard University, July 1990.
46. *Ibid.*, Table 2.
47. *U.S. Statistical Abstract 1989*, Table 304, p. 366. Other real welfare payments per recipient, such as food stamps, and Medicaid, have also declined, although to a lesser extent. See *U.S. Statistical Abstract 1982* Table 517, p. 319, and *U.S. Statistical Abstract 1989*, Table 580, p. 353.
48. U.S. Bureau of the Census, *U.S. Historical Statistics*, p. 50.
49. Alan J. Auerbach and Laurence J. Kotlikoff, "Demographics, Fiscal Policy, and U.S. Saving in the 1980s and Beyond," in National Bureau of Economic Research, *Tax Policy and the Economy*, vol. 4, 1990.
50. *Ibid.*
51. *Business Week*, May 20, 1991, p. 76. This interesting factoid about U.S. divorce rates—that the U.S. rate is almost twice the rate of most West European countries and four times the rate of Japan—appeared in the July 9, 1991, issue of *USA Today*.
52. Jane E. Brody, "Children of Divorce: Steps to Help Can Hurt," *New York Times*, July 23, 1991, p. C1.
53. *Ibid.*
54. See Laurence J. Kotlikoff and John Morris, "Why Don't the Elderly Live with Their Children? A New Look," National Bureau of Economic Research, *Issues on the Economics of Aging*, 1990, and Laurence J. Kotlikoff and John Morris, "How Much

Care Do the Aged Receive from Their Children? A Bimodal Picture of Contact and Assistance," National Bureau of Economic Research, *The Economics of Aging* (Chicago: University of Chicago Press, 1989).

55. U.S. Bureau of Labor Statistics, "Employment and Earnings," *Monthly Labor Review*, November 1989, and unpublished data.

56. There are a number of reasons for the trend toward earlier and earlier retirement. First, at least until recently, each successive postwar cohort has had a higher lifetime income than its predecessor, thus providing each successive cohort with greater economic means to retire early. Second, many private pension defined-benefit plans have been structured to provide very significant incentives for retiring early from one's principal job. (See Laurence J. Kotlikoff and David Wise, *The Wage Carrot and the Pension Stick*, W. E. UpJohn Institute for Employment Research, 1989. And third, as will be discussed in Chapter 7, those generations retiring in the last four decades received significant net transfers (to be payed by subsequent generations) from the government; those transfers helped provide the means to finance an early retirement.

57. *U.S. Statistical Abstract*, various issues.

58. Randy will have to wait until age sixty-seven if he wants to collect normal retirement benefits. Note that today one needs only to reach age sixty-five to be eligible to collect Social Security's normal retirement benefits.

59. This statement assumes, of course, that the prior law would not otherwise have been altered. While the new legislation cut benefits of baby boomers, it may have improved the chances that boomers would actually collect even this smaller amount of benefits in the future. As will be described in Chapter 5, even with the 1983 Social Security legislation, the baby boomers' children face fiscal burdens that are quite high relative to those faced by current generations. Had the 1983 legislation not been enacted, the burden to be placed on these and subsequent generations of paying for the baby boomers' Social Security benefits might have been too high to be sustained by the political process.

60. These figures are based on data reported in Committee on Ways and Means, U.S. Congress, *The 1990 Green Book: Overview of Entitlement Programs*, Ways and Means CP 101–29, 101st Cong. 2d Sess., June 5, 1990, p. 26, as well as additional information provided by Dr. Jane Gravelle of the Congressional Research Service.

61. John F. Fitzgerald and John A. MacDonald, "Aging Baby

Boomers Face Older and Stingier Social Security," *Hartford Courant*, February 17, 1991, p. A1.

62. A recent study—Barry Bosworth, Gary Burtless, and John Sabelhaus, "The Decline in Saving: Evidence from Household Surveys," in *Brookings Papers on Economic Activity*, 1991— shows a pronounced decline in the saving rates of baby boomers in the 1980s, but an even larger decline in the saving rates of older cohorts. Analysis of the change over time in the age-consumption profile by John Sabelhaus and Laurence J. Kotlikoff suggests a somewhat larger role of the baby boomers in raising national consumption and lowering national saving. Unfortunately, there does not appear to be an easy explanation for the drop in saving in the 1980s. For an analysis of the puzzling drop in saving in the 1980s, see the above cited study and Alan J. Auerbach and Laurence J. Kotlikoff, "Demographics, Fiscal Policy, and U.S. Saving in the 1980's and Beyond," in *Tax Policy and the Economy*, NBER vol. 4, 1990.

63. "The New Way to Get Rich," *U.S. News and World Report*, May 7, 1990, pp. 27–36.

64. Board of Governors of the Federal Reserve System, "Balance Sheets for the U.S. Economy, 1949–88," Balance Sheets, Flow of Funds, October 1989, pp. 17, 20.

65. Alan M. Garber, "Financing Health Care for Elderly Americans in the 1990's," mimeo, Stanford University Medical School, August 1989.

66. *1990 Annual Report of the Board of Trustees of the Federal Hospital Insurance Trust Fund* (Washington, D.C.: U.S. Government Printing Office, 1990), p. 9.

67. Garber, "Financing Health Care."

68. David M. Cutler, James M. Poterba, Louise M. Sheiner, and Lawrence H. Summers, in "An Aging Society: Opportunity or Challenge," Brookings Papers on Economic Activity, vol. 1, pp. 1–56, 1990, report average nursing home costs at $23,600 per resident per year as of 1985. Since 1985 health care costs have increased dramatically, well in excess of the roughly 30 percent increase in the overall consumer price level.

69. *U.S. Statistical Abstract 1990*, p. 112.

70. For an analysis of the saving disincentive represented by Medicaid's 100 percent asset tax, see Laurence J. Kotlikoff, "Health Expenditures and Precautionary Savings," in Laurence J. Kotlikoff, *What Determines Savings?* (Cambridge, Mass.: MIT Press, 1989), Chapter 6, pp. 141–62. In the last few years private long-term care insurance policies have begun to be marketed by the insurance industry. The widespread avail-

ability of such insurance could limit the saving disincentives of Medicaid. Even in the absence of private long-term care insurance, one can question the strength of the medicaid saving disincentive. Since many higher-quality nursing homes effectively circumvent the system by requiring an up-front fee (usually a year's private pay) to gain admittance for patients who will ultimately go on Medicaid, there is an incentive to save to cover the up-front fee. In addition, by transferring assets to children and other relatives prior to applying for Medicaid, one can avoid surrendering one's assets, while at the same time enrolling in Medicaid.

71. See Alan J. Auerbach, Jinyong Cai, and Laurence J. Kotlikoff, "U.S. Demographics and Saving: Predictions of Three Saving Models," Carnegie-Rochester Conference Series, 1991. Note also that young people do not vote as frequently as the middle-aged and the elderly.

72. For a detailed examination of the opportunities as well as potential problems arising from near-term social security surpluses see Carolyn Weaver, ed., *Social Security's Looming Surpluses: Prospects and Implications* (Washington, D.C.: The AEI Press, 1990).

73. Federal Old-Age and Survivors Insurance and Disability Insurance Trust Funds, *Communication from The Board of Trustees* (Washington, D.C.: U.S. Government Printing Office, April 26, 1989), Tables 23 and F2.

74. A variation on this theme involves permitting Medicare to meet its projected shortfall of receipts later this decade not by asking boomers for more money, but by borrowing from the boomers' Social Security trust fund.

75. Note that the U.S. Treasury can, and often does, borrow directly from the Social Security Trust Fund.

3. Blame It on the Deficit

1. Firms borrow part of the money they invest in new plant, equipment, and other forms of capital. If the expected return to this investment is higher, they will be willing to pay higher interest rates to borrow the funds to invest. Competition between different firms, each of which is borrowing by selling bonds in the bond market, ensures that interest rates reflect the profit that firms can earn on their investments.

2. Forward by Paul Samuelson to Paul Krugman, *The Age of Diminished Expectations* (Cambridge, Mass.: MIT Press, 1990).

3. Krugman, *Age of Diminished Expectations,* p. 68.
4. *Ibid.* Emphasis in original.
5. *Ibid.,* p. 43.
6. *Ibid.,* p. 48.
7. Benjamin Friedman, *Day of Reckoning* (New York: Vintage Books, 1988), p. 174.
8. *Ibid.*
9. *Ibid.,* p. 184
10. Alan Greenspan, "Statement to the Deficit Commission," *The Federal Reserve Bulletin,* January 1989.
11. David Alan Aschauer, "Fiscal Policy and Aggregate Demand," *American Economic Review,* vol. 75, March 1985, pp. 117–28; Roger C. Kormendi, "Government Debt, Government Spending, and Private Sector Behavior," *The American Economics Review,* vol. 73, December 1983, pp. 994–1010; and John J. Seater and Roberto S. Mariano, "New Tests of the Life Cycle Tax Discounting Hypotheses," *Journal of Monetary Economics,* vol. 15, March 1985, pp. 195–215.
12. Gerald P. Dwyer, Jr., "Inflation and Government Deficits," *Economic Inquiry,* July 1982, p. 327.
13. Paul Evans, "Do Large Deficits Produce High Interest Rates?" *The American Economic Review,* vol. 75, no. 1 (March 1985), pp. 68–87, and *idem,* "Interest Rates and Expected Future Budget Deficits in the United States," *Journal of Political Economy,* vol. 95, no. 1 (February 1987), pp. 34–58. See also Charles Plosser's article, "Government Financing Decisions and Asset Returns," *Journal of Monetary Economics,* vol. 9, 1982, pp. 325–52, for equally negative findings on the relationship of federal deficits to nominal interest rates and Paul Evans's "A Test of Steady-State Government-Debt Neutrality," in *Economic Inquiry,* vol. XXVII, January 1989, pp. 39–55.
14. Paul Evans, "Do Budget Deficits Raise Nominal Interest Rates? Evidence from Six Countries," *Journal of Monetary Economics,* vol. 20, 1987, pp. 281–300.
15. Paul Evans, "Is the Dollar High Because of Large Budget Deficits?," *Journal of Monetary Economics,* vol. 18, 1986, pp. 227–49.
16. Paul Evans, "Do Budget Deficits Affect the Current Account?" mimeo, Ohio State University, June 1990.
17. Peter L. Bernstein, and Robert L. Heilbroner, "The Relationship Between Budget Deficits and the Saving/Investment Imbalance in the United States: Fact, Fancies, and Prescriptions," in James M. Rock, ed., *Debt and the Twin Deficits and Debate* (Mountain View, Calif.: Mayfield Publishing Company, 1991).

18. One might wonder who the Keynesians believe actually voluntarily purchased the $3 trillion worth of outstanding government bonds. One might also ask them why employers would set aside almost $3 trillion of workers' earnings as contributions to pension funds if those workers were so desperate to consume every dollar they could get into their physical possession.

19. Presumably, households receiving interest on loans made to the government are not the liquidity-constrained consumers of Keynesian economics, so the interest component of the deficit doesn't tell us about the size of disposable income available to liquidity-constrained, Keynesian-type consumers.

20. Although federal taxes are almost 40 percent larger than those of state plus local government, federal spending on goods and services is less than two-thirds the corresponding state plus local figure. *The Economic Report of the President 1991*, pp. 380, 381.

21. *Ibid.*, pp. 310, 380, 381.

22. *Ibid.*, pp. 286, 310.

23. In considering these figures it is also worth noting that the slight rise in the 1980s in the ratio of disposable income to NNP primarily reflects a decline in corporate taxation. Keynesian households should be less responsive to corporate taxes than to other taxes, because corporate tax breaks aren't handed directly to the supposedly grubby little hands of American consumers. In the 1980s corporate taxes represented only 8 percent of total government taxes. For purposes of comparison, they represented 11 percent of total taxes in the 1970s. *Ibid.*

24. See Michael J. Boskin, Laurence J. Kotlikoff, Douglas Puffert, and John Shoven, "Social Security: A Financial Analysis Within and Across Generations," *The National Tax Journal*, March 1987.

25. Economists are as guilty as anyone in taking seriously the official private–government division of national income. Indeed, economists took Edward Denison's 1958 observation—in "A Note on Private Saving," *Review of Economics and Statistics*, vol. 40, August 1958, pp. 261–67—that the official private saving rate changed little over time, and proclaimed it "Denison's Law," and then proceeded to write articles—e.g. Paul David and John Scadding, "Private Savings: Ultrarationality, Aggregation, and 'Denison's Law'," *Journal of Political Economy*, vol. 82, no. 2, Part I, (March–April 1981), pp. 225–49—explaining why such a law is true. Fortunately, the

failure of Denison's Law in the 1980s has put a damper on this research on the government's vocabulary.

26. Alan Greenspan, "Statement to the Deficit Commission," *The Federal Reserve Bulletin*, January 1989.

27. Given that millions of Americans are co-owners (shareholders) of Japanese, European, and other foreign companies, and millions of Japanese, Europeans, and other foreigners are co-owners of American companies, the distinction between an "American" and, say, a "Japanese" firm is unclear. If there is a useful foreign-domestic distinction between firms it is probably not the nationality of the owners, but the nationality of the top managers. Even this distinction may be disappearing. Citicorp, the largest U.S. banking company, is now owned by Saudi Prince al-Waleed bin Talal. According to the *New York Times*, February 22, 1991, Prince Waleed "will not be represented on Citicorp's board and has promised not to try to gain control over the company." Some day we may see American presidents of companies like Honda, and Japanese presidents of companies like IBM and General Electric. When that day comes all firms will be truly international; no one will make a fuss about the nationality of the managers of firms buying or selling Rockefeller Center, just as today no one in Missouri cares whether the purchaser of a Missouri firm happens to be from Texas rather than Missouri.

28. I am very grateful to Professor Eisner for providing an updated version of the deficit series reported in Robert Eisner, *How Real Is the Federal Deficit?* (New York: Free Press, 1986), pp. 84, 87.

29. These data come from *The Economic Report of the President 1982*, p. 104.

30. The period under discussion here is 1970–90. The comparison is between total federal debt (*The Economic Report of the President 1991*, p. 384) and the closed group unfunded liabilities of Social Security's OASDI programs reported in Social Security Office of the Actuary, mimeo, September 4, 1990.

31. One recent exception is OMB Director Richard Darman's presentation of alternative budgets in the appendix to *The Budget of the United States Government FY 1992* (Washington, D.C.: U.S. Government Printing Office, 1991).

4. Figures Lie and Liars Figure

1. There are a variety of nondistorting ways of changing the net payments of different generations. Since essentially everyone

is now covered by Social Security, one way is simply to subtract from each individual's current or future (if they aren't
yet retired) Social Security benefit a fixed amount (lump-sum
amount, in the language of economics) equal, in present
value, to the required uniform percentage reduction multiplied by the present value of the individual's lifetime net
payments.

2. These figures are based on the National Income Accounts definition of government consumption; but correcting these numbers for government investment would only strengthen the
conclusion that government consumption spending as a share
of NNP did not increase in the 1980s.

3. The public's saving rate equals $1 - [C/(NNP - G)]$, where C
stands for personal consumption expenditures and G stands
for government consumption. Since C, NNP, and G are well-
defined economic concepts, the public's rate of saving is also a
well-defined economic concept.

4. The ratio of federal spending to NNP was .086 in 1980 and
grew to only .087 in 1990.

5. Thanks to the superb, dedicated work of Dr. John Musgrave of
the U.S. Department of Commerce, who over the years has
made careful measurements of federal, state, and local capital
stocks, we have all the data necessary to measure government
consumption properly. The reader should also understand
that the classification of government investment as government consumption is not a practice followed by most developed Western economies.

6. Thus, in the course of correctly measuring spending policy,
we would need to do the type of capital accounting recommended by the General Accounting Office (GAO) in its recent
study of government budgeting. General Accounting Office
report, "Managing the Cost of Government: Proposals for
Reforming Federal Budgeting Practices," Washington, D.C.,
October 1989.

7. See *The Economic Report of the President 1991*, p. 293, and Ali-
cia H. Munnell, "How Does Public Infrastructure Affect Regional Economic Performance?" Federal Reserve Bank of
Boston's *New England Economic Review*, September–October 1990, pp. 11–32. One plausible defense of the lower rate of
U.S. infrastructure investment is that less is now needed because of the near completion of the interstate highway system.

8. This is a conservative estimate based on a 6 percent real discount factor. The $16,500 is a simple average of the predicted
present value loss of $21,000 for 1989 male newborns and
$9,000 for 1989 female newborns, increased by 10 percent to

adjust for inflation between 1989 and the present. The source for these figures are Appendix Tables 1 and 2 in Alan J. Auerbach, Jagadeesh Gokhale, and Laurence J. Kotlikoff, "Generational Accounts: A Meaningful Alternative to Deficit Accounting," in David F. Bradford, ed., *Tax Policy and the Economy*, National Bureau of Economic Research vol. 5 (Cambridge, Mass: MIT Press, 1991), pp. 55–110. See also Michael J. Boskin, Laurence J. Kotlikoff, Douglas Puffert, and John Shoven, "Social Security: A Financial Analysis Within and Across Generations," *The National Tax Journal*, March 1987.

9. See Alan J. Auerbach, and Laurence J. Kotlikoff, *Dynamic Fiscal Policy* (Cambridge, Eng.: Cambridge University Press, 1987), for an in-depth examination of the generational implications of changing tax bases. See also Lawrence H. Summers, "Capital Taxation and Capital Accumulation in a Life Cycle Model," *American Economic Review*, vol. 71 (1981), pp. 533–44.

10. The top effective, as opposed to nominal, marginal federal income tax rate today is 34 percent. See Ridge Multop, "Fiscal Policy and Tax Policy, 1991–1995," Committee on the Budget, U.S. House of Representatives, mimeo distributed at WEFA Inc. Conference, November 15, 1990.

11. One caveat is that those members of young and future generations who inherit such appreciated assets, rather than having to purchase them, will not be adversely affected.

12. To be precise, capital purchased in the past and depreciated under old law is not grandfathered under new law stipulating more attractive investment incentives. Purchasers of pieces of "old capital" (as distinguished from purchasers of the title to old capital, as in a sale of stock) are eligible to use the most recently legislated investment incentives, but the seller of the old capital must pay a recapture tax, which leaves the seller, from a tax perspective, in the same position as selling his title to old capital at a discount.

13. The capital loss to existing capital arising from investment incentives appears to have been first recognized by Robert E. Lucas, Jr., and Edward Prescott in "Investment Under Uncertainty," *Econometrica*, vol. 39, 1971. The issue was also discussed by Lawrence H. Summers in "Taxation and Corporate Investment: A q Theory Approach," *Brookings Papers on Economic Activity*, vol. II, January 1981, pp. 67–127. For a dynamic general equilibrium analysis of capital losses due to investment incentives and their generational consequences, see Alan J. Auerbach and Laurence J. Kotlikoff, "Investment Versus Savings Incentives: The Size of the Bang for the Buck and

the Potential for Self-Financing Business Tax Cuts," in Laurence H. Meyer, ed., *The Economic Consequences of Government Deficits* (Boston: Kluwer-Nijhoff Publishing, 1983), p. 121–54, and Alan J. Auerbach and Laurence J. Kotlikoff, *Dynamic Fiscal Policy* (Cambridge, Eng.: Cambridge University Press, 1987), Chapter 9.

14. This discussion abstracts from the costs to the new buyer of locating another building and spending time acquiring and assembling the needed equipment. Because of the existence of such "adjustment" costs, the sixty-year-old seller and the thirty-year-old buyer might strike a deal whereby the seller loses, say, only 25 percent of the original sale price.

15. This is based on research in progress by the author and Professors Andrew Abel of the University of Pennsylvania and Douglas Bernheim of Princeton University.

16. Especially if one measures the millionaire's current income inclusive of his unrealized capital gains.

17. For an analysis of the lifetime progressivity of social security see Michael J. Boskin, Douglas Puffert, and John Shoven, "Social Security: A Financial Analysis Within and Across Generations," *The National Tax Journal*, March 1987.

18. Capital income taxes can also affect labor supply decisions, as shown in David F. Bradford, "The Economics of Tax Policy Toward Savings," in George M. von Furstenberg, ed., *The Government and Capital Formation* (Cambridge, Mass.: Ballinger, 1980).

19. For 1980 the U.S. Treasury Office of Tax Analysis reported a 29.1 percent effective federal average marginal tax rate on labor income. It reported a 21.7 percent tax rate for 1990. The gap between those two numbers is 7.4 percent. A total of 2.1 percentage points of this gap were eliminated by the 1.9 percentage point increase in the Social Security OASDHI tax rate combined with the reduction in the rate at which the employer component of this tax could be deducted from federal income taxes. (Note that the calculation here assumes that 60 percent of labor income is reported on tax returns that itemize their deductions.) This leaves a gap of 5.3 percentage points. Of this gap, 1.5 percentage points were eliminated by the ending in 1986 of the deductibility of sales taxes from federal income taxes, which raised the labor-tax-equivalent effective sales tax from 9.2 percent to 10.7 percent. This brings the remaining gap down to 3.8 percent points. Another 1.6 percentage points was eliminated by the increase in state and local wage and income taxes relative to labor income (measured as state and local personal tax and nontax receipts relative to national in-

come) plus the reduction of the federal marginal tax rate at which these taxes could be deducted. Now we are down to a gap of 1.6 percentage points. The remainder of this gap easily disappears if one factors in the reduction in future Social Security benefits and the projected future increase in federal taxation of Social Security benefits. These reduced benefits mean that each extra dollar earned yields less back at the margin in the form of future Social Security benefits than was previously the case. In 1990 the total (all taxes and all governments) average effective tax on labor income was 50.8 percent, not counting the reduced return of Social Security benefits in exchange for tax contributions.

20. To be technically accurate, the 1983 Social Security amendments mean that every additional dollar earned (up to the Social Security covered earnings ceiling) will lead to less in terms of future Social Security benefits than previously; that is, Social Security benefits are formally linked not to actual payroll taxes paid, but rather to the level of workers' earnings on which payroll taxes are collected.

21. Author's calculations.

22. See Jane G. Gravelle and Laurence J. Kotlikoff, "Corporate Taxation and the Efficiency Gains of the Tax Reform Act of 1986," National Bureau of Economic Research working paper no. 3142, 1989. The 23 percent figure was provided by Dr. Gravelle in a telephone conversation.

23. See Alan J. Auerbach, "Corporate Restructuring: Tax Incentives and Options for Corporate Tax Reform," in *The Tax Lawyer*, vol. 43, no. 3 (1990), pp. 663–91, Table 4. Legally, employer pension funds are, except in the cases of pension-plan default, assets of the employer. But since most corporate pension funds are not overfunded—see Laurence J. Kotlikoff and Daniel Smith, *Pensions in the American Economy* (Chicago: University of Chicago Press, 1983)—virtually all the assets held by these funds will eventually be paid out to current and past workers.

24. See Alan J. Auerbach, "Inflation and the Choice of Asset Life," *Journal of Political Economy*, June 1979, pp. 621–38; Alan J. Auerbach and Dale Jorgenson, "Inflation-Proof Depreciation of Assets," *Harvard Business Review*, September–October 1980, pp. 113–18; and Mervin King and Donald Fullerton, eds., *The Taxation of Income from Capital* (Chicago: University of Chicago Press, 1984).

25. Many of these studies will prove invaluable to improved generational accounting and distribution analysis.

26. Alan J. Auerbach and Laurence J. Kotlikoff, *Dynamic Fiscal*

Policy (Cambridge, Eng.: Cambridge University Press, 1987), provides one example of a dynamic overlapping generations model of the economy.

27. James M. Poterba, "Is the Gasoline Tax Regressive?" in David F. Bradford, ed., *Tax Policy and the Economy*, NBER vol. 5 (Cambridge, Mass.: MIT Press, 1991) pp. 145–164. See also James Poterba, "Lifetime Incidence and the Distributional Burden of Excise Taxes," *American Economic Review*, vol. 79 (1989), pp. 325–30, and Richard Kasten and Frank Sammartino, "The Distribution of Possible Federal Excise Tax Increases," Congressional Budget Office, 1988.

28. Two important earlier discussions of the use of consumption rather than annual income as the reference point for assessing distribution are David F. Bradford, *Blueprints for Basic Tax Reform*, 2d ed. (Arlington, Va.: Tax Analyses, 1984), and James B. Davies, France St-Hillaire, and John Whalley, "Some Calculations of Lifetime Tax Incidence," *American Economic Review*, vol. 74 (September 1984), pp. 633–49.

29. Michael J. Boskin, Laurence J. Kotlikoff, Douglas J. Puffert, and John B. Shoven, "Social Security: A Financial Appraisal Across and Within Generations," *National Tax Journal*, vol. XL, no. 1 (March 1987), pp. 19–34; also see, for example, Anthony Pellechio and Gordon P. Goodfellow, "Individual Gains and Losses from Social Security Before and After the 1983 Amendments," *Cato Journal*, Fall 1983.

30. Daniel Patrick Moynihan, "Statement of Senator Daniel Patrick Moynihan on the Social Security Tax Cut Act of 1991," January 14, 1991.

31. One caveat to that statement is that the relationship of longevity to lifetime income is poorly understood. Since the amount one gets back from Social Security depends on how long one lives, the system is less progressive to the extent that the lifetime rich live longer than the lifetime poor.

32. For a different discussion of the arbitrary nature of the distinction between taxes and negative subsidies see David F. Bradford, "Tax Expenditures and Problems of Accounting for Government," in Neil Bruce, ed., *Tax Expenditures and Government Policy* (Kingston, Ont.: Queen's University, John Deutsch Institute for the Study of Economic Policy, 1988), pp. 427–34.

33. *The Economic Report of the President 1991*, pp. 380–82.

34. *Ibid.*

35. See Michael J. Boskin, Laurence J. Kotlikoff, and John Shoven, "Personal Security Accounts: A Proposal for Social Security Reform," in Susan Wachter, ed., *Social Security and Private Pensions: Providing for Retirement in the 21st Century*

(Lexington, Mass.: Lexington Books, 1988), for a proposal to reform Social Security for those under age forty.

5. Generational Accounting

1. The source for these tables is Alan J. Auerbach, Jagadeesh Gokhale, and Laurence J. Kotlikoff, "Generational Accounts: A Meaningful Alternative to Deficit Accounting," in David Bradford, ed., *Tax Policy and the Economy*, NBER vol. 5, 1991, pp. 55–110.
2. This is meant to be a pretax discount rate. See *ibid.*, for a justification of these choices of the discount and growth rates.
3. For an analysis of the sensitivity of generational accounts to alternative growth and interest rate assumptions, see *ibid.*
4. If the present value of money, say $300, paid at some date in the future is not a familiar notion, think of it as the amount of money that you'd have to place in a savings account today so as to have $300 at that date in the future. This amount—this present value—will depend on the interest rate your savings account is paying. The higher the interest rate, the less money you need to put in the bank today to end up with the $300 at the date in the future; hence the higher the interest rate, the smaller the present value of $300 at the date in the future.
5. The two-thirds figure is based on calculations by the author using the U.S. Census Bureau's Survey of Income and Plan Participation.
6. Precise details are available in Auerbach, Gokhale, and Kotlikoff, "Generational Accounting."
7. The average rate here is defined as all federal, state, and local income taxes divided by NNP. The data are from 1989.
8. The average federal income tax rate is 11.8 percent for 1989. It is measured as federal labor plus capital income taxes divided by NNP.
9. The average payroll tax rate is defined as total federal, state, and local payroll taxes divided by total U.S. labor income. The data are from 1989.
10. The average sales/excise tax is defined as total federal, state, and local indirect business taxes divided by U.S. personal consumption expenditure. All data used in the calculation are from 1989.
11. The average capital income tax rate is measured as total federal, state, and local capital income tax revenue divided by total U.S. capital income. All data are from 1989.
12. Unlike an increase in payroll taxes, increasing capital income taxes makes the current elderly also pay to help correct the

245

generational policy imbalance. For a given amount of additional annual revenue, the present value of the payments of all current generations combined is larger under the capital income tax than under the payroll tax; raising the capital income tax raises the current elderly's present value of projected net tax payments, but also the projected present value net payments of the current young and middle-aged, who will pay these higher capital income taxes in the future. Thus one can collect fewer dollars from the capital income tax and still equalize generational burdens, because each dollar raised under the capital income tax does double duty in raising the present value of net payments of those currently alive.

13. These and other policy-induced changes in generational accounts discussed in this book do not take into account the feedback effects of the policies on the economy's saving, growth, wages, and interest rates. As analyzed in Alan J. Auerbach and Laurence J. Kotlikoff, *Dynamic Fiscal Policy* (Cambridge, Eng.: Cambridge University Press, 1987), these feedback effects can be important and can themselves serve to redistribute across generations. They occur, however, quite slowly. In addition, in almost all cases, their consideration reinforces the changes in generational accounts calculated without feedback effects. Incorporating feedback effects is an important goal for future research on generational accounting.

14. Females at a given age pay roughly the same excise taxes as males, despite the fact that their lifetime earnings are much lower. The explanation is that married females share in the total household expenditures, which are based on the couple's combined income.

15. The additional taxes are set equal to the product of the additional accumulated debt and a growth-adjusted interest factor equal to the assumed 6 percent interest rate less the assumed 0.75 percent growth rate.

16. These are real 1990 dollars.

17. See Michael J. Boskin, *Too Many Promises: The Uncertain Future & Social Security* (Homewood, Ill.: Dow Jones/Irwin, 1986).

18. Actually, there is an escape hatch in the new law that permits non-"pay-as-you-go" changes in Social Security, provided such changes are originated in the Senate.

6. Deficit Delusion

1. Chapter 7 will show that for many younger Americans the Reagan "tax cuts" were, in present value, more than outweighed by tax increases and benefit reductions, some of

which occurred in the mid- and late 1980s and some of which will occur in the future. For older Americans, the Reagan "tax cuts" of the early 1980s also provide the wrong description of the policy. They understate the present value change in net lifetime payments to the government.

2. Suppose Sam gives zero on net to the government at age forty and gets zero on net at age fifty. This could, as an example, be described as the government taxing Sam $23,000 at age forty and lending him $23,000 at age forty. The zero net amount Sam receives at age fifty would then be described as Sam's repaying the government $23,000 on his loan and receiving a $23,000 transfer. There is no requirement that each of these four transactions be conducted with Sam. The government could "tax" Sam $23,000 at age forty and lend the funds to, say, Jane (no relation to Sam), and use Jane's repayment on her loan to "transfer" $23,000 to Sam at age fifty.

3. For an excellent discussion of the economic equivalence, but cash flow differences, of FSAs and IRAs, see Jane G. Gravelle, "The Federal Budget and Long-Term Decision-making." testimony presented to the Senate Finance Committee, April 12, 1991.

4. Even the legal distinction is blurry, since the government does not force us on pain of imprisonment or worse to earn income or buy goods or do anything that triggers a tax payment; in some, admittedly weak, sense our tax payments can also be viewed as voluntary.

5. *The Economic Report of the President 1991*, pp. 310, 380, and the National Balance Sheets of the Federal Reserve System, 1989.

6. Daniel T. Slesnick, "Gaining Ground: Poverty in the Post-War United States," mimeo, Kennedy School of Government, Harvard University, July 1990.

7. See Fumio Hayashi, "Tests for Liquidity Constraints: A Critical Survey and Some New Observations," in Truman F. Bewley, ed., *Advances in Econometrics, Fifth World Congress*, vol. 2 (Cambridge, Eng.: Cambridge University Press, 1987), for a technical analysis of why credit markets would adjust to changes in the timing of government taxes even in contexts in which large segments of society are cash-constrained.

8. Table 5.8 of *The Economic Report of the President 1982* reports the revaluation of net financial debt through the 1970s. The $500 billion estimate assumes that at least three-quarters of this revaluation reflected the impact of inflation driving up nominal interest rates and thereby driving down the market value of outstanding debt.

9. Thus, rather than give a "front-loaded" IRA tax deduction or a "back-loaded" FSA tax exemption, the government could give a tax break some years after one's contribution to such saving accounts, but some years before the withdrawal of funds from these accounts.
10. Presumably the credit given would be per dollar contributed to the account.
11. Note that the incentive per dollar contributed can be set equal in each of the cases.
12. In recent years the U.S. federal government has limited, but not eliminated, taxpayers' abilities to take losses on their investment income.
13. It would also represent a windfall to those earning over $5,000, since they will receive a subsidy even if they fail to increase their earnings.

7. Postwar Generational Policy

1. Recall that the NIPA deficit includes Social Security.
2. The National Income and Product Accounts of the U.S. Department of Commerce report state and local as well as federal government deficits back to 1929. They do not, however, report a corresponding series on the level of state and local debt or, indeed, on the level of federal debt. (The federal debt figures cited in this chapter are based on federal budget data.) Since no series on the stock of total government debt is available, a series was constructed by assuming that the stock of debt in 1928 was zero and then summing the annual combined government deficits, as calculated by NIPA, to form the stock of debt for each year after 1928. Sources for the federal as well as state and local deficit series back to 1929 are *The National Income and Product Accounts 1929–1982* and *The Economic Report of the President 1991*, p. 379.
3. Recall that the present value burden on future generations equals the present value of government spending, less government net worth, less the present value of net tax payments of existing generations. Thus, holding fixed the present values of net payments of existing generations, if the present value of government spending rises by more than government net worth declines, the burden on future generations will increase.
4. The definition of government spending on goods and services used here differs somewhat from that in the NIPA. It treats government pension and disability payments to civil servants, members of the military, and veterans as government spending rather than as a transfer payment. Such payments are part

of the compensation the government pays to hire the services of civil servants and members of the military. As such it represents a purchase by the government of services. This modified definition of government spending does not materially affect the inferences about changes in generational policy over time.

5. The spending increases during the Eisenhower years were bad news in the sense that younger and future generations were hit with much of the bill for the additional spending. But this "bad news" abstracts away from the "good news" that may have been associated with these spending increases to the extent that this spending benefited members of these generations. A careful imputation to different generations of the benefits of government spending remains to be done.

6. The hypothetical Social Security policy considered in Table 5–4 is a 20 percent benefit increase. Since Social Security benefits are currently 7.4 percent of NNP, a 20 percent benefit increase would raise that ratio by 1.5 percentage points. But in the 1950s Social Security benefits relative to NNP rose by 2.1 percentage points. The ratio of 2.1 to 1.5 is 1.4.

7. These and subsequent numbers in this chapter concerning tax-induced capital gains and losses are based on calculations done by Jane Gravelle and reported in Jane G. Gravelle, "The Effects of Changes in the Taxation of Income from Capital on Stockholders' Wealth," mimeo, Congressional Research Service, September 22, 1982.

8. After 1999, Social Security benefits remain 2.1 percentage points higher relative to the economy's output than they would otherwise have been.

9. There are six different features of this hypothetical exercise. First, government spending is increased by 7 percent of NNP, and this increase is financed by an equal percentage increase in all average tax rates. Second, the shares of labor income taxes (other than payroll taxes), sales plus excise taxes, and capital income taxes are adjusted in accordance with changes in these shares during the 1950s. Third, Social Security benefits are increased, as well as the payroll taxes needed to pay for them, so that the benefit increase equals the 2.2 percent of NNP. Fourth, adjustments to inframarginal and marginal capital income taxes are made to account for the 4 percent capital loss induced by the 1954 investment incentives. Fifth, real welfare payments are altered gradually over the course of the decade so that the change in real welfare payments relative to NNP after ten years equals the change actually observed between 1950 and 1959. These welfare changes are assumed to be financed on a pay-as-you-go basis by equal proportional

changes in all taxes other than payroll taxes. Finally, to capture the reduction in official government debt over a ten-year period, all tax rates are increased for ten years by a percentage such that in the tenth year, the debt-to-NNP ratio has declined by 0.33. From the eleventh year onward, all tax rates are reduced by a fixed percentage so that the new ratio of debt to NNP is maintained through time.

10. Were it not for the redistributive policies summarized in the second column, the generational accounts in Column 1 would be those listed less the corresponding values in Column 2. For example, sixty-year-old males would have seen their remaining lifetime bill rise, on average, by $21,900, which is the $5,700 listed in Column 1 less the negative $16.2 thousand listed in Column 2.

11. The figures are the simple average, across males and females, of the division of the numbers in the first column of Table 7–1 by the corresponding numbers in the first column in Table 5–1.

12. There are two problems with fine-tuning. First, it takes Congress time to pass new fiscal legislation, with the result that when the new laws take effect the problem they were meant to fix may no longer exist. A second and more fundamental concern was identified by the University of Chicago economists Robert Lucas and Thomas Sargent. Lucas and Sargent pointed out that the public will catch on to the government's fine-tuning policies and wait for these policies to be enacted before responding. Thus if the country is in a recession and everyone expects the government to, say, subsidize new investment to stimulate economic activity, business will hold off on its investment until those subsidies are enacted. This waiting game, of course, lowers investment during the pre-subsidy period, and, as a consequence, makes the shortfall in investment, and the recession, that much worse.

13. Joseph A. Pechman, *Federal Tax Policy*, fifth edition (Washington, D.C.: The Brookings Institution, 1987).

14. Through the course of the 1960s, the consumer price index increased by almost 25 percent.

15. "1989 Annual Report of the Federal Old-Age and Survivors Insurance and Disability Insurance Trust Funds," p. 55, and "1990 Annual Report of the Board of Trustees of the Federal Hospital Insurance Trust Fund," p. 39.

16. This liberalization arose from the elimination of a basis adjustment.

17. Of course, not all the owners of capital held onto their capital throughout the 1960s. Hence, some owners suffered net capital losses, and some enjoyed net capital gains.

18. The larger check given to the seventy-year-old female compared with that given the seventy-year-old male reflects the point that seventy-year-old males experienced larger absolute tax increases in this period than did their female contemporaries. In contrast, seventy-year-old females experienced somewhat larger increases in the present value of their Social Security (including Medicare) benefits, due to their greater life expectancies. Recall that generational accounting discounts for mortality risk as well as interest.

19. This figure is based on multiplying, for each year in the 1970s in which investment incentives were changed, Dr. Jane Gravelle's estimate of the tax-induced change in asset value by the Commerce Department's estimate of the value of the capital stock in the corresponding year. These changes in capital value were then valued in current dollars and summed.

20. In fairness, both houses of Congress were controlled by Democrats during the Nixon and Ford presidencies.

21. This time a Republican Administration was assisted by a Republican Senate.

22. Of course, the capital losses produced by Nixon, Ford, and Reagan were, in large part, visited on different people.

23. As mentioned in note 2, the National Income and Product Accounts, while they report annual deficits for both the federal government and state and local governments, do not tabulate series on either federal or state and local debt. The reason they do not report such a series appears to be that they do not have an initial 1928 value of federal or state and local debt from which to start their debt accumulation. In the absence of any published NIPA series with the clear-cut heading "federal debt," many commentators have simply used the gross federal debt series in discussing the buildup of federal liabilities. The initial levels of federal and state and local debts in 1928 appear to have been tiny when measured against the postwar deficits. Hence, treating them as zero, as is done here, and then adding together the annual NIPA deficits to arrive at total debt figures, seems reasonable. While the derived NIPA debt series seems less silly than the gross federal debt series (there is no corresponding gross state and local debt series), the NIPA deficit has been faulted by those who take deficits seriously for excluding certain government transaction, such as the ongoing S&L bailout.

24. The increase in federal debt here is that measured by the National Income and Product Accounts.

25. The ratio of HI benefit payments to NNP was .0103 in 1980 and .0129. *Economic Report of the President 1991* and the HI Trust Fund Report, 1990.

26. Feldstein, Martin S., "Social Security, Induced Retirement, and Aggregate Capital Formation," *Journal of Political Economy*, vol. 82, 1974.
27. In paying unwarranted attention to the official labeling of receipts and payments, the politicians have misread the true economic picture and, in many instances, have compounded problems they were trying to allieviate. This is the sense in which labels have mattered for economic outcomes.
28. For example, compare for newborns the present value of their future projected payroll taxes reported in Table 5–1 with the table's corresponding present value of Social Security OASDI and HI benefit receipts.
29. The rate of return that is relevant for this comparison is the economywide pretax real return to capital.
30. Another "balanced budget" intergenerational redistribution mechanism is tax-financed increases in government spending where that spending is targeted to specific age groups, e.g. spending on school lunches.
31. For an analysis of different determinants of saving see Laurence J. Kotlikoff, *What Determines Savings?* (Cambridge, Mass.: MIT Press, 1989).
32. See, for example, Alan J. Auerbach and Laurence J. Kotlikoff, *Dynamic Fiscal Policy* (New York: Cambridge University Press, 1987).

8. Social Security and the Baby Boomers

1. See Gregory Mankiw, "The Baby Boom, the Baby Bust, and the Housing Market," *Regional Science and Urban Economics* (Vol. 19, No. 2, May 1989, pp. 235–58).
2. Finis Welch, "Effects of Cohort Size on Earnings: The Baby Boom Babies' Financial Bust," *Journal of Political Economy*, vol. 87, no. 5, Part 2 (October 1979), pp. S65–S98.
3. See Alan J. Auerbach and Laurence J. Kotlikoff, *Dynamic Fiscal Policy* (Cambridge, Eng.: Cambridge University Press, 1987), Chapter 11. Since the demographic transition is an international phenomenon, occurring in Japan and all the major West European countries, rates of return worldwide will fall, as will asset values. See Alan J. Auerbach, Giuseppe Nicoletti, Robert Haggerman, and Laurence J. Kotlikoff, "The Economics of the Demographic Transition: The Case of Four OECD Countries," in *OECD Staff Papers*, 1989.
4. See, for example, Auerbach and Kotlikoff, *Dynamic Fiscal Policy*, Chapter 11.
5. See Joseph Altonji, Fumio Hayashi, and Laurence J. Kotlikoff,

"Is the Extended Family Altruistically Linked?" National Bureau of Economic Research working paper, May 1989, for an empirical study suggesting that adult children would not offset dollar-for-dollar government transfers to themselves and away from their parents.

6. See, for example, Peter Ferrara, *Social Security—The Inherent Contradiction* (Washington, D.C., The Cato Institute, 1980).

7. See Alan J. Auerbach and Laurence J. Kotlikoff, "The Adequacy of Life Insurance Purchases," *Journal of Financial Intermediation*, 1991, and Alan J. Auerbach and Laurence J. Kotlikoff, "Life Insurance of the Elderly: Adequacy and Determinants," in *Work, Health, and Income Among the Elderly* (Washington, D.C.: The Brookings Institution, 1987).

8. This is roughly the difference in the present value of Social Security and Medicare benefits less the present value of taxes for seventy-year-olds listed in Table 5–1.

9. For an excellent volume discussing Social Security's surpluses, see Carolyn L. Weaver, *Social Security's Looming Surpluses* (Washington, D.C.: American Enterprise Institute, 1990).

10. *The 1989 Annual Report of the Board of Trustees of the Federal Old-Age and Survivors Insurance and Disability Insurance Trust Funds* (Washington, D.C.: U.S. Government Printing Office, 1989), p. 9.

11. To the extent the economy grows, the income tax rate won't need to rise as much as would otherwise be the case.

12. *The 1989 Annual Report*, p. 132, Alternative II-A.

13. *New York Times*, April 11, 1988, p. A18.

14. *Ibid.*

15. *New York Times*, Sunday, June 9, 1991, p. 16.

16. Darman, Richard, "Introductory Statement: The Problem of Rising Health Costs," presented before the Senate Finance Committee, Executive Office of the President, Office of Management and Budget, April 16, 1991, p. 6.

17. *Ibid.*, Chart 18, p. 14.

18. *Ibid.*

19. *Ibid.*

20. *Ibid.*, p. 15.

21. Specifically, the reduction in Medicare benefits after 2020 equals interest (less an adjustment for growth) on the additional accumulated (with interest) Medicare expenditures through 2020 arising from higher Medicare growth in the 1990s.

22. See Michael J. Boskin, Laurence J. Kotlikoff, and John B. Shoven, "Personal Security Account: A Proposal for Funda-

mental Social Security Reform," in Susan Wachter, ed., *Social Security and Private Pensions: Providing for Retirement in the 21st Century* (Lexington, Mass.: Lexington Books, 1988). Another example is the recent ill-fated attempt to provide a limited amount of catastrophic health insurance to the elderly, with the premium for this insurance to be paid primarily by the elderly. This policy, the Medicare Catastrophic Coverage Act of 1988, which was repealed in 1989, met with opposition from a substantial segment of the elderly, many of whom were in good health and did not see why they should pay for the health care of their contemporaries, many of whom were already in bad health; in other words, many of the elderly correctly perceived the policy as, in large part, ex-post redistribution rather than as ex-ante insurance. Had the authors of the policy enacted it for those generations under, say, age fifty, it may well have met with universal acceptance, since all contributors to the program would understand that they were truly purchasing insurance against catastrophic illness in old age.

9. Whither Generational Accounting?

1. Senator Bill Bradley of New Jersey, Chairman of the Senate Finance Committee's Subcommittee on Deficits, Debt Management, and International Debt, and Representative Bill Gradison of Cincinnati, Ohio, the ranking Republican on the House Budget Committee and member of the House Ways and Means Committee, have formally requested the General Accounting Office to evaluate generational accounting. Senator Bradley has also made this request to the Congressional Budget Office.
2. In U.S. deficit accounting, infrastructure expenditures and other government investments are not distinguished from government spending on current consumption.
3. As of this writing, the Bank of Italy, in concert with the author and Dr. Jagadeesh Gokhale of the Federal Reserve Bank of Cleveland, is engaged in the construction of generational accounts to describe the fiscal actions of the Italian government.

INDEX

Age distribution, 54
Age of Diminished Expectations, The (Krugman), 44, 66–67
Agricultural labor force, 40
American Economic Review, The, 72
"Animal spirits," 42–43
Arbitrariness of deficit accounting: *See* Labeling of receipts and payments
Argentina, 44
Aschauer, David, 72
Asset markets, running generational policy through, 99–101

Baby boom generation
   demographic dilemma of, 53–55
   economic dilemma of, 55–62
   saving shortfall and, 2–3, 56
   Social Security legislation and, 24–25
   Social Security policies and, 193–215
   trustworthiness of Social Security Trust Fund and, 59–62
Banking system, 41
Bankruptcies, 40

Bernstein, Peter, 73
Blinder, Alan, 38–39
Boston Globe, 43–44
Budget agreement of 1990
   fiscal policy fundamentals and, 91–92
   impact on generational accounts, 132, 139–141
Budget deficit
   analyses of impact of, 68–74
   arbitrary nature of: *See* Labeling of receipts and payments
   cash-constrained consumer issue and, 31–34
   as deficient measure, 18–20, 22, 23, 31, 62–63
   economic problems blamed on, 6, 65–68
   Eisner high-employment definition, 83–85
   vs. generational accounting, 23, 138–139
   "Golden Rule" of, 7–8, 60, 62
   government spending and, 5–7, 94–95
   Gramm–Rudman targets, 5–6, 12, 13
   interest rate levels and, 66, 67, 72–73, 79–83

Budget deficit *(cont.)*
  Keynesians and, 8, 30–33, 42
  multivariate analyses of impact of, 71–74
  National Income and Product Account (NIPA), 9, 11, 69–71, 84–86, 163, 180, 181
  in the 1950s, 166–167
  in the 1960s, 174
  in the 1970s, 176–177
  in the 1980s, 180–182
  proposed corrections to, 83–86
  public opinion on, 17
  reasons for popularity of, 30–32
  recessions and hysteria about, 41–42
  saving level and, 66–70, 74–79
  size of, 4–5
  "Smoke-and-Mirrors" game of redefining, 12–18
  unified, 12, 19, 60
  variety in definitions of, 9–12
Burden on future generations, 126–130
  calculation of, 28–30, 120
  equalization of, 127–130
Bush, George, 17, 37–38, 181, 182

Capital income taxes
  equalization of burden on future generations and increases in, 128–130
  in female generational accounts, 118–119
  in male generational accounts, 116–117
  in the 1950s, 169
  in the 1960s, 174
  in the 1970s, 177
  as saving disincentives, 103, 105
Capital/labor ratio, 49, 50
Cash-constrained-consumer issue, 31–34, 153–156
Cash-flow measures of economic policy, 31
Congress
  budget deficit definition and, 11–17, 23–24
  investment incentives of 1980s and, 178–179
  legislative time bombs of, 24–25
Congressional Budget Office (CBO), 12, 219
Consumption, 3, 21, 26, 27, 52
  cash-constrained-consumer issue and, 31–34, 153–156
  government spending policy, 91–95
  in Keynesian model, 31–33, 76
  in neoclassical model, 33
  studies of deficit impact on, 72

Darman, Richard, 208
Day of Reckoning (Friedman), 44, 67–68
Deficit Reduction Act of 1982, 105
Depreciation allowances, 105–106
Disposable income, 31–33, 75–76
Distortionary policy, 91, 102–106

Distribution policy, 91, 101–102, 108–111
Divorce rate, 54
Dollar, value of, 66, 67
Dunn, Paul, 39
Dwyer, Gerald, 72

Economic policy measures
  budget deficit: *See* Budget deficit
  generational accounting: *See* Generational accounting
  Who will pay? question, 20–21
Economic Recovery Tax Act of 1981, 179
Economic stabilization policy, 21
Economic uncertainty, 25
Education, 4
Eisenhower Administration, 166–173
Eisner, Robert, 10, 83
Eisner high-employment deficit, 83–85
Elderly population
  generational accounts of, 117, 119, 122–123
  health care expenditures on, 58
  reliance on children by, 54–55
Erdman, Paul, 43
Europeans, investment of savings in U.S., 3
Evans, Paul, 72–73
Excise taxes
  equalization of burden on future generations and increases in, 128–130
  in female generational accounts, 118–119

in male generational accounts, 116–117
as work disincentives, 103

Family Savings Accounts (FSAs), 152, 159
Federal debt: *See* Budget deficit
Federal Savings and Loan Insurance Corporation (FSLIC), 14–15
Feldstein, Martin, 9, 188
Fertility rate, 53–54
Financial crowding out, 80–82
Financial markets
  impact on generational accounts of redistribution through, 132, 135–139
  stability of, 41
Financing Corporation, The (FICO), 15–16
Fiscal policies, recommended fundamentals of, 89–113
  comprehensive nature of measurement of, 111–112
  as conceptually distinct, 91
  distortionary policy, 91, 102–106
  distribution policy, 91, 101–102, 108–111
  generational policy: *See* Generational policy
  government spending policy: *See* Government spending policy
  intertemporal nature of, 106–107
  potential benefits of measurement of, 113
  practical interrelation of, 91–92

Food stamp payments, 173
Food stamp receipts
  in female generational ac-
    counts, 118–119
  in male generational ac-
    counts, 116–117
Ford, Gerald, 178
Foreign investment, 3, 45–48
Friedman, Benjamin, 44, 67–68
Friedman, Milton, 28
Fringe benefits, 50, 51
Full employment deficit, 30,
  69–71
Furstenberg, Frank F., Jr., 54

Gasoline tax, regressivity of,
  110
General Accounting Office
  (GAO), 219
*General Theory of Employ-
  ment, Interest, and Money*
  (Keynes), 8
Generational accounting, 96–
  97, 101, 115–141, 217–220;
  see also Generational policy
  advantages of, 23–26, 113,
    219–220
  baseline accounts, 115–122
  budget deficit vs., 23, 138–
    139
  burden on future genera-
    tions: *See* Burden on fu-
    ture generations
  comprehensive nature of,
    111–112
  concept of, 22–23
  construction of accounts,
    125–126
  defined, 22

goal of generational balance
  and, 218–219
interpretation of accounts,
  122–125
male vs. female accounts, 122
policy-induced changes in accounts: *See* Generational
  accounts, policy-induced
  changes in
understanding, 26–28
Generational accounts, policy-
  induced changes in, 131–
  141
  budget agreement of 1990,
    132, 139–141
  deficit-induced tax cut, 131–
    134, 138, 139
  federal debt policy vs. all
    1950–1980 policies, 185–
    187
  investment incentive elimina-
    tion, 132, 135–139
  1950s policies, 170–173
  1960s policies, 171, 175–176
  1970s policies, 171, 178
  Social Security policies, 132,
    134, 138, 175, 176, 201–205
  tax base change, 132, 134–
    135
Generational policy, 91, 96–
  101, 113, 165–191; *see also*
  Fiscal policies, recom-
  mended fundamentals of
  baby boom generation and,
    194–196
  comprehensive manner of
    studying, 166
  importance of, 107–108
  national saving and, 190–191
  in the 1950s, 166–173
  in the 1960s, 171, 173–176

in the 1970s, 171, 176–178
in the 1980s, 171, 178–184
policy-makers' misjudgment
of, 188–190
Generation-specific policies,
215
Gimmickry, 12–18
"Golden Rule of Deficits," 7–8,
60, 62
Government labeling of receipts and payments: *See*
Labeling of receipts and
payments
Government saving, 76–79
Government spending
budget deficit measurement
and, 10, 11
budget deficit size and, 6–7
generational accounting
and, 24, 26
Gramm–Rudman Act and, 5
Keynes and, 8
Social Security policies and,
199–204
Government spending policy,
91–95
in the 1950s, 167–173, 175
in the 1970s, 177
in the 1980s, 182–183
Gramm, Phil, 6
Gramm–Rudman deficit tar-
gets, 5–6, 12, 13
Gramm–Rudman–Hollings Act
of 1985, 5
Great Britain, 44, 73, 207
Greenspan, Alan, 5, 68, 80
Greenspan Commission, 59

Health care: *See* Medicare
Heilbroner, Robert, 73
Heller, Walter, 37

Hicks, John, 8
Hollings, Ernest, 6

Income
disposable, 31–33, 75–76
future, 33
per capita, 45, 51
real, trend in, 50–52
Income distribution, 52
Income taxes
equalization of burden on future generations and in-
creases in, 128–130
in female generational accounts, 118–119
impact on generational accounts of cuts in, 131–134
impact on generational accounts of financing Social
Security with, 202, 206
in male generational ac-
counts, 116–117
in the 1950s, 169
in the 1960s, 173, 174
in the 1970s, 177
in the 1980s, 183
as saving disincentives, 103,
105
as work disincentives, 102–
104
Individual Retirement Ac-
counts (IRAs), 152, 159
Inflation
adjustment of deficit for, 11
generational accounting
and, 25
indexing of Social Security
against, 24, 25
labeling of receipts and payments and, 156–157

Inflation *(cont.)*
  studies of budget deficit impact on, 72
Inheritances, 57
Interest payments, 75
Interest rates, 66, 67, 72–73, 79–83
Investment, 3–4
  budget deficits and level of, 65–68
  foreign, 3, 45–48
  public, misclassification as public consumption, 95
  rate of: 1950–1990, 45, 46
Investment incentives
  impact on generational accounts of elimination of, 132, 135–139
  labeling of receipts and payments and, 160–161
  in the 1950s, 170
  in the 1960s, 174–175
  in the 1970s, 177–178
  in the 1980s, 179–180
IS-LM model, 8

Japan, 3, 43–46, 48, 49, 73, 206
Journal of Monetary Economics, The, 72
Journal of Political Economy, 72

Keynes, John Maynard, 8, 42
Keynesians, 6, 8, 30–33, 42, 74–76, 189, 204
Koppel, Ted, 5, 10
Kormendi, Roger, 72
Krugman, Paul, 44, 66–67

Labeling of receipts and payments, 18–20, 77, 96–101, 123–124, 143–164, 166
  counterarguments to case study, 149–161
  deficit-as-irrelevant case study, 144–149
  in the 1980s, 181–182
  nonrelationship between marginal and average net tax payments, 161–162
  Social Security, 18–20, 77, 123–124
Labor force, 40, 51, 55
Labor income taxes
  equalization of burden on future generations and increases in, 128–130
  in female generational accounts, 118–119
  in male generational accounts, 116–117
  in the 1950s, 169
  in the 1960s, 174
  in the 1970s, 177
  in the 1980s, 183
  as work disincentives, 102–104
Legislative time bombs, 24–25
Local government policies, combined treatment with federal policies, 112
Lucas, Robert, 32

Malkin, Lawrence, 5, 50
Manufacturing, employment in, 40
Marginal tax rates, 104–105, 161–162
Mariano, Robert, 72
Medicaid, 58
Medicare
  baby boom generation and, 197, 208, 212–214

changes in generational accounts from policies of, 209–212
in female generational accounts, 118–119
growth in expenditures, 58, 125, 174, 177, 183, 206–214
in male generational accounts, 116–117
Microeconomic concept of generational accounting, 26–28
Mills, Wilbur, 24
Mitchell, George J., 111
Mitchell, John N., 89
"Morning After, The" (Peterson), 44
Moynihan, Patrick, 9, 11, 110–111
Social Security proposal of, 198–205
Multivariate analyses of budget deficit impact, 71–74

National Income and Product Account (NIPA) deficit, 9, 11, 69–71, 84–86, 163, 180, 181
National saving, 69–71, 76–79, 93, 190–191
Neoclassical economic theory, 18, 22, 31–33
Net disposable income, 75–76
Net liabilities, U.S., 10
Net worth
household, 57
U.S., 10, 26, 33
New Republic, The, 38
New York Times, The, 204
Nixon, Richard, 24, 178
"No Free Lunch" dictum, 24

"Notch babies," 24
Nursing homes, 58

Overseas Fund of Fidelity Investments, 48

Pay-as-you-go tax-transfer schemes, 21–23, 97–98, 188–190
changes in generational accounts from Medicare policies and, 210–212
expansion in Eisenhower years, 169
impact on generational accounts of, 134, 138
Moynihan proposal of, 199
Payroll taxes
equalization of burden on future generations and increases in, 128–130
impact on generational accounts of cuts in Social Security taxes, 198–204
impact on generational accounts of shift to excise taxes from, 132, 134–135
Per capita income, 45, 51
Peterson, Peter, 38, 44
Poterba, James, 110
Poverty, 52–53
Power of Being Debt-Free (Schuller and Dunn), 39
Present value
in calculation of burden on future generations, 28–29
concept of, 26–27
of receipts and payments in generational accounts, 116–121
Private pension plans, 56

Private saving, 79, 93–94
Productivity growth, 48–50
  adjustment of deficit for, 11
  annual: 1950–1990, 49
  budget deficits and level of, 70
  investment and, 3–4, 49–50
Progressivity, 101–102, 109–111, 205–206
Property taxes
  in female generational accounts, 118–119
  in male generational accounts, 116–117
Psychological factors in recessions, 41–43
Pure public goods, 168

Reagan, Ronald, 7, 37, 40, 104, 105, 178–179, 181, 182
Real wages, 50–52, 66
  growth in, 4
Recessions, psychological factors in, 41–43
REFCORP, 16
Reich, Robert, 50
Reischauer, Robert, 13
Resolution Trust Corporation (RTC), 16
Retirement, early, 2–3
Retirement programs
  budget deficit measurement and, 10
  Social Security: See Social Security
Revenue-neutral changes in tax base, 98–99
Revenue sharing, 112
Ricardo, David, 8
Rudman, Warren, 6

Sales taxes
  equalization of burden on future generations and increases in, 128–130
  impact on generational accounts of increases in, 132, 134–135
  as work disincentives, 103
Samuelson, Robert, 38, 66
Sargent, Thomas, 32
SAT test scores, 4
Saving, 2–3, 26
  baby boom generation and, 2–3, 56
  budget deficits and level of, 66–70, 74–79
  disincentives, 103, 105
  distortionary policy and, 102–106
  government, 76–79
  incentives, 159–160
  in Keynesian model, 32
  lifetime progressivity and, 101–102
  national, 69–71, 76–79, 93, 190–191
  in neoclassical model, 27
  private, 79, 93–94
  rate of: 1950–1990, 45, 46
  trade deficit and, 47
Savings & Loan bailout, 9, 12–16
Schuller, Robert, 39
Seater, John, 72
Seignorage
  in female generational accounts, 118–119
  in male generational accounts, 116–117
Service sector, employment in, 40

Slesnik, Daniel, 52
Smith, Adam, 8
"Smoke-and-Mirrors" game of
  redefining the deficit, 12–18
Social Security
  arbitrary nature of labels
    and, 18–20, 77, 123–124
  baby boom generation and,
    24–25, 193–215
  budget deficit measurement
    and, 9, 11–12, 23–24, 85–86
  in female generational ac-
    counts, 118–119
  impact on generational ac-
    counts of changes in poli-
    cies, 132, 134, 138, 175,
    176, 201–205
  labor earnings treatment
    and, 161
  legislative time bombs and,
    24–25
  in male generational ac-
    counts, 116–117, 121
  Medicare financing and, 208–
    209
  Moynihan proposal, 198–205
  1950s policy, 169, 170
  1960s policy, 174–176
  1970s policy, 177
  1980s policy, 182–183
  pay-as-you-go: See Pay-as-you-
    go tax-transfer schemes
  progressivity of, 110–111
  reductions in benefits, 3, 56,
    104, 196
  surpluses, 23–24, 30, 60, 196–
    205
  taxation of benefits, 104
  trustworthiness of Trust
    Fund, 59–62

Social Security Amendments
  of 1983, 56, 182–183
Spending policy: See Government spending policy
State government policies,
  combined treatment with
  federal policies, 112
Supply-siders, 73–74

Tax base changes
  impact on generational ac-
    counts, 132, 134–135
  in the 1970s, 177
  revenue-neutral, 98–99
Tax cuts, 11, 32–33, 96, 104
  impact on generational ac-
    counts of, 131–135, 138,
    139, 198–204
  by Reagan Administration,
    181, 182
Tax Equity and Fiscal Responsibility Act of 1982, 105,
  179
Taxes; see also names of spe-
    cific taxes; Tax policy
  distortionary policy, 91, 102–
    106
  equalization of burden on fu-
    ture generations and, 128–
    130
  federal taxation offset by
    state and local taxation in
    1980s, 75–76
  in generational account cal-
    culation, 26–29, 116–122,
    125–126
  in Keynesian model of house-
    hold economic behavior,
    74–75
  labeling issue and: See Label-

Taxes *(cont.)*
    ing of receipts and pay-
      ments
Tax increases, 10, 11
  by Bush Administration,
    181, 182
  equalization of burden on fu-
    ture generations and, 128–
    130
Tax policy
  in the 1950s, 167, 169
  in the 1960s, 173–175
  in the 1970s, 177–178
  in the 1980s, 179–180
  tax cuts: *See* Tax cuts
  tax increases: *See* Tax in-
    creases
Tax rates, marginal, 104–105,
    161–162
Tax Reform Act of 1969, 173
Tax Reform of 1986, 23, 104,
    105, 179, 180
Technological change, 49, 50
Thurow, Lester, 44
Trade deficit, 3, 46–48, 66, 67,
    71
Transfer payments
  generational accounting
    and, 26
  Social Security: *See* Social
    Security
Twin deficit theory, 67

Uncertainty, labeling of re-
    ceipts and payments and,
    156–158
Unemployment insurance
  in female generational ac-
    counts, 118–119
  in male generational ac-
    counts, 116–117

Unified budget deficit, 12, 19,
    60
U.S. economy, 37–63
  baby boomer demographic
    dilemma, 53–55
  baby boomer economic di-
    lemma, 55–62
  background on malaise of,
    37–39
  budget deficit: *See* budget
    deficit
  consumption, 3, 21, 26, 27,
    31–34, 52, 72
  erosion of world position of,
    43–45
  federal debt: *See* Budget defi-
    cit
  income: *See* Income
  investment: *See* Investment
  net liabilities, 10
  net worth, 10, 26, 33
  parallels between 1980s and
    1930s, 39–41
  productivity growth: *See* Pro-
    ductivity growth
  psychological factors in re-
    cessions, 41–43
  saving: *See* Saving
  trade deficit, 3, 46–48, 66, 67,
    71
  two-tier society issue, 50–53
U.S. News & World Report, 57

Volcker, Paul, 43

Wages, decline in, 4, 50–52
Wealth of Nations (Smith), 8
Welfare payments
  decline in, 53
  in the 1950s, 170
  in the 1960s, 173–174, 176

in the 1970s, 177
in the 1980s, 183
Welfare receipts
  in female generational accounts, 118–119
  in male generational accounts, 116–117
Work disincentives, 102–105, 161

World economy, integration of, 40–41

Zero deficit target, 7–8
Zero Sum Society, The (Thurow), 44

Printed in the United States
By Bookmasters